Carnival King: The last Latin Monarch

by

Brent Alan James

Floricanto Press

ISBN: 978-0-915745-78-4

Floricanto Press
650 Castro Street, Suite 120-331
Mountain View, California 94041-2055
www.floricantopress.com

Carnival King

Excerpt from an unpublished manuscript belonging to Geoffrey Powell, an employee of the Consulate of the United States of America in Rio de Janeiro, Brazil.

Evening, 24 February, 1993.

In these streets the powerful and the meek shall finally meet, though, for today, all such distinctions will be forgotten. A senator no more important than this snack vendor, a banker no more worthy than that domestic servant, for tonight they are stars that shine equally bright in a spectacle of the world's most sublime public theater.

In these streets the asphalt serves as stage, upon which will traipse the most unlikely procession of kings – many queens! - and other contemporary nobles.

It is a spectacle some accuse to be exhibited for the eyes and ears of outsiders alone, and – it's true – we gringos have arrived in droves from every corner of the world to witness the avenues overflowing with bodies that drip with a sweat that is perhaps only possible here in the tropics, it is that intense. Above, banners hang from buildings and signposts throughout the city, while below the streets pulse beneath a cat's cradle of green and yellow as miniature flags run from one open window to another. Under this canopy, music blares from stereo speakers tied precariously to the surfboard racks of cars, and - as if these vehicles didn't create enough noise and confusion – a band of drummers follows close behind chanting a refrain that varies with each new group. As the rush of people pushes through these narrow colonial streets, they are showered with confetti as residents lean from their balconies and windows to watch the parade go past.

Oh, no! This is not Carnival. If only this party were so organized as that infamous celebration! Tonight's mayhem is of a completely different sort, for, in Brazil, tomorrow is Election Day.

PART ONE

I

Once upon a time there was a king. In fact, throughout the years there have been quite a few, but only three who could ever claim the tropics of Brazil as the seat of their empire. The first arrived here from Portugal to escape the troops of a certain Junot that, under General Napoleon's orders, were swiftly advancing upon his coastal European capital, eager to strip him of his velvety robe and crown as they would soon do to his Castilian counterpart. The second, always more interested in the affairs of a certain Marchioness than in those of his empire, remained in these warmer climes for as long as he could, prolonging what he must have considered as a holiday from his extended European family. The third simply made Rio de Janeiro his home for he had known no other, though he too eventually returned to Europe.

They all returned home, leaving behind a country that had changed considerably since their arrival, but a land that would have changed without them. One might even argue that, if not for the bastards the second monarch left behind, there would be little trace of the royal family's eighty-year presence here in Brazil. What's that? Yes, you're correct to point out the existence of that nearly infinite array of statues and monuments that adorn the parks and squares of our downtown, catching one king or another in his perpetually gallant pose, as if a monarch never had occasion to slump, letting the hands fall to his side like the rest of us. We might also add, since you've brought it up, the royal lineage reflected in the names of those parks and squares, and in the city streets that connect them. But is it not true that, regardless of whether he resided here or abroad, these monuments would still have been built to remind loyal subjects to honor their king? And, besides, most of those street names - far more malleable than marble or stone - have now been changed to reflect more recent heroes and conquerors; the town square that once celebrated the first kingdom of the Americas, now heralds its last-to-bloom Republic, and streets once evoking the memory of Brazil's royal family now bear the names of Presidents as diverse as Vargas, Wilson, and Roosevelt. What ingratitude on this city's part, but, really, History can be so unforgiving.

And yet, the memory will not be totally erased, for no matter how demanding you may be, dear listener, no one enjoys a riveting story as much as a nation. Therefore, the country will choose to preserve those elements that best fit its own unique plot, tucking them away inside libraries and museums whose sole purpose for existing is to guard those artifacts that, proudly or not, remind us that we once shared the same humidity with members of Europe's most prestigious royalty. For some strange reason, it will be these musty halls that most effectively recall Brazil's past, as no marble emperor on horseback ever could. Room after dust-covered room filled with letters and other royal scribble carefully arranged atop mahogany bureaux – desks fashioned not from brazil wood, but instead imported from France, England, or the Carolinas of North America. Halls peopled by a family of mannequins frozen amongst these documents and fine furniture, and adorned with clothing that has by now been reduced to mere tatters by the thick marine layer that permeates this port city. If blessed with a literary bent, one of these dolls might wish to peruse an aging manuscript, falling back onto the settee to rest her aching feet after the tourists have all gone home. And there she would find proof of the three kings' stay.

But we needn't imagine such fanciful scenes to prove that history can, at any moment, spring to life from its solemn surroundings. Tonight, for example, the specter of ages long passed has returned to guide the future of a nation for, were it not for its imperial legacy, the choice of Monarchy would never have been presented to the Brazilian citizenry. The very idea would seem as ludicrous as, well, as it actually is, and any legislator who dared approach the podium on the floor of Congress to suggest that such an option be included in today's public referendum would be laughed off this and every future political stage.

Referendum is the word lawmakers have chosen over the more correct plebiscite – which carries within it the unsavory root of plebe, and so quickly reminds one of plebeian. No, Congress has instead decided to emphasize the act of referral and disguise the embarrassment they feel in having to seek the opinion of maids and taxi drivers.

From a fanciful idea to transfer an entire monarchy and its court to a southern colony, through nearly a century of imperial rule, half a century of dictatorship and another fifty years of representative democracy, we are back again to that recurring whim that plagues all nations: to trade the devil in our midst for the demon as yet unknown. In this case, to substitute a rather bland executive officer whose only prominent characteristic until today has been his ability to disagree with the legislative branch, and replace him with maybe a prime minister and matching parliament, or with a king and that infamous moderating power of his, an influence that lies somewhere between totalitarianism and pure ceremony.

At this hour of night in which our story begins, the citizens have already decided the nation's fate. Their ballots lie resting inside large metal boxes, which look more like pirates' chests meant to purloin their votes rather than shelters to preserve their integrity. Few voters bother staying awake for the results, most have long ago tucked their children into bed with a kiss on the forehead, perhaps even reading the first pages of a bedtime story until they can verify that the closed eye lids are not just blinking, can see the grip upon a beloved toy slowly loosen. Others have settled down on couches with loved ones, watching this country's version of the late-night talk show, a genre that replicates itself with amazing ease and therefore looks the same no matter where you go in this world. Here, a smartly-dressed overweight man opens with a few timely jokes, announces the evening's guests, and blows a kiss to the audience as the jazz band barrels into a Gershwin tune. Having been taped earlier in the day, and not wanting to draw attention to this well-known practice, the host does not even hint at the referendum that is about to change the lives of so many. Some much more than others.

February 25, São Paulo, Brazil.

"WE BEGIN TONIGHT'S campaign hour with a word from the Brazilian Popular Movement for a Just and Equitable Monarchy, " a voice from the television announced. No, not from our late-night comedian, but from one whose act is not intentionally humorous, although it is, without a doubt, the most entertaining show to have aired in years - since the last election, we might safely say. You have arrived to this story on Election Day. A bit late – if you'll pardon my candor – for if you had been here less than twenty-four hours ago you could have enjoyed the campaign in its full splendor. Lucky for you, now that the voting has ended, the news outlets are again permitted to air the appeals made to the public by the various interested parties, which they've woven together as part of their election night recap.

"Once there was a king," another voice began. "In fact, throughout the years there have been many, but only three – yes, only three – who could ever claim Brazil as the seat of their empire.

"I ask you, fellow citizens, how many monarchs have graced the arid pampas of Argentina, the mountains of Bolivia, the jungles of Peru? Not a one! Yes, Brazil is the only Southern nation to give birth to a king!

"Sadly, they all returned home, but not before leaving behind a country that had been transformed since their arrival. So, while these naysayers claim that it is by coincidence alone that Brazil became home to royalty, I ask you to examine our behavior since their departure. Do we not continue to think and dream on a majestic scale? How many times during your day have you wandered by a 'King of Televisions and VCRs' wholesale warehouse? An 'Empire Cleaning Goods and Supplies'?

"My fellow Brazilians, should we not honor our royal legacy by raising our voices once again in favor of monarchy? Please be sure to mark your ballot 'King.' Thank you and good night."

"And now a word from the National Association of Parliamentarists," the first voice from the television again spoke.

"The people of this country are complete idiots."

No, that wasn't our newly-introduced NAP spokesman, but a young man complaining to another between sips of coffee. The statement seems harsh, but not unexpected for one witnessing these absurd speeches for the umpteenth time; tonight transmitted over a small television suspended from the ceiling in the corner of the room.

For those who lack a young one to lull to sleep or a loved one with whom to cuddle tonight, there is always the consolation of politics. And so it is not surprising that at this hour we should find these two young men seated inside a tiny room in the upper floors of an imposing skyscraper, just one of so many erected at the center of this sprawling network of people and machines they named, perhaps for irony, after a saint: São Paulo. We say men out of politeness, since the two seated here across from each other are boys, really, too young to tuck children into beds, too immature to have that soothing voice a lullaby requires.

"Idiots? Present company excluded, I assume," the other confirmed, paying considerably less attention to the election night hype.

"I mean think about it," Paulo invited his friend to reflect. "Our history, this referendum... we're capable of almost anything."

"I guess you mean that in a bad way?" Marcos wondered, raising his eyebrows. "Oh, come on," he continued, without waiting for a response. "We're not that bad."

Before the other could respond, their attention was again drawn to the television where, as the screen darkened, the words "PRESIDENTIALISM! We'll get it right this time!" appeared in white over a black background. The image faded and a third, stiff-suited gentleman appeared.

"Yes, once there was a king," he began. "But, we begged and begged, and fought and fought, and he finally left us alone! And now we want to invite him back? It's true we haven't had the best of luck with democracy in the twentieth century, but a new millennium is just around the corner and we mustn't lose hope."

"Anyway," Marcos shrugged, turning from the TV and returning to the conversation, "one has to respect the vox populi."

"Papa who?" Paulo asked.

"The voice, or the will, of the people. Familiar with the concept?" Marcos chuckled.

"I've heard something about it," Paulo said dismissively.

"Well, if we can't respect it we're right back to a dictatorship, which I assume you'd rather avoid?"

"Tough call, my friend. What I do know is that democracy is definitely over-rated."

"Over-rated?"

"Sure, look," Paulo said. "Why do we keep putting the nation's destiny in the hands of people that have never studied the issues involved? They don't understand politics, how the government works, the demands of a global economy," he pointed out. "For Christ's sake, a quarter of them don't even know how to read!"

Before Marcos could respond, a telephone resting upon the table began to ring.

"Hello? Hi Juliana," Marcos greeted the caller. "Yeah, still at the office. Here with Paulo, awaiting the results. How's your father, is he nervous?"

"Nah, not really," a young woman responded, seated inside a white, cushiony living room in another part of the city. "He seems to have accepted defeat," she added, referring to her father, Senator Antonio Cruz.

"Me too," Marcos confessed. "How totally crazy is this? A king, who would've thought?"

"So you'll be stopping by later, to console me after defeat?"

"Ah, momô, I don't know. There's still a lot to do around here."

Paulo flashed his friend an incredulous look, for the two's activities had been limited to watching TV and gulping down stale coffee for the last several hours.

"But you'll try...?" Juliana suggested.

"But I'll try," Marcos repeated unconvincingly.

"Make an effort this time, Marcos. I miss you."

"I miss you too, momô. We'll talk later, then."

"Fine." Puckering her lips, Juliana made a loud kissing sound, although one that was mostly voice and therefore lacked any convincing amount of emotion. Under his breath, an absurd attempt at secrecy in a room so small, Marcos murmured "kiss, kiss" in return and hung up.

"Was that Juliana — or should I say 'momô'?" Paulo chuckled.

"It was. She says the Senator isn't holding out much hope that his initiative will pass."

"Ai, for the love of God," Paulo moaned. "So what, then?"

"So a monarchy, I guess," Marcos shrugged.

"That's it, I give up!" Paulo declared, slamming his hand down hard upon the table. "I think I'll go live with my cousin in Miami. Half the country's there already. Wait," he said, pausing. "They don't have a monarchy there, too, do they?"

"No," Marcos laughed. "They've got a President just like we have. Had," he quickly corrected himself.

"Well, even if they did have a monarchy, at least it would be cool," Paulo decided. "You know, with that babe Diana as queen. Instead we get some Portuguese dude. You name me one Portuguese person that's cool," he challenged Marcos.

"Magellan was pretty cool."

"One person that's still alive?" Paulo clarified.

"Look," the other shrugged, "I don't really keep up with —"

"You're ok with this whole thing, aren't you?" Paulo asked.

"What whole thing?"

"With the monarchy thing, with going back to being subjects of the Portuguese?"

"Subjects of the ... Oh, come on. Relax," Marcos told him. "This Portuguese fellow isn't out to take over Brazil. He's just looking for some nice tropical getaway. Besides, it's the congress that governs in this country, always has been."

"Oh, really...?" Paulo murmured, unconvinced.

"Sure. The President spends half his time attending galas and entertaining foreign diplomats. A king would have to do even more of that kind of thing," he pointed out. "Very little will change around here, you'll see."

Distracted by something on television, Paulo grabbed the remote control and turned up the volume. A news anchor was announcing the results of the referendum:

"Much to the surprise of both politicians and we in the media," she began, "a majority of voters has tonight decided to give monarchy another try. This after nearly one hundred years since Pedro the Second left our shores and returned to Portugal, thereby ending the first ever experiment with monarchy in the Americas."

"And it is again Brazil that will give it a try," her colleague and fellow anchor chimed in. "Amazing turn of events," he concluded.

"Our Lady, Mother of — !" Paulo despaired. Again, the phone began to ring.

"Hello?"

"Marcos, it's me." For Senator Antonio Cruz no further announcement was needed.

"Hello, sir. We're watching the news right now," Marcos said, as he rose from his chair. "I'm sorry, sir," he consoled him.

"No need for condolences," the Senator assured him. "This

decision changes very little around here. Our projects in the Senate will go on as planned, without interruption."

"I agree, sir, I agree," Marcos repeated, absent-mindedly, as he leaned over the table to scribble a message to himself on the tiny notepad he always kept at his side. MONARCHY?!?, it read. "So, what's the next step?" he asked his boss, pacing nervously about the room.

"Well, the Senate will contact Mr. Teixeira in Lisbon and he should be moving to Rio quite soon, perhaps within the month."

TEIXEIRA, Marcos again scribbled in his notepad.

"But believe me, Marcos," the Senator continued, "things won't change for us. So, why don't you two go on home and get some sleep," he suggested. "It's almost midnight," he pointed out.

"Thank you, sir. Well, until tomorrow then. Good night."

As Marcos stood there, rather pensive, above his head the images on the muted television screen behind him created a strange pantomime, as reporters and news anchors continued to gesticulate between charts and other polling statistics. It was an act whose peculiarity would prove impossible to follow, evidenced by its interruption of this evening's interview with the late-night talk show's second guest, an up-and-coming actor whose storied rise to fame will now have to wait a few days. Republicanism, it seems, was not the evening's only victim.

II

The handful of folks that knew always thought it strange the king should carry 'round a baked chicken leg in his vest pocket, but to your gran'pa it was a simple matter of life 'n' death. And to think that he come all this way 'cross the Atlan'ic Ocean to get away from ol' Napoleon when the real threat was right inside his home: the Queen Carlota. You laugh, but the king had plenty of reason to worry; she had killed before. Sure, not with her own hands – a Queen would never stoop that low – but do such particulars really matter when one lives day-to-day under fear of attack? Was it that boiling hot Spanish blood that made her give in to all manner of passionate an' bloodthirsty desires? Or was the syphilis finally working its way to her brain? Didn't matter, really. Why bother speculating over a whole bunch of causes that would all wind up producing the same effect? Regicide, the law called it when she finally got to him many years after.

Your gran'pa didn't expect the queen would use maybe a bullet or a sword on him, no, 'cause the emperor's passing on had to be consistent with a death by nat'ral causes. That left poison as the most likely weapon. Dom João recognized this so he gone an' made arrangements to have his meals prepared separately by only one man in the whole kingdom, fella that'd come over with him from Portugal an' had many a time proven his trustworthiness. Now this loyal servant would row his skiff out into the bay real early in the morning an' meet the merchants before they docked. That way he could make sure the product wasn't tainted in any way; see to it that the queen hadn't somehow got to the chickens first. Only chickens in history, I figure, to receive a royal escort onto land. Anyways, folks started noticing this fella that was so anxious to get his chickens an' they took to calling him the Fowler, though I don't suspect they knew he was a royal fowler. Anyways, returning to the palace the fowler would slaughter, an' clean, an' do up the meat all by hisself an' begin his watch over the pot night 'n' day, since the king might stop by at all manner of hour to replenish his stash.

Sounds like a perfect system, don't it? Well, it wasn't. Not even a king is meant to have vi't'als always at his beck and holler, an' with that delicious aroma rising up to his nostrils, wasn't long 'fore the emp'ror was digging his hands down into those pockets, front of comp'ny and everybody. Folks started whispering 'mongst themselves, complaining 'bout the king's greasy hands an' fingers, an' the newspapers couldn't resist teasing him 'bout how his belly kept pressing tighter and tighter against that vest. And with those poor chicken legs trapped there inside. They looked like handles to the giant kettle your gran'pa was becoming. All this chatter didn't bother the king too much, though. Mostly, he just missed eating from a plate.

They say a man is like to marry the woman most like his mother, an' your gran'father was no exception. In his case, both of 'em were completely crazy. Even before arriving here in the New World, the Queen-Mother had started seeing visions of Napoleon, firm upon his stead, sword outstretched like so an' heading her way. I think she imagined him a good bit taller than he really was, which didn't help none. Then, after landing in Rio, the visions changed to the ghost of an old Independence leader, fella who'd long ago been drawn and qua'tered for his crimes against the Empire. With blood just a dripping from where his arms used to be, the ol' rebel would limp up an' down the hallways of the City Palace, chasing Dona Maria from room to room an' finally into the confines of her tiny, sweltering hot bed chamber. As her only defense against these spirits, she took to screaming. And she took to it good, I s'ppose, 'cause folks could hear from all the way out into the bay. Kept the port safe from enemies, sailors used to laugh.

As you might imagine, times were plenty when your gran'pa couldn't stand it no longer inside that haunted castle, so he always made up some sort of story to get outside into the fresh air. He'd summon up his carriage an' head out to survey his new kingdom, traveling 'long the beaches of Boqueirão, Lapa, Glória, an' finally past the beautiful Sugarloaf mountain. It was a fine landscape for an Empire to come to rest in, no doubt about it. But even way on past the palace gates, poor João's troubles seemed to find him. Passing by the Royal Chapel one day, the king was reminded of the hours Carlota spent with that young vicar who was busy creating, rather than hearing, his wife's confessions. Then, at the Rua das Laranjeiras, he stumbled upon the street corner where the wife of Dr. Carneiro Leão was shot dead in broad daylight. The good doctor had treated the queen on various occasions, an' treated her mighty well, by most folks' accounts, for he an' Carlota had... well, never mind. Anyways, I s'ppose the doctor's wife found out 'bout the whole thing and took to limiting his hours of examination, which didn't please Carlota none, no sir. Sure, they convicted a slave man for act'ally committing the crime, but the king, he was no dummy. He could smell the hot Castilian blood behind the murd'rous plot.

Anyways, only a blame fool could ignore the facts of the case, which your gran'pa was forced to become, no disrespect intended. You see, son, a king is mighty powerful an' can always make arrangements for separate meals an' separate bedchambers. But no man can split up the Iberia' Peninsula. So when the king thought long an' hard over his situation on those rides through the city, he always did come back to that same conclusion: Carlota would stay his wife, else the Empire get ready for war with Spain.

When he come back to the palace later that day, the king felt kinda guilty 'bout all the plotting 'gainst his wife, so he thought he'd visit with her for a while. But the folks at the palace told him that the queen had gone out for another round of her confessions. Meanwhile, upstairs, turned out Napoleon had recruited that no arms and no legs rebel an' they were both now coming after the Queen Mother – together on the same horse! With his mother's screams growing louder an' louder in the background, all your gran'pa could do was sigh to hisself, pass by the kitchen to grab another chicken leg or two from the Fowler, an' stuff 'em into those coat pockets as he headed on back to his carriage for another few moments of peace. Remember this, child, it ain't always so easy being king.

III

If Charles de Gaulle were to enter the offices of the Supreme Court at this early hour perhaps he would recant his infamous statement that Brazil is not a serious country. For - look General! - it's the morning after the referendum, a night of unprecedented excitement, and already a young woman is hard at work here inside this cluttered office. Looking quite serious indeed, a black thick-rimmed pair of eyeglasses perched at the end of her nose, she has been studying a document that appears legislative in nature. Intently reading, something suddenly catches her attention as she looks up and calls out, "Judge?" But there is no response.

"Judge Barbosa?" she tried again, looking about and finding only empty office space around her. She rose and began to search for someone throughout the halls of the government building, a structure whose 1960s architecture seemed strangely equipped to produce a hollow, reverberant echo to her call.

"Judge Bar– Ah, here you are," she said upon entering a small meeting room where legislative texts and bulky legal tomes lined the shelves. A bald man, already in his sixties, looked up from his reading.

"Yes? What is it?" he asked her.

Veronica approached her boss with the legislative documents in hand, opening them out onto the conference table.

"Sir, I've been looking over the legislation regarding the referendum, in particular the clause that pertains to an eventual choice in favor of monarchy."

"Yes," the Judge again said, removing his eyeglasses, and slowly becoming more interested.

"Well," Veronica continued, "I noticed that the legislation — for the referendum, that is — doesn't explicitly mention the nature or functioning of the monarchy, it just references a clause from the old Imperial Constitution. Curious, I decided to look it up."

"Very good. And?"

"The clause clearly states that the monarch, even if he or she is the modern day heir of the royal family, cannot be a foreigner." Looking down at the document, she read: "'The presumptive heir of the Empire shall succeed to the throne in accordance with the normal order of primogeniture, preferring always the earlier lines to the later'... here it is: 'No foreigner shall be able to succeed to the crown of the Empire.' It makes it very clear, no room for interpretation really."

"Yes, well..." the Judge sighed, pondering the situation as he nibbled the end of his eyeglasses. "At that time the descendants of the royal family were still part of the Empire of Brazil, since no political distinction was made between Portugal and its colonies. But, after independence, that of course changed." The Judge paused for a second before continuing: "So how is it that no one noticed this restriction before?"

Veronica, also perplexed, shrugged her shoulders.

"I know the possibility of returning to monarchy was considered remote throughout the referendum debates, but do you really think that no one bothered to consult the original legislation?" she asked. Then, removing her eyeglasses, she continued: "And what about this Portuguese fellow who's already begun looking for a condo along Ipanema Beach?"

"Right. I hope he hasn't already put down a deposit," the judge laughed. "Well, it looks like the Court will need to intervene in this process and oblige the Senate to locate the Brazilian heir, if one even exists. Do me a favor, call the President of the Senate and tell him what we've – you've – found."

"Yes, sir. I know one of his staffers, a friend from college."

As she was leaving the room, the Judge called to Veronica.

"Yes, sir?" she asked, poking her head back through the door.

"I applaud your curiosity. Nice work."

"Thank you, sir," she smiled, pushing the heavy black frames back against her face.

No young man in his mid-twenties should own more than ten ties and five business suits. Marcos Antonio, however, owns some fifteen of the former, six of the latter. One suit above the expected one-per-each-day-of-the-week, for he has prepared for the unfortunate possibility that there may pass five consecutive work days in which he is too busy to make it to the dry cleaners, which is unlikely since it is located just steps from his apartment. Yet, there it hangs: the sixth suit. All six dark blue, by the way, while the ties vary in color from dark green to a deep red, this last one so audacious as to flaunt a shower of yellow sunflowers. Having arrived late to his apartment because of the previous night's excitement, Marcos lay still asleep as his mobile phone began to ring. Confused and only half-awake, he looked about the room in search of this portable device, which in 1993 was a good deal easier to find, for most were twice as large and twice as heavy as today's models.

"Hello?" he mumbled into the awkward contraption after the fourth or fifth ring.

"Marcos? It's Veronica." Drinking coffee alone in a small café, she heard no response at the other end of the line. "From USP," she added, mentioning their alma mater.

"Of course, of course. Veronica, how's it going? Up so early?"

"It's ten-thirty already," Veronica noted, looking down at her watch. "Were you asleep?"

"Yeah. I was up pretty late last night, what with the vote and all."

"Right, right. Actually, that's why I'm calling. We've discovered a, let's say, complication and I wanted to give you a heads-up before I have to notify your boss."

Marcos, now out of bed, secured the phone with his shoulder while trying to pull on a pair of pants. "Wait a sec, Veronica. What do you mean 'complication'? And who's 'we'?"

"The Court."

"The Supreme Court's gotten involved?"

"I guess you could say that. It's just that we noticed a clause in the old Imperial Constitution that regulates a possible second monarchy, with stipulations and everything."

Marcos, frozen with his pants still unbuttoned, dared to ask: "And...?"

"And... it stipulates that a future monarch cannot be foreign-born. It can't be this Mr. Ribeiro."

"Teixeira," Marcos corrected her. "His surname is Teixeira."

"Yeah him. He can't be king. The Judge is going to officially inform the Senator this morning, I just wanted to warn you first. I imagine he's gonna be in some kind of mood."

"No kidding. Jesus, I'm screwed. Well, anyway... thanks for the heads-up."

"Sure thing, Marcos. If you need anything, let me know, ok?"

"Yeah, of course. Thanks again."

"Hugs," she added in parting.

"Huh? Oh, right. Hugs," he replied as a formality, obviously distracted.

Veronica hung up the phone, shrugged her shoulders at her friend's response, and finished off in a single gulp what was left of her double espresso. Meanwhile, Marcos walked to his desk, grabbed his notepad, and wrote NOT before the name TEIXEIRA. Underneath, he asked himself: THEN WHO?

IV

'Brazil?' the young girl asked. 'Oh, father, since childhood I have dreamt of visiting the tropical paradise of the Americas. Its gentle hills,' she sighed as she began to dance around the room, 'the exotic flora and fauna, gigantic rivers, plummeting waterfalls, enchanted forests! Yes, father,' she agreed, dropping to her knees. 'I will marry Dom Pedro of Brazil!'

'Easy now young'n,' I woulda told her. 'You marrying the man, not his country.' But that was the kind of answer the great Emperor Franz the First of Austria got when he asked your mama if she would like to become the wife of the heir to the Portuguese Empire. I s'ppose she was old enough to know the difference between man and country, but even so, she couldn't get it out of her noggin that Brazil would be a mighty nice place to call home.

Leopoldina, the ladies' version of that mighty name Leopold, which comes from Leo, which I guess you know means lion. Perfect name, too, if you remember that a lion is the king of the jungle. That's exactly what her gran'pa was, King Leopold the Third of the Holy Roman Empire. Besides him, the young girl had kings and queens in her family spread out all the way to Spain, Italy, Poland, Germany, and of course, Austria, where she was from. People even said she was related to Marie Antoinette of France, you know, the one that got her... well, nevermind, that's another story altogether. Anyways, with a name like that and a family to match I s'ppose Leopoldina might seem like a young girl who had ev'rything. But, no, she didn't have ev'rything. Your mother was, let's see, how can I say this to you? Son, your mama wasn't pretty. Now I don't mean that she was ugly, don't get me wrong. I'm jus' saying that folks gen'rally preferred eyeing the other daughters. So when the king of Portugal came knocking at the door, looking for a wife for one of his children way off in Brazil, ol' Franz figured he'd better marry off the older and more homely of the bunch first. That meant Leopoldina would go while Princess Carolina would stay, in case there was a better offer on down the road. Dom João didn't care. 'Any old one will do!' your gran'pa told the Austrians. He was jus' happy some family in Europe had agreed to his request. You see, not all of royalty was so fascinated with the Americas like Leopoldina was. Most wouldn't even consider setting foot here on holiday, much less moving here permane'tly. On this occasion, ol' João received a double helping of good luck, for his son's reputation was also well-known round Europe. With rumors circulating 'bout woman-chasing and other gallivanting south of the equator, Pedro the First didn't exactly make for the ideal son-in-law. But, like I said, Franz's worse nightmare was for Leopoldina to go unmarried, so in the end he agreed.

And once he agreed, the preparations could begin. And my word how they did begin! The young Prince and Princess started up a three-month courtship that went on across the seas, can you believe it, without them ever even once seeing each other? All thanks to Dom João's Ambassador, the Marquis of Marialva. From the day he arrived in Vienna with a procession of forty-one carriages to the day he escorted the Princess away in a procession of forty-two, there was nothing but parties and fancy dinners for the entire royal family, all paid for by your gran'pa. He even threw a ball for more than two thousand of Europe's most prestigious aristocracy; heads a state and ambassadors from places like England, France, and Spain. The party was so grand, they say an orchestra even played for the townspeople gathered outside the palace gates.

Every day during those three months Leopoldina would receive a bouquet of flowers, or other gifts, an', once and a while, she even got a letter from the Prince hisself. But the best gift of all was when she was presented with a diamond-studded portrait of your father. After all, it was the first time she had seen his face. And the young woman wasn't disappointed. Your papa was a real looker! Dark eyes, dark moustache, and well-tanned skin; not like anything she was used to in frigid ol' Vienna.

Now, it wasn't like your father wasn't getting a pretty good something out of this deal as well. 'Cause, for just twenty years old, the Princess was smart as a whip! She spoke all kinds of foreign languages – was learning Portuguese, too, even though people warned her it wouldn't ever come in useful; even in Brazil most of the folks she'd be around already spoke French. She loved art and books, and had a special liking for the nat'ral sciences. 'What are my future husband's preferred areas of study?' she asked the Ambassador one day over dinner. That poor Marialva almost spit his wine clear across the table for wont of laughing. Dom Pedro study? Trying to think quick on his feet, and also trying not to lie to the girl too much so that she wouldn't be completely disappointed when she finally met the Prince, the Ambassador called upon his best diplomatic skills and blurted out: 'Anatomy.'

'Anatomy?' the Princess repeated. The Ambassador sat frozen in his chair, praying the answer would satisfy her. 'Biology, then. How wonderful! I also love the natural sciences,' she smiled, allowing the Ambassador to finally exhale.

Meanwhile, the entire city of Rio was busy preparing for the Princess' arrival. When they heard the news that Princess Leopoldina of the Hapsburg Empire was coming, folks took to the streets to celebrate, chanting Te Deum Laudamuses in the chapels to give thanks to the good Lord for such a singular blessing. Flags hung from the ships out in the harbor and from every building in the city, and they placed luminaries along every street after they got done washing the bricks clean of all the garbage that city folks 'ccumulate. The beaches, too, got a good cleaning up. I guess you could say that folks sure was hopeful that this new princess would be nicer than ol' Carlota, and they wanted to make a good first impression on her.

Out by the bay they built a big ol' pavilion so that the couple would have something pretty to walk under when she arrived. It was the first of a whole bunch of arcs the young lovers would pass through that first day. Funny things, those arcs, rising up from the ground outta nothing. Shaped like a bridge 'cross the top, 'cept that it didn't connect one darn thing to another. A big ol' gateway that didn't seem to lead nowhere, just to the other side of the arc, like they forgot to put up the rest of the building. Anyways, after they arrived a big procession of carriages carrying dignitaries and soldiers on horseback was to escort them from the Rua Direita all the way to the Royal Chapel. At the head of the parade was the cavalry battalion, followed by other guards on horseback, musicians, flagmen, heralders, folks whose only job far as I could tell was to keep watch over the fancy clothes and other costumes. Then came the butlers, stewards, each with their own set of helpers, lackeys on foot ahead of the lieutenant and captain of the Royal Guard, and finally the royal family, their carriages surrounded by chamberlains on each side. Kinda funny, 'cos I s'ppose the guards were there to make sure that folks who entered the procession had a right to be there, but they was more folks in the parade than was left to watch it!

Anyways, back in Vienna, the night before she left, the Princess spent many hours alone with her younger sister Carolina, trying to convince the young girl that they would see each other again soon. You see, this would be the first time the two sisters had been apart. Leopoldina told her that a Princess sometimes has to sacrifice her own comfort for the well being of the nation. So no matter how much Leopoldina wanted to stay, she was happy to be able to help with an alliance that was pleasing to both her father and her future husband's people. Carolina would be married one day herself and be honored to do the same. And, besides, Leopoldina had always felt that strange attraction to the Americas, like it was her destiny to one day make that journey 'cross the ocean. And now that day had come.

On the fifth of November, 1817, the vessel Dom João VI entered Guanabara Bay. Early that next morning, Leopoldina was transferred from the big ship to a smaller boat and rowed ashore, where she stepped off the skiff and placed her tiny feet, for the first time ever, on Brazilian soil. Hundreds of boats were swarming all around the marina, so filled up with folks trying to get a better look at the bride-to-be it's a miracle they stayed afloat. The king rushed to escort his future daughter-in-law into the pavilion, just a kissing her hand and secretly thanking her for picking the Braganzas out of all the other possible choices for marriage. Behind him a military band had started to play while folks threw confetti out of windows, church bells rang out, and shots were fired from the forts all along the beach. Finally, over the king's shoulder, your mama caught sight of the Prince.

Now, I don't want you to think her ungrateful, but Leopoldina shed a tear that morning in spite of all the happiness she felt gazing upon her new husband and his beautiful country. I can't know for sure, but I s'ppose your mother was sorry she had lied to Carolina. I guess she somehow knew she wasn't ever gonna see her folks back home again.

V

When one thinks of South America, he or she may imagine those lush tropical scenes of arching palms reaching towards the sea as its waves lap soothingly against a snow white strip of sand; scenes peppered with dark-skinned inhabitants that sip slowly from decapitated coconuts while swaying their hips to the gentle lull of a steel drum, or to the staccato thumping of the bongo. Outside of a vague image of the majestic Andes, one rarely pictures the more frigid and inhospitable landscapes, where mountains rise up abruptly to arrest one's view, spilling forth powerful waterfalls that pound the rocks below. Yet, now several days after the referendum, such is the landscape in which we find Marcos, aide to Senator Cruz, and loyal companion to this esteemed legislator's daughter as well. A curious triangle, indeed, for occasionally, after a night out with Juliana, Marcos has found himself pondering the micro-economic phenomenon whereby the salary he receives from the Senator is then distributed back into the Cruz family via the daughter. This digression is not meant to suggest that he resents spending money on his loved one, really, he ponders this economy with curiosity alone. Pressing the buttons on his mobile telephone – a task made all the more dangerous while driving his red convertible along the winding roads that carve their way through the hills – Marcos realized that he could no longer pick up a signal.

Must be the mountains, he decided. Or the distance, for nearly four hours had passed since he'd left São Paulo when Marcos finally saw a sign that read:

Welcome to Cruzília

Population 4,738

Below, carved into the wood in cursive writing, were the words: "Brazil's diamond in the rough."

Upon entering the quiet country town, the young man spotted a pay phone at the corner of a quaint little plaza and parked the car. Approaching the booth, he dropped some change into the slot, and dialed.

"Hi love, it's me," he said into the receiver. Juliana wasn't in so he left a message on her answering machine, reading aloud the phone number just above the number pad and cracking a joke about the size and remoteness of the town that wasn't funny enough to record here on paper. "It's just after 11 o'clock, right now," he told her, "11:05, more or less. If you get home in the next, let's say, ten minutes you can try to reach me here. Lots of love, bye bye."

As Marcos waited beside the phone booth, he cast a look about the deserted city and the rugged mountains that surrounded it. Dusty and jagged old things these were, most unlike the gentle, rolling hills he could expect to find in Rio, but beautiful nonetheless. The town's man-made structures, however, had not fared as well amid the ruggedness around them. The streets seemed as though, at one time, they had been paved, but were now slowly losing the battle against nature and its relentless assault of wind and sand. And there was not a single building in sight that was more than two stories tall, so different from São Paulo, where there is no building less than two stories tall. Once again, Marcos opened his notepad and read:

REGINALDO SANTOS

CONJUNTO BELA VISTA, 147

CRUZILIA (MG)

Strange to think of a king actually having a street address, he thought. And stranger still to imagine the monarch making his home so far out here in the countryside. Had he, or one of his ancestors, fled persecution? It seemed the only reasonable motive to settle in such a desolate place. As he reached back into the car for the map he'd kept beside him on the passenger seat, a woman standing in the doorway of a small café, some fifty meters away, began to call to him.

"You hungry?" she yelled.

"No, thank you," Marcos politely replied.

Nearly screaming because of the distance, the woman tried again: "You thirsty? What about a drink?" she suggested.

"No, really, thank you!"

"Don't even wanna sit down?"

"It's just that I'm -"

"What?" she interrupted him.

Finding it absurd to scream back and forth in the middle of such a quiet town square, Marcos approached the café.

"It's just that I'm waiting for a call," he explained.

"Ah, you can hear that old thing ringing from here easy," the woman assured him. "Come, c'mon in. I make an excellent side of pork ribs with whipped potatoes."

"Whipped potatoes?" Marcos wondered, turning his head to look back at the pay phone, fearful of missing Juliana's call. "Is that like puréed?"

"Uh huh," the woman confirmed.

"Well, alright," he finally agreed. "I never could resist potato purée."

While the owner of the café began to unleash upon Marcos an almost interminable stream of chit chat and other small talk, behind him a young woman entered the plaza carrying a shopping bag in each arm. As she passed the booth, the phone began to ring. Looking around and seeing no one, she placed her bags down and decided to answer.

"Hello?" the young woman timidly asked.

"Marcos?" a voice responded from the other end.

"Ugh..." the girl stammered, glancing nervously around the plaza.

"Marcos Antonio? Could I please speak with Marcos?" the voice again demanded.

"I... I'm sorry," she stuttered. "I only answered because no one..."

Before the young woman could finish, Juliana hung up. Perplexed, this otherwise innocent passerby shrugged her shoulders, grabbed her bags, and continued on her way. Over at the café, Marcos tried his best to break the verbal grip in which the owner held him in order to steal an occasional peek in the direction of the phone booth. Polite to a fault, he heard nothing and didn't notice the girl pass by.

The young woman turned down a narrow, brick-paved street, stopping occasionally to say a word or two to the friends and acquaintances that pass the quiet country hours sitting just inside their front windows, the heavy wooden shutters thrown open towards the street with neither glass nor screen to prevent one from kissing or embracing the occasional passerby. Arriving at one of these modest homes, she pushed a short wooden gate open with her foot and entered the front yard, placing her bags down on the front step. Instead of entering the house, she began removing several plants from the bags as she surveyed the garden, pondering where they might best fit in. Having decided, the young woman walked to the side of the house to grab a hand shovel and a pair of gloves before hiking up her dress as she knelt down in the garden and set about her work.

After nearly half an hour had passed, she heard a car pull up outside the gate. As she rose to see who it might be, Marcos called out: "I'm sorry, I don't mean to interrupt."

"Not a problem," she assured him. "Can I help you?"

"Well, I hope so," he told her, stopping just outside the gate. Then, consulting his notepad, he added: "I'm looking for a Mister... Reginaldo Santos. Is this the right address?"

"Sure is, but he's not here at the moment."

"I see."

"I'd guess he's either at the library or the supermarket," she said, pulling off her gloves.

"Yes, well, it is a pretty small town," Marcos noted.

"Small, but it's got everything he needs: a hobby and a stable job to survive," she pointed out.

"Simple folk, eh?"

"Simple, but not stupid," she coldly responded.

"Sorry, I didn't mean to offend."

"That's all right."

Having survived his first gaffe, Marcos quickly committed another: "Are you his maid -"

"A friend," she corrected him. "The fool spends all day with his head in the clouds, while the poor plants here on earth go neglected," she explained, motioning towards the garden. "I've adopted them, like they were orphans, I suppose. Were you looking to speak with Reggie?" she added after a pause.

"Reggie?" Marcos wondered, confused. "Oh right, Reginaldo. Yes, I was. You wouldn't be able to direct me a bit here in the city, at least point me in the direction of that library or supermarket?"

"Sure," she agreed. "Come on in a second while I wash up," she said, opening the gate.

"Thanks," he smiled, passing by her and into the yard.

As Marcos followed her into the house, he inadvertently noticed her well-tanned legs and that pitch black hair, features he'd always found attractive; pigments of his imagination that are, after all, common enough here in Brazil. And yet something's different about her, he reflected, but was embarrassed at the triteness of the thought. Wisely, Marcos pushed the issue to the back of his mind, and returned to the task at hand.

"Kind of strange asking for directions in a town smaller than my neighborhood back in São Paulo," he admitted, speaking loudly now that the young woman had entered the kitchen to wash her hands.

"Don't worry, if it makes you feel better I won't tell anyone," she joked, approaching him while drying her hands. "Can I ask, sir, why you..."

"It's Marcos," he told her.

"Isabel, a pleasure," she smiled as the two cordially shook hands. "Can I ask why you've come all the way from São Paulo to speak with Reggie?"

As Senator Cruz exited his office building in downtown São Paulo, the reporters gathered on the sidewalk began to call for his attention. Finally, one of them managed to make her question heard: "Is it true, Senator, that the Portuguese heir has been disqualified by the Supreme Court?"

Hands raised to quell their clamor, the Senator offered a well-scripted answer: "Yesterday I received a phone call from the Honorable Joaquim Barbosa of the Supreme Court informing the Senate that the constitution prohibits any foreign-born person from assuming leadership of our government. I agree completely with the Court's decision and I ask for forgiveness from the Brazilian people for the confusion and uncertainty during this historic moment in our nation's history. But I can assure you that we are establishing contact with members of the royal family here in Brazil and soon this will all be resolved. Now, if you'll excuse me, I need to return to the Capital. Thank you."

The Senator darted quickly into a black sedan as the reporters continued to shout their questions into the windows of the car, but to no avail.

"Vultures," the Senator sighed as he eased into the leather seat. "From here on out I'm going to really need your help," he said, turning to Paulo, who was waiting for him there inside the car.

"Of course, sir."

"Marcos has gone to fetch our new king - so strange to say that word 'king', isn't it?"

"Very strange, sir," Paulo agreed.

"Well, don't worry. We're prepared."

"Prepared, sir?"

"You see, Paulo," the Senator began, turning towards him with that tone of voice that signals an impending lecture. "You see, one can never rely on the public's judgment, and you certainly can't count on any stirs of civic duty."

"Right," Paulo said, nodding his head in agreement, as the

Senator continued:

"It's just that, even in a democracy, the power of the people is extremely limited. Frustrated, angry, I don't know which, they will always try to squeeze the most advantage out of the little power they do possess. Not to vote for someone or for something they actually believe in, no," he laughed. "They will instead try to trip up the plans of those actually in power."

"Screw up the workings of the government," Paulo offered as an interpretation.

"Exactly. It's a weakness of democracy, I suppose. The rule of all," the Senator chuckled to himself, "as if this, or any, country were made up of scientists, economists, lawyers, men with real intellectual training. No, the reality is that the majority are at best beer guzzling lie-abouts, at worst common crooks. Can you imagine," he said, turning to Paulo, "if we were to place the destiny of this nation in their hands? We're here to protect them from themselves!" he said emphatically.

"I've been trying to tell Marcos the same thing," Paulo murmured, shaking his head.

"So we have to expect that, when they do exercise their power," the Senator continued, "they will try to cause the most damage possible to our power – voting for a monarchy, for example – and use this to our advantage. Don't hope for the best," he concluded, "manipulate the worst."

"Right... right. And so you'll be needing my help?" Paulo confirmed.

"Huh, ah yes. What with Marcos in Rio..."

"He's going to Rio?"

"Sure. He'll have to help the king out quite a bit these first few weeks, moving him into the former royal palace, orienting him to the day-to-day activities of a monarch, insuring that he's comfortable in his new surroundings. Who knows, perhaps they'll even have time to enjoy the beauty of Rio's beaches," the Senator smiled.

"Maybe the king will even learn to surf," Paulo joked.

The Senator, finding little humor in this thought, dropped his smile and stared blankly at the young man.

"Sorry, sir," Paulo mumbled, lowering his head.

"YOU'RE KIDDING, RIGHT?" Isabel asked, seated in the passenger seat of Marcos' convertible.

"Nope."

"Reggie, a member of the royal family?"

"Look," Marcos explained, "the branches of that family tree are pretty weak here in Brazil. He probably doesn't even know he's a descendant."

"Oh, I'm positive he doesn't know."

"It's possible he's not actually a legitimate heir," he continued, "more likely a descendent of an ex-lover of Pedro the First. I'm pretty sure the legitimate family members all returned to Portugal. Only the lovers and the 'fruits of their encounters,' let's say, stayed behind."

"A country full of bastards," Isabel concluded. "Sorry," she added, slightly embarrassed.

"No problem," he assured her. "I'm proud of the fact. A country of rebels, independent since the beginning, without the hang-ups of an imperial power."

"That's one way to interpret our history. I like it," she smiled.

When the two pulled up outside a small library, Isabel got out and entered the building alone. Walking up to the circulation desk, she greeted an older woman seated there behind the counter.

"Hi Edith. Reggie hasn't been by today, has he?"

"Not yet, honey," the woman answered, looking up from her paperback. "Care to leave a message for him?"

"No, that's all right. I'll look for him at work. See ya."

"Bye bye, now."

"He must be still at work," Isabel told Marcos, returning to the car. As the two pulled away, Ms. Edith abandoned her paperback for a moment in order to steal a peek through the front window, curious after seeing Isabel with a stranger in such a flashy car.

"IT DOESN'T MAKE SENSE," the journalist remarked, as she paced from side to side, smoking more heavily than usual – even for a member of the press. Here inside the offices of Rio's Tele-Journal, a local television reporter, Flavia Moraes, was conversing with a colleague, her camera operator Gustavo. "I knew Senator Cruz was an idiot, but not this stupid," she added.

"God dammit," Gustavo complained, seated behind a cheap metal desk, fumbling with an even cheaper computer. "The connection went down again."

"Stop playing around and pay attention," Flavia told him, creating quite a bang as her fist came crashing down hard upon the desk. Looking up, Gustavo made a half-hearted attempt to divide his attention between Flavia and the little message windows that kept popping up on the screen before him. "How is it," she continued, "that the President of the Senate is not going to know about a fundamental clause in our constitution?"

"Ah, you know politicians these days, Flav. All they know how to do is campaign," Gustavo scoffed. "For them it's a matter of choosing the right people to write their speeches, others to apply the right amount of make-up for the cameras... the politicians themselves hardly know a thing about the actual functioning of the government."

"No, with this bastard it's different. He's hiding something," she concluded.

"I thought the media was supposed to be unbiased," Gustavo observed. "Why're you getting so worked up?"

"Forget it, let's go."

"What?! I'm trying to look something up here."

"C'mon, you can search for porn later."

"I wasn't - "

"Now! Hurry! We have to research this piece of shit of a constitution," she told him.

"Flavia, I've never met a girl with a mouth as dirty as yours, you know that?" Gustavo reflected. "It's pretty sexy," he concluded.

"Pervert... c'mon," she motioned to him, opening the office door.

Gustavo stood up and grabbed a bulky set of keys from the desktop. "So, where we headed?" he asked.

"To a place you've certainly heard of, but probably never visited," Flavia said in a sarcastically dramatic tone. "The library."

CLIMBING THE STEPS of Rio's National Library, Flavia and Gustavo passed quickly between its brick columns, through the doors, and directly towards the Information Desk.

"Hi Milena, how's it going?" Flavia whispered to the young girl behind the counter.

"Hi Flavia, Hi Gustavo," she answered.

"Hello Milena. How have you been?" Gustavo added, smiling and flirting a bit. "I've missed you, you know."

"All you've gotta do is come look up a book, I'm always here."

"Oh, too bad he can't read," Flavia cut in. "Look Milena, can you help us find some legislative documents?"

"What kind? Local, state or federal?"

"Federal."

"Let's see, federal...," Milena echoed as she searched her memory. "That'd be letters NA through NF. Around there."

"Incredible!" Gustavo exclaimed. "Beauty and intelligence!"

"Anything in particular you're looking for?"

"The constitution? Something that sets out the rules for this whole monarchy business?" Flavia guessed.

"Got it," Milena winked. "Grab a table, I'll bring them out."

"Thanks a million," Flavia smiled. "I owe you."

"Dinner," Gustavo chimed in. "We'll owe you dinner, I'd say," he decided.

"I accept."

"Come on, Don Juan," Flavia said, dragging Gustavo away.

"YOU ASKED TO SEE ME, SIR?" the Chief of Rio de Janeiro's police department asked as he poked his head into the Mayor's office.

"I did. Please, have a seat," the Mayor answered, extending an arm in the direction of one of two leather chairs that faced his desk.

"Look, Viana, I'll get right to it. As I'm sure you're aware," the Mayor began, "not only has the future of this nation changed because of this referendum, but our city's future has changed very dramatically as well. From one day to the next we've been capitulated from a state capital to —"

"You mean 'catapulted,' sir?" the Police Chief interrupted.

"Right, catapulted. What did I say?"

"I think you said 'capitulated.'"

"No, Viana, catapulted," the Mayor began again, "launched from being a mere state capital to the capital of the nation. And while this city has always been a major player on the world stage - and even been the nation's capital before, I might add - it doesn't mean that we won't have to make some important changes and adjustments around here."

"I agree completely, sir," Viana said, bobbing his head. "Did you have anything specific in mind?"

"Not really," the Mayor confessed. "We should of course work to keep the crime rate down, but I think we need to do even more than that, something on a more fundamental level."

Receiving a baffled look from his Chief of Police, the Mayor stood up and began to pace back and forth behind his desk. "Something that shows we deserve this privilege," he continued, "that we are not a capital by chance, but by right. And we're not merely a capital, Viana. We are the seat of an Empire, home to a king."

"Right, we should project to the world a king-like glory!" Viana awkwardly proclaimed.

"Exactly, Viana, an imperial aura that will surround our city," the Mayor summed up, as he again took a seat and leaned forward, resting his elbows upon the desk.

"Exactly," Viana echoed, his eyes beaming. "So... how do we do that?"

"Well, quite frankly, I considered it your job to figure that out," the Mayor told him.

"Me?" Viana wondered. "But I'm just the Chief of Police."

"Sure, Viana, I realize that. But the streets are your domain. Can't you see that, in this battle to define the city's image, you're on the front lines?"

"I am?" the Chief frowned.

"Yes. And I'll need a proposal as soon as possible. The coronation is less than two weeks away."

"Yes, sir. I'll have a list of proposals on your desk as soon as possible," the Chief assured him.

The two sat facing each other for several seconds, each expecting the other to speak when, finally, the Mayor broke the uncomfortable silence.

"That'll be all for now, Viana. I look forward to your

suggestions."

"Yes, sir!" the Police Chief barked, as he rose to take his leave. "Proposals are on the way! We'll speak again soon."

"Yes we shall," the Mayor sighed with a slight shaking of his head as he watched the door close behind this, his top cop.

Presiding over a collection of legislative texts, Flavia and Gustavo talked quietly while they gathered the documents to return to Milena.

"Hey Gus, what time is it?"

"Almost noon. You hungry too?"

"No, it's not that. We've been here, what?" Flavia asked, "maybe fifteen minutes and we've already found the clause regarding the monarchy."

"If you're thanking me for my help, you're welcome."

"What I'm saying is that, with a restriction so obvious, it's almost impossible the Senator wouldn't have known that the Portuguese heir would be disqualified."

"Yes... hmm..." Gustavo murmured, bobbing his head slightly.

"Maybe, just maybe, the Senator was expecting this confusion in order to install some ally of his to the throne?" Flavia speculated. "Perhaps he's in cahoots with the Brazilian heir?!"

"Sure, could be." At the thought of such possible cunning on the Senator's part, a smile broke across Gustavo's face. "That rascal," he laughed.

"Someone in his confidences, perhaps," Flavia continued, "to facilitate or cover up some sort of corruption... a royal heist, no pun intended."

"But who?" Gustavo wondered. "I mean, after all, who is the king?"

"That is the question, my friend," Flavia nodded, looking over at her colleague with all the mystery and intrigue of a private detective. "Just who is our king?"

VI

The future king of Brazil can be found on aisle nine, between the pre-packaged baked goods and an infinite array of salted snacks. He is Reginaldo Santos, a man in his mid-thirties with blond wisps of hair marked for certain extinction. Beneath a green apron, which bulges slightly to accommodate his paunch, he wears a loosely knotted tie and cardigan, a combination he adopts so faithfully that customers of the *Mercado da Serra* take it for a uniform required by the management. While arranging packages of crackers and chips on a supermarket shelf, Reginaldo began to hum what one would assume to be a jazz ballad, although the sounds emanating from his puckered lips were far from comprehensible. Making their way slowly through the supermarket, Isabel and Marcos followed the strains of Reginaldo's song.

"Over here..." Isabel said, indicating the direction with a jerk of her head.

Reginaldo grabbed the broom at his side and clutched it as if it held a microphone. Eyes closed, he began to sing somewhat louder. Smiling, Isabel and Marcos made their approach.

"Reggie?"

"Da te da, la te da..."

"Psst! Reggie?"

"Isabel? Isa, my dear!" Reginaldo finally answered, interrupting his song. "What brings you here? How are the plants?" he asked before Isabel could respond. "The poor girl feels obliged to labor hours and hours since I can't help but dehydrate any and every sign of life that appears in that garden," he explained to Marcos.

"But what a surprise," he sighed looking back to Isabel, "you caught me trying out a new..." Finally, Reginaldo registered Marcos' unfamiliar presence. Turning to him again, he asked: "And you are...?"

"Reggie, this is Marcos," Isabel answered. "He works for the government."

"The government..." Reginaldo echoed as he paused to contemplate this new development. "So then, you all received my request for funding to restore these beautiful churches you no doubt noticed on your way into town?" he asked Marcos. "It's our nation's cultural heritage that's at stake, you realize?"

"Sir, that's not exactly why I —"

"Then you're here about the museum I proposed?"

"No, that's not it either..."

"The Special Collections wing for the municipal library?"

"Sorry," Marcos winced, shaking his head.

"I don't understand, then," Reginaldo said, looking to Isabel.

"I intend to explain," Marcos told him, looking around the supermarket before adding: "Is there any way we could step outside to talk?"

"I suppose so," Reginaldo shrugged. "But only for five minutes," he was quick to add. "I'm working, you see."

"I see," Marcos replied sarcastically, glancing down at the broom that had so recently contributed to Reginaldo's song.

The three exited the supermarket and came to rest at a small concrete table, where Marcos was first to break the silence.

"Sir," he began, "are you very familiar with your family his-"

"Piggy Crisp?" Reginaldo interrupted.

"I'm sorry?" Marcos asked, confused.

"Would you care for a Piggy Crisp?" Reginaldo repeated, thrusting in Marcos' face a plastic bag of fried pork rinds he had grabbed from the shelves as he exited the store.

"No thanks, I just ate."

"Suit yourself," Reginaldo shrugged. "You were saying?"

"I was wondering," Marcos continued, picking up where he'd left off, "if you were familiar with your family history."

"On the contrary, I know very little," Reginaldo admitted. "What I do know comes from my mother's side. She's from the town of Leopoldina and moved here shortly after I was born," he explained. "I really don't know anything about my father, since Mother raised me all on her own. In May it will be nine years since she passed away."

"I'm sorry to hear that," Marcos told him. "And her parents?"

"Well, I know that my grandmother was fairly old - for the standards of the time - when she became pregnant with my mother. Mother was an only child, you see."

"Yes, well..."

"Yes," Reginaldo interrupted, obviously enjoying this opportunity to talk about himself. "Mother never spoke much about her family. I suppose she was still pretty hurt due to the... well, due to the separation."

"Separation?" Marcos asked, taking the bait.

"Imagine, the only child, pride of her parent's heart, becoming pregnant out of wedlock."

"I see..."

"But they didn't send her away, no," Reginaldo was quick to add. "Mother left on her own to spare them the shame. And you?"

"Me?" Marcos asked, surprised.

"Sure," Reginaldo confirmed. "What's your story?"

"Hmm, my story..." Marcos repeated, contemplating the question. "I'm also an only child, but Mister Santos," he said, interrupting himself.

"Oh jeez, please," Reginaldo laughed, "no one calls me that. You can call me Reggie."

"Ok then, Reggie, we should probably skip my story for now and get to why I'm here," Marcos suggested.

"I think he's right," Isabel agreed.

"Fine," Reginaldo shrugged. "So, why are you here?"

"I'm here," Marcos began, "because my boss - or the federal government, I guess I should say - has concluded that you are the most likely descendent of the former royal family here in Brazil. Now, I have to warn you," he quickly added, "that I don't have any specific data on me right now since I had to leave São Paulo in a bit of a hurry. I assume, sir - sorry - that you, Reggie, were not previously aware of this?"

"Me... a descendent of the royal family?" Reginaldo asked, confused. "Does this have anything to do with the referendum vote?" he continued after a pause.

"Everything to do with it. The federal government is prepared to declare you the new king of Brazil."

Reginaldo rose from the concrete bench and began to circle the tiny table.

"Isn't it fantastic, Reggie?!" Isabel exclaimed, turning her head to follow his orbit around them.

"How do they know this?" Reginaldo asked Marcos, ignoring Isabel's excitement.

"I don't know exactly," Marcos admitted. "I imagine they researched it a bit in the nation's birth records, the Senator really didn't say." Pulling the small notepad from his shirt pocket, he continued: "He just left me your name, address, and a map of the region."

"Will I have to move to Brasília?" Reginaldo worriedly asked.

"No, to Rio!" Marcos informed him.

"Rio de Janeiro, Reggie!" Isabel cried.

"Rio?" Reginaldo wondered. "Since that was the capital of the former monarchy?"

"That's right," Marcos nodded.

"Will I have to wear a crown?"

"I don't think so."

"Some kind of special clothing?"

"Only if you really want to."

From the door of the supermarket, the manager called out to Reginaldo.

"Coming!" he shouted in response. "I should really get back," he told Marcos. "We can talk about this later. Karaoke tonight at the Apolo?" Reginaldo asked, looking to Isabel.

"Sure," she shrugged.

"How about you?" he wondered, looking next to Marcos.

"How about me what?"

"Can you sing?" Reginaldo asked him. "Actually," he added, without waiting for an answer, "it doesn't matter. Come along with us to the Apolo," he said, throwing a heavy arm across Marcos' shoulders. "Besides the best selection of karaoke tunes in town they make an excellent pork rib plate with a side of whipped potatoes," Reginaldo smiled.

"Pork ribs and whipped potatoes, you don't say..." Marcos grimaced, still too full from his lunch.

"Well, until later then," he nodded to them both, smacking Marcos on the back.

"See ya, Reggie."

"Goodbye," Marcos murmured, slowly recovering from the jovial slap.

As Reginaldo walked back into the supermarket, Marcos and

Isabel looked to each other, both somewhat surprised.

"He seemed to take that pretty calmly," Marcos shrugged.

"I'll say."

Although he would perhaps never admit it to himself or to others, Police Chief Viana believed that the locomotive mechanism of the human leg was somehow intimately related to the proper functioning of the brain. Wasn't it, in fact, integral to his profession? Hadn't millions of officers before him walked their "beats" before patrol cars were used? And so, after exiting the Mayor's office at City Hall, Viana decided to leave his vehicle behind and walk east towards Guanabara Bay in order to better reflect on the recommendations that had just been requested of him. True, he might find himself at a distinct disadvantage if a crime were spotted and a chase to ensue, but not having to deal with Rio's appalling traffic left the Chief free to let his thoughts wander.

And wander, they did, for this new task left him feeling strangely empowered, even slightly intoxicated, as if faced with the dizzying task of erecting an entire city from the ground up. As Viana looked North towards the hills that surround the bay, he did not see the hodge-podge collection of concrete buildings and poorly built houses, but instead imagined a lush green verdure that must have, surely at one time, carpeted the hillside and valleys in between. Viana then began, in his head, to lay out the first network of roads that would cut through the flora, descending into the heart of Rio as the fingers of a river approach the delta. And after this image lingered for a few seconds in his noggin, Viana realized that he was picturing roads of concrete, when surely they had been originally made of cobblestone? Right, cobblestone streets, he corrected himself. Just like those that one finds in any of the old colonial towns farther inland and along the coast. It then occurred to Viana that, instead of faithfully imagining what the city of Rio de Janeiro had looked like in the past, perhaps it would be wiser to spend his energies deciding what the city must in the future become.

That's the problem with history, Viana mused. One can't just start over from scratch, you have to work with what you've got and just make the best of it. So, no matter how much he enjoyed it, Police Chief Viana decided he had better abandon his historical reconstructions for the moment and instead concentrate on bringing the Mayor a recommendation that addressed the city's current predicament. Thus resolved, Viana confidently raised his head and was surprised to find himself already facing the bay.

"How do you feel about pork, Marcos?" Reginaldo asked, peeking over the top of his dinner menu. He and Isabel were seated across the table from their new friend, as the sounds of karaoke singing invaded their conversation.

"I like it all right," Marcos hesitantly replied, unsure as to where the conversation was headed.

"This part of the country is a pork lover's paradise," Reginaldo explained. "We've got crackling, you know, pork skin cooked over an open flame, or even fried; Tutu, which we mix with beans and manioc meal; sarapatel, and of course the Hot Dog, which I'm sure you city folk are already familiar with."

"I'm relatively familiar with all of those, at least by name. Except the sarapatel. Never heard of that one before."

"No?" Reginaldo asked. "Oh, it's quite the delicacy."

"Really?" Marcos laughed.

"Sure. You throw pepper, garlic, onion, and some other odds and ends into a blender and mix well. Meanwhile, you've been boiling the entrails of the pig - primarily the stomach - with salt and lime. Then, you'll want to stuff those first ingredients into the stomach and let it sit overnight in the refrigerator. Now, here's where it gets a little tricky. You're going to bring about two cups of pig's blood to a boil, then mix in your seasoned tripe. And you need to let it simmer over a low flame for five or six hours in order for it to be just right. Then, on a bed of white rice, just fluff and serve!"

By the time Reginaldo finished, Marcos' face had contorted into a most dreadful expression. "I guess delicacy is one way to describe that," he grimaced.

"Oh, our cuisine here in Cruzília, and throughout the state of Minas, is really something to marvel at. Although, I must warn you, it can be a bit fattening," he added, placing a hand over his paunch. Suddenly becoming quite serious, Reginaldo asked: "What's the food like in Rio? Being a coastal town, I imagine they eat lots of fish. I don't really care much for fish," he confessed, turning up his nose.

"They eat a lot of fish," Marcos conceded, "but they also have lots of barbecue houses," he told him, reminding himself to make note later of the town's strange fascination with pork.

"I would imagine the king could request whatever food he likes," Isabel suggested.

"Is that true, Marcos?" Reginaldo asked, losing interest in the menu before him. "Can I request any food I want and they'll make it right there in the palace kitchen? It is a palace I'm going to be living in, yes?"

"Yes," Marcos replied, tiring of so many questions. "You'll be living in a wing of the ancient palace and, sure," he guessed, "I'm sure they'll be glad to whip up whatever dish you like in the kitchen there. How does that sound?" he added, somewhat tersely.

"So good it's almost dangerous," Reginaldo admitted. Then, noticing something over Marcos' head, he smiled: "Ooh, here comes the waiter."

A waiter arrived. This one, however, to deliver a fresh bottle of beer to Flavia and Gustavo who were seated at a small open-air bar in Ipanema.

"So, when's he going to arrive?" Gustavo questioned her.

"Who, the king?" Flavia asked in return, pouring the beer as a cigarette dangled precariously from her lips. "We don't even know who he is. Look," she said, taking the cigarette from her mouth.

"Tomorrow we'll begin our stakeout, set up camp outside the palace and stay glued there night and day."

"Tomorrow?" Gustavo worried. "But tomorrow's Sunday."

"Yeah, so? You religious all of a sudden?"

"No, it's just that I always eat lunch with the family on Sundays, watch a little football, that kind of thing."

"Fine," she agreed, clearly frustrated. "We'll start on Monday."

"So, we're gonna stakeout the palace gates, waiting in the car with binoculars and short-wave radios? Just like private eyes?"

"I don't know, I haven't decided yet," she grumbled. "You own any binoculars?"

"No."

"Yeah, me neither," Flavia reluctantly admitted.

Every February, while the rest of Brazil celebrates Carnival, Senator Antonio Cruz and his wife, Melba, travel to the premier city of Latin America: Miami Beach, Florida. The pre-Lenten mayhem and the oppressive heat of São Paulo are convenient excuses for a trip whose main purpose is to buy the latest fashions for Juliana, an array of household appliances for Melba, and five or six bottles of Chivas Regal whiskey for the Senator, which he purchases just before his departure back to Brazil at the Duty Free Shop inside the Miami International Airport. The Senator has often joked with his wife, saying "Mel" - he calls her Mel - "there's no reason for me to even leave this airport." He's right, by the way, for Miami International is one of the few airports that hosts a very fine hotel inside its terminals. But Antonio Cruz is a respected legislator, and therefore a family man, so while on vacation his family will be seen together. For, while one may successfully escape the heat of a Brazilian summer, you can never completely avoid its press corps.

Now in March, some two or three weeks after Carnival, the Senator emptied the last drops of the first bottle of Chivas Regal into an ice-filled glass for himself and the two friends that have assembled here inside his home. One is a fellow senator, his junior in rank, the other a childhood friend whose profession we might describe as "banker," although the term has become increasingly complicated these days. In silence, the three enjoyed a simultaneous sip from their glasses, their thoughts too preoccupied upon other matters to suggest a toast.

"With all due respect, Antonio," the friend began after swallowing his whiskey, "you tell me not to worry but I can't understand your calm. The opposition isn't likely to disappear from one day to the next."

"Fernando," the Senator sighed in a mildly condescending tone, "when there's no President, there are no allies of the President to cause trouble in the Senate."

"He's right," the other lawmaker added. "Do you believe the government's supporters in the Senate are opposed to banking reform for ideological reasons? They were just repaying favors from the last election. I think we'll be able to fill their leadership vacuum."

"I don't need to believe anything, my friends," the banker laughed. "It's you politicians that have to worry about ideological matters. But, I can assure you that if the reforms aren't passed, banks will fail, citizens will loose their savings and, after a trip to the polls, well-intentioned Senators will have to arrange other means of support."

In another part of the house, a door closed and feminine voices filled the otherwise stuffy air. Shortly afterwards, Juliana entered the room.

"Daddy?" she remarked with surprise. "I thought you'd gone back to Bras'lia."

"Decided to stay another day," he smiled to her, taking her hand and kissing it.

"Good evening, hi," she greeted the other men. "Daddy, Tatiana's gonna spend the night, is that ok? We have to study for exams," she explained.

"That's fine, sweetie."

"Where's Mom?"

"Upstairs, I suppose. Perhaps we can all three sit down for lunch tomorrow before I leave?"

"Of course, Daddy," she agreed, kissing him on the forehead. "Well, good night then. Oh," Juliana remembered as she was leaving the room. "Did Marcos call?"

"No, sweetie, not yet."

"Alright, good night."

After the two girls could be heard climbing the stairs, the men returned to their conversation. "Antonio," the banker said, "I don't mean to sound threatening, but... this is the picture we're looking at."

"I know, I know," the Senator said, dismissing his friend's worries. "We'll see to things."

"You smoke, Reggie?" Marcos asked, exiting the bathroom in Reginaldo's house where he'd seen, abandoned on the windowsill, a pack of cigarettes.

"Huh? Ah, no... just in there," Reginaldo explained. "When I have to... you know," he added, scrunching up his nose. "It masks the -"

"Got it," Marcos said, raising a hand to halt the need for Reginaldo to elaborate. "Let's see," he murmured to himself, laughing and glancing down at his watch. "Ten-thirty. Mind if I use your phone? My mobile's not working out here," he explained.

"Sure. I was about to jump in the shower so take your time."

As Reginaldo headed down the hall, Marcos grabbed the phone and dialed.

"Juliana! Finally," he sighed.

"Oh, love! How are you?" she sighed in return, falling onto her bed as her friend Tatiana read at the desk nearby. "I called that number you left on the machine but someone else answered."

"Yeah, I'm sorry. A woman from this café wouldn't stop talking my ear off."

"So, how's everything going out there? Did you already meet the new king? What's he like?" she excitedly asked.

"Is he cute?" Tatiana yelled from the corner.

"He's... different," Marcos stuttered in response to Juliana's question.

"A total hunk?" Tatiana asked over Juliana's shoulder. "Body of a god, tall and tan, the whole thing?"

The two girls laughed.

"Tatiana wants to know if he's got the body of a god, totally buff and all."

"The body of a god?" Marcos asked. "Buddha, maybe," he suggested, beneath his breath.

"Say what?"

"Nothing. Look, babe, I should be getting into Rio on Monday. I'll call you from there and we can plan your visit for later this month. How does that sound?"

"Fantastic, my little teddy bear. Sweet dreams, ok?"

"Ok, good night."

Marcos hung up the phone and sat for a few minutes on the sofa with his eyes closed when he suddenly noticed a unique smell to the house. Keeping his eyes shut, so as to strengthen his olfactory senses, he tried to decipher the mysterious odor, which was neither pleasant nor unpleasant, merely familiar. Finally, he opened his eyes and cast a glance over a room in which every possible surface area, be it counter-top or table, had proved the perfect candidate for a stack of books. But not your everyday paperback, mind you. These were old books, ancient dusty things that were in most cases falling to pieces. Walking towards the wall of bookcases, Marcos stopped in front of a small coffee table and, with his index finger, gently lifted the front cover of the first of four small, matching volumes. *El Ingenioso Hidalgo Don Quixote de la Mancha* he read, as the cover fell open and broke away from the spine.

"Shit!" he whispered at the same moment the bathroom door opened.

"Unfortunately, Marcos," Reginaldo called from down the tiny hallway, "I don't have a guest room. You're sure the sofa will do?"

"Of course. I'll be fine," Marcos assured him, leaning down to pick the tiny cover up from the floor.

Reginaldo grabbed a pillow and blanket from the linen closet and returned to the sitting room wearing a large white robe. Still drying his hair with a towel, he settled into a chair beside the sofa.

"Whatcha doing?" he asked Marcos, who was now leaning over the book trying to return the front cover as if it were a puzzle piece that would slide neatly back into place.

"I broke your book," the young man apologized.

"Broke my book?" Reginaldo asked. "You've rendered it illegible?" he joked.

"Just the front cover, but it seems pretty old. I hope I haven't ruined its value."

"Let's see," Reginaldo said, getting up and walking towards the scene of the crime. "Oh, the man from La Mancha. No worries, he's seen worse."

"You're sure?"

"Of course. One shouldn't be prohibited from opening a book, no matter its age."

"Quite a collection you've got here," Marcos noted, looking around the house.

"Yes, well, I've been at it for years."

"Where d'you find all these old books?"

"To be morbidly honest, I pick them up when people die," Reginaldo admitted. "The family members don't realize what they're worth and they practically give them away just to tidy up after the poor soul's passed on. Take this four-volume edition of *Don Quixote*, for example. Printed in 1814. Sure it's not in great condition, but I think my dinner that evening cost me more."

"How's your Spanish?" Marcos asked, leafing through the pages after having worked up the courage to handle the book again.

"Non-existent. But that's the great paradox of the bibliophile," Reginaldo explained. "He's hardly read half his collection. He looks at books as more than just the author's words on a page. He sees the humanity in the production of the book itself. That's the problem with paperbacks," he scoffed. "No history, no soul. Just mass-produced like so many Ford automobiles. I prefer the time when each edition told its own fascinating story, above and beyond the one between its pages."

"Interesting," Marcos nodded. "So, you know the story behind all of your books here?"

"Unfortunately, no," Reginaldo sighed. "But what I don't know, I like to imagine. Take this edition of *Candide*, for example," he said, walking towards the bookshelf and pulling down a slender, incased volume of Voltaire's classic. "Count the number of naked women pictured in this edition," he said, pulling the book from its case and handing it to Marcos.

"Naked women?"

"Uh huh. Go ahead," Reginaldo nodded.

"Alright then, let's see. Whoa, there's two already!" Marcos laughed. "Even before the title page. Ok... oh, there's another one at the top of Chapter One. With horns?" he asked, surprised.

"Keep going."

"Here's another one. This one doesn't have horns, but she's

wearing high heels in the middle of a battle scene, which can't be very comfortable," Marcos laughed. "So that's four, right?"

"Yep. Four so far," Reginaldo agreed.

"Here's another already," the young man noted. "Poor thing, she's got some pirate hanging off of her, copping a feel, no doubt. You know," he said, looking up from the book, "I read *Candide* and I don't remember any of this stuff happening. So that's five... Oh, here's number six. And this one's clever," Marcos pointed out. "The artist has some wizard-looking guy with his hands covering up her private parts. Don't know why he chose to cover them now after all the others. Does this one count?" he asked Reginaldo, holding up to him another illustration. "It's just her backside, really, but it is naked," Marcos argued.

"Alright, I guess that's enough —"

"Really?" Marcos asked, somewhat disappointed. "How many more are there?"

"I don't know exactly, but you get the point."

"I do?" the young man wondered.

"Well, you will. So tell me," Reginaldo challenged him. "When was the edition published? You didn't cheat by looking, did you?"

"No, I swear. But how am I supposed to know when it was published? By the binding," Marcos asked, turning the book over in his hands. "How yellow the pages are?"

"Those are possibilities," Reginaldo conceded, "but I think the pictures offer a more reliable answer."

"Oh yeah? How's that?"

"Look at the date. On the other side of the title page."

"1930," Marcos read. "So?"

"So?" Reginaldo echoed. "Look more closely at the naked women."

"Sure," Marcos obliged, turning to one of the illustrations. "What about them?"

"The haircut, the women's style of dress."

"She's naked, Reggie."

"Accessories, I mean," he clarified.

"Ok, the hair... the accessories," Marcos nodded.

"Don't they remind you of the flappers of the 1920s?"

"The flappers?" Marcos wondered.

"The women of the gay twenties? The slicked-back hair, bodies thin as rails."

"Yeah, I see what you mean," Marcos agreed. "The jewelry, the necklaces."

"So the mystery is solved. The text of Voltaire's novel was re-imagined inside a 1920s brain. And here's the result!" Reginaldo announced, holding up another, especially piquant, illustration, this one involving a friar. "A *Candide* born in the year 1930!"

"Yeah, that's neat," Marcos acknowledged, trying, but quite clearly failing, to match Reginaldo's level of excitement.

"Well, quite a day," Reginaldo sighed, changing the subject of conversation.

"Uh huh," the young man nodded.

"I keep imagining how exactly I'm descended from the royal family, uhm... what was their last name?"

"Wasn't it Braganza?"

"That's it... it went something like John Doe the Fifth of the House of Braganza. I should really read up on my ancestors. Yes...," Reginaldo began to speculate, "perhaps my grandmother's mother was married to a man that was the son of the woman that was the daughter of Pedro the Second."

"I don't mean to offend," Marcos warned, "but I think you may descend from a less than legitimate branch of the family tree. The result of a royal indiscretion, shall we say?"

"So I'm the great-great-great grandson of Pedro the First, the infamous womanizer?" Reginaldo joked.

"Probably," Marcos smiled.

"My dear mother, poor thing," the other sighed, shaking his head. "Part of a long tradition of single mothers, as if it were her destiny. It's a shame she's not here, she would get a kick out of this whole thing. What about you, Marcos? You mentioned you're an only child as well."

"Yes, I am. My father's retired. My mother, no. She continues to take care of the house and him," he joked. "The others — cousins, aunts, and uncles — all live in São Paulo. Actually," Marcos corrected himself, "I do have a cousin down in Buenos Aires. She married an Argentine guy," he explained.

"It's always the women that have the courage to leave home," Reginaldo sighed in a somewhat dramatic tone. "Setting out when love calls, or when an early pregnancy demands," he added, before becoming quiet, as if observing a moment of silence. The unexpected interruption in the conversation left Marcos bobbing his head, unsure as to what he should say in response, or if he should even speak at all.

"So, need anything?" Reginaldo finally asked after the pause.

"No, I'm fine."

"Well, then. Until tomorrow."

"Good night," Marcos smiled.

As he turned towards his bedroom, Reginaldo took a slight detour past one of the bookcases and grabbed a volume from the shelf. *American Emperor*, the spine read. Satisfied with his selection, he turned out the living room light and entered his bedroom, leaving the door slightly ajar behind him. Through the sliver of light that remained, Marcos couldn't help but notice Reginaldo's bedtime preparations, as he made his own there on the couch. Luckily for the young man, when Reginaldo dropped his robe he was wearing beneath it a light blue pajama shirt and shorts. But the scare was enough to convince Marcos that he had better close his eyes and rest for the busy days ahead. Lying down, he grabbed his notebook in order to reflect upon the day's events and perhaps add a few more notes. Next to the entry PORK RIBS & "WHIPPED" POTATOES, he remembered to write in parentheses before it (LOTS OF), reflecting the eating habits of the region, which he found quite interesting, if not redundant. And beneath that line, he added: ISABEL, which he traced over several times, even though the first pass of the pen had worked just fine. ISABEL. It was the last thing Marcos saw that night before finally closing his eyes to sleep.

After sliding into bed and pulling the covers snugly up around his chin, Reginaldo opened his book and took a deep breath, inhaling with pleasure the musty smell of its pages. Thus prepared, he began to read: *In the early morning hours of the second day of December, salvos were sent out above the Palace. Salutes boomed in response from the guns of warships and forts along the bay and church bells rang out joyfully. Lights appeared in the houses, as citizens climbed out of bed to watch the sky. Two blazing rockets for a girl, they remembered; three for a boy. They counted. First one, then two, then — after what seemed an interminable pause — a third! A prince was at last born; the future Emperor! His name: Pedro de Alcântara João Carlos Leopoldo Salvador Bibiano Francisco Xavier de Paula Leocadio Miguel Gabriel Raphael Gonzaga of the House of Braganza, but to the citizens of Brazil who welcomed the first monarch to be born in their land, the child was known simply as little Pedro.*

PART TWO

VII

It was well past midnight, but Assemblyman Castro was still unable to sleep. He was anxious and felt that gnawing desire Mrs. Castro had never quite been able to quell. Lifting his torso gradually, so as to avoid any possible creaks from the aging wooden bed frame, he looked across the nightstand to his wife's bed to verify that she was sound asleep.

"Love?" he whispered, but no response came. "Dear," he repeated, slightly louder this time. Still, Mrs. Castro did not stir. So, slowly drawing his legs from beneath the covers, the Assemblyman placed his feet onto the cold hardwood floor, and was soon upright and slinking quietly towards the door. As he passed her bed, Castro again stopped, this time waving his arms in the air to see if she might notice the movement in the room. Nothing.

Negotiating the flight of stairs was an even more painstaking task, but this was not the first time the Assemblyman had performed this somnolent journey from the master bedroom to the slave's quarters. By now he knew full well just which step groaned the loudest and where to place his foot to avoid such protestations and similar treasonous tendencies the house harbored against his enjoyment. Arriving at the bottom floor, the Assemblyman quickened his pace in the direction of the kitchen, reaching the entrance of Clara's tiny room before the swinging door could close behind him. Clara, a name the slave girl's mother had decided upon at birth when she saw for that first time the infant's light complexion that differed so much from her own. Clara, a name at first so lovely, now a painful and ironic reminder of a fate that was all too dark.

"Clara," the Assemblyman whispered through the door. "Clara, open up."

The young girl's blood no longer froze upon hearing that voice, for she had long ago grown accustomed to these late-night interruptions. She rose mechanically from her cot and unhooked the flimsy latch that served as merely an illusion of a barrier between her and the Castro home. Pushing through the door, the Assemblyman entered and immediately wrapped his arm around the slave girl's tiny waist, drawing her closer and placing his mouth firmly to her neck. He rarely kissed her full on the mouth, preferring instead this canine-like investigation of the crevices and folds of her skin. Castro himself was unsure as to which he most savored, the taste of that strange flesh or the smell so different from all the other women he had caressed in his life.

Certainly the smell, he thought to himself as he inhaled deeply the scent that lingered just behind Clara's ear. While the Assemblyman sniffed and slobbered along the length of her neck, Clara felt his left hand slowly pull her thin white gown down over her shoulder and across her right breast, which he then began to knead with the exaggerated force of either lust or anger. Meanwhile, his other hand had begun to lift the hem of her nightdress as he clutched the taut flesh at the cusp where her buttocks met the back of her thigh. Castro would rarely lift her dress immediately, deciding instead to prolong the feeling of anticipation, as if he were gently wooing a reluctant partner.

Clara never resisted, but would instead stare into a distance located somewhere far beyond the walls of her tiny room as her body grew limp. She knew these episodes would not last for more than half an hour. She would soon be able to return to her sleep, after first kneeling over the small wash basin in the corner of the room to wipe away the fluids the Assemblyman always left sticking to her stomach and thighs. With the skirt of her nightdress pulled above her waist and her knees scraping against the stone floor, Clara would straddle the basin and splash the water onto her body, often surprised to find herself wishing the devil would just finish still inside of her, instead of withdrawing early and leaving her feeling like the dirty linen it was her job to wash.

Suddenly, a shot rang out in the night.

"Jesus Christ, what in the hell was that?" the Assemblyman whispered in shock. Clara remained quiet, taking advantage of the interruption to push down the skirt of her nightdress. Seconds later, another shot was heard.

"Dear Lord, are we under siege?" the Assemblyman again cried as he began to button his pajamas.

What else would you call this?, Clara thought to herself, but bit her tongue to stifle the insubordinate response. Then, again, a third shot rang out.

"Oh, for Christ's sake," the Assemblyman grumbled as he reluctantly interrupted his parting caresses. Knowing that his wife would soon come running down the stairs to see about the disturbance, the Assemblyman quickly left Clara's room and hurried across the kitchen towards the parlor. Pushing open the swinging door he came face to face with his wife whose surprise at the sound of gunfire was soon replaced by that of seeing her husband downstairs at such an hour.

"So, dear, you heard the shots as well?" the Assemblyman was quick to ask.

"What are you doing down here?" Mrs. Castro responded as she pushed past her husband and entered the kitchen.

"I... I was feeling hungry," he stuttered, "so I came down for a little nibble."

"I see," his wife mumbled underneath her breath, spotting the slave girl in the doorway at the other end of the room. Without turning her eyes from her mistress, Clara closed the door to her room, fastening the latch behind her.

"And the shots?" the Assemblyman again asked, seeking to divert attention from his wanderings.

"They came from the palace," his wife answered coldly.

"The palace! Is there some sort of disturbance?"

"Of sorts, I suppose. A king has apparently been born."

"A king!" the Assemblyman responded, surprised. "How do you know? Are you sure?"

"For one who works so closely with the Court, you sure are ignorant of its affairs," she scoffed. Mrs. Castro was an avid reader of the city's weekly journals, but the Assemblyman rarely followed such gossip. In his opinion, women read while men discussed, for anything important could never be trusted to the printed page. "The Empress Leopoldina was expected to give birth at any moment," she explained. "The shots are surely a salute to the new sovereign."

"And it's an heir?" the Assemblyman asked his wife.

"Yes, silly, the three salutes confirm it's a boy."

From her bed, Clara could hear the celebration taking place outside in the streets and found herself laughing at the thought of a similar fuss being made upon her arrival in this world, fifteen — or was it sixteen? — years ago. She imagined the mid-wife coaching the mother with her breathing, telling her to push just a little bit harder, then harder still. The patch of hair around the vagina seemed to lift itself up as if awakening from a life-long slumber, as the child's head poked through amid a rush of liquids that had kept it alive for these nine long months. Taking the newborn from the mother's womb, a fellow slave woman severed the umbilical cord and lifted the child triumphantly to the stars as shots and cries filled the night air. A group of ladies had gathered in an intimate circle around the tiny cot, women who had protected the mother as a child inside a different sort of womb. They wiped the infant clean as it passed from bosom to bosom, showering it with kisses and proclaiming that it was surely a gift sent directly from the gods themselves. But, after having passed from the womb, infant slaves didn't always make it back to the comfort of their mother's arms. So when at last this child was returned to her, Clara held it tight and looked down into the eyes that had suddenly stopped crying and now opened wide to take in its surroundings. How many women before her had regretted the act of giving birth, had wished they could protect the child, not a mere nine months, but a lifetime? An immense sadness passed over Clara, for she had never in her life felt so vulnerable. It was one thing to experience the enslavement of your own body, but to expose such a helpless creature to that same fate was quite another nightmare. Only the childless celebrate birth; mothers, however, know the perils.

Clara soon regretted such dire thoughts, for she saw in the boy's face a peace that seemed almost unnatural to her, and certainly unwarranted, but it calmed her nonetheless. The young woman made a vow to always protect the child, but she knew her promise was made without guarantee. For no particular reason, or perhaps to dispel a young mother's foolish worries,

Clara decided she would call this child by a name that had always soothed her ears: Jacob.

VIII

Excerpt from John Henry Stuart, *An Englishman's Travels to the Spanish and Portuguese Settlements of Brazil, the Argentine, and further inlands of the River Plate* (1809).

I believe never shall I again witness a spectacle more absurd than a king and his court passing beneath the limp palms of the Southern tropics. Yet, since the Portuguese crown's recent arrival at its colonial port city of Rio de Janeiro, mine eyes have accustomed themselves to this quotidian scene, such processions being a daily ritual of this roving royalty as it gradually surveys its new home. Either before midday or in the early evening to avoid the stifling heat, the royal family slowly make their way along the yawning arc of Guanabara Bay, rarely venturing into the city's interior, where the streets become more narrow and more filthy, the stench rising up to assault tender European nostrils.

Upon João IV's arrival, the local government and the city's more wealthy residents surrendered their most valued possessions to accommodate the court and its entourage. City dwellings, country homes; all were offered up to the crown as one might offer bread to a weary traveller. Strangely, an edifice once used to contain those accused and convicted of criminal behavior was chosen for His Majesty, and hastily emptied and readied for its royal tenants. Chosen presumably for its size, the structure offers little that might please the eye, conveying instead a rather sober and lifeless air – a mere collection of right angles and flat surfaces. Furthermore, the placement of this newly anointed *Paço Imperial* is unbefitting as well, being entirely too near the bay and its whir of constant commercial transactions and the din of heavy labour. The mundanity of their surroundings has not escaped the royal family, for they seem more concerned than ever to reiterate their magnificence, and therefore insist upon these outings. Little realizing that such excess of ceremony and ornamentation renders the spectacle of their tropical presence ever more absurd.

"See anything?" Gustavo asked. The Tele-Journal cameraman was seated at a small luncheon café along the Rua da Assembléia, eating a sandwich and drinking a beer, while his colleague Flavia stared intently through a brand new pair of binoculars, scanning the various points of entry into Rio's Imperial Palace.

"No, Gus. Not yet," she murmured in response.

Between bites, Gustavo grabbed a limp sheet of paper from the table, obviously a facsimile.

"According to the Senator's press release, the king is from the Minas countryside, a city called Cruzília."

"I know, Gus. I read it already," Flavia coldly responded, still looking through the binoculars.

"Cruzília... Senator Cruz..." Gustavo pondered. "Strange coincidence, don't you think?"

"I thought so too," Flavia admitted, finally lowering the binoculars and looking back at him. "We need to investigate this town of Cruzília, maybe the Senator has some sort of business interest there, a factory or mining —"

"Hold on, I think someone's coming," Gustavo interrupted, noticing something in the distance.

Flavia grabbed the binoculars. "It's them, let's go!" she yelled, bolting from the café. Struggling to pull from her pocket a small tape recorder, she ran towards the building. With considerably less haste, Gustavo finished off what was left of his beer, grabbed the camera and tripod, and followed. Stepping into the street he noticed a stream of other journalists pour forth from the nearby cafés and diners — some with cameras, others holding microphones, one or two with just pads of paper – who also ran towards the palace. All descended simultaneously upon Marcos' car, pushing microphones and recorders into Reginaldo's face so that they seemed to sprout from his chin.

"What is your full name, sir?" a reporter called out.

"What does Your Highness plan to do while..." another interrupted.

"My name is Reggie, and I guess I would like to..."

"His name is Reginaldo Santos of the House of Braganza," Marcos cut in. "We will explain everything to the press in a few days during an organized," he said, stressing the word, "I repeat, an organized press conference that will most likely take place here at the palace. In the meantime, we appreciate your patience. Thank you."

"Your Highness, were you aware that you were the Brazilian heir?" Flavia yelled, but before Reginaldo could respond he was swept inside the building.

Rio's *Paço Imperial*, its formal imperial palace, is located in the downtown *Praça XV*, just blocks from the equally majestic Guanabara Bay. And, while in the past it was home to royalty, it now housed more modest tenants; that is, a revolving collection of contemporary art.

Marcos led the king beneath the portico and up the steps into a lobby that was nearly empty, with only a struggling plant and leather couch as furnishings. Waiting there, lined up, was the palace staff — several workers in starched-white kitchen aprons, two maids and a young woman wearing a backpack.

"Reggie... Your Highness," Marcos corrected himself, "this is your wait staff. They'll be here to help provide your meals, and see that you're comfortable."

Marcos was speaking as if they'd arrived at a hotel, but no

one present could ignore the fact that they were standing in an empty museum lobby. Perhaps sensing this absurdity, the young man quickly pressed on.

"And... you would be the secretary?"

"Uh huh," the young woman with the backpack responded through a mouth full of chewing gum. "I'm Bebel," she added, this time remembering her manners and taking the gum out of her mouth with her left hand as she offered Reginaldo the other for a handshake. "At your service, sir... uh, Your Highness, I mean," she said, returning the gum to her mouth after having dispensed with the formality. The other staff members greeted the king with bows, murmuring "welcome" and "at your service."

"Well, shall we see your new... home?" Marcos suggested to Reginaldo, searching for the correct word.

"Sure," the king shrugged.

"Shall we?" the young man repeated, motioning beyond the lobby, but looking directly at the young woman. "Bebel..."

"Yeah? Oh, right," she started, finally registering her cue, as she led the two men down several corridors to a suite of offices usually reserved for the museum staff.

"My office is in here?" Marcos verified, motioning to one side.

"Yes, and this here is my desk," Bebel proudly announced.

"And this one here is yours, Reggie," Marcos said, pointing to the largest office. Inside, a leather sofa rested against the left wall, and along the back, facing the door, there sat a large desk and matching leather chair. Behind the desk, a window looked out onto a quiet courtyard, safely cloistered from the bustling *Rua 1 de março* beyond.

"So... what do you think?" Marcos expectantly asked.

"It's nice," Reginaldo conceded, "but where will I sleep?"

"Follow me," Bebel said.

Outside, the journalists had begun setting up tiny camps in the *Praça XV* near the palace entrance as they dug in and prepared for future live, breaking news opportunities.

"Did I miss him?" Gustavo asked as he approached his colleague.

"Don't worry," Flavia scoffed. "You didn't miss much." She took from him the tripod and began setting it up.

"So, now what?" Gustavo asked her.

"What do you mean, now what? We're gonna wait it out," she informed him.

"Wait it out? You really think the king's gonna walk out here and start answering questions with all these people here."

"He has to come out sooner or later. And when he does...," she said, smiling as she slammed her fist hard against her palm, "I'll be waiting for 'im."

"Ok...," Gustavo sighed. "Think I'll head back for another beer, then." Placing the camera atop the tripod, he headed off once again towards the tiny café, weaving between reporters as they spoke into television cameras, announcing the arrival of the king.

UPSTAIRS, INSIDE THE re-anointed palace, Marcos passed from room to room as Reginaldo followed close behind.

"This room will serve as the living room," he announced as Reginaldo plopped down upon a sofa to test its spring and resistance.

"And this one as your bedroom," Marcos continued. Reginaldo carried out the same experiment on the bed, this time lying completely back.

"Very comfortable, Marcos," he said, staring up at the ceiling.

"And through here is the dining room," Marcos said, exiting the bedroom. Hearing the words "dining room," Reginaldo jumped up and followed quickly behind.

"The dining room?" he verified.

"Uh huh. Through this door here," Marcos pointed.

"The kitchen, Marcos," Reginaldo said with exaggerated solemnity. "When can we see the kitchen?"

Returning to the first floor, the two pushed through two large swinging doors into a tiny kitchen where the staff was busily washing the dishes and counters. Having served, for the last one hundred years, mere ceremonial purposes – museum receptions, mostly – the tiny alcove seemed ill-equipped to provide for the appetite of a king - especially this new one.

"Hello, once again," Marcos greeted the workers.

"Which one's the cook?" Reginaldo whispered to Marcos.

"It's me, sir," a young man responded, stepping forward. "At your service," he bowed.

Reginaldo approached the chef and shook his hand. "It's truly a pleasure," he smiled to the young man. "What is your name?"

"Felipe, sir."

"A pleasure indeed, Felipe. Felipe... is that French?"

"I believe so, sir."

"Please, Felipe, you can call me Reggie. Are you, or either your parents, French?"

"No Reggie sir, we're Brazilian. From the Northeast."

"Interesting," Reginaldo murmured. "How's the food in the Northeast? Lots of fish?"

"A fair amount of fish, Reggie sir."

"I don't care much for fish," Reginaldo explained to the young man. "You know, I'm also in the food service business and -"

"Your Highness," Marcos interrupted, "we really should get going and let the staff finish preparing dinner."

"Oh, of course. Well, see you soon, Felipe. I'd still like to chat with you about your culinary influences, maybe we could even trade recipes sometime."

"It would be a pleasure, sir," the cook nodded.

When the two finally returned to the office designated as the king's, Reginaldo fell into the bucket seat of the leather chair and swiveled around to look out onto the courtyard. Marcos exited and was soon back with a crown in his left hand, some papers in the other.

"Look here, Reggie," Marcos announced with the excitement of a child. "Your crown! Well, actually it's just a model the museum had in a back room."

"Is the real one going to be this big?" Reginaldo asked, taking it in his hands and turning it around.

"I'm not sure."

"Marcos," Reginaldo said, already losing interest in the crown and placing it off to the side. "Where are you going to stay? Here with me?" he suggested.

"I still don't know. But I'm glad you mentioned it because I need to run speak with a woman about an apartment for rent in Ipanema."

"You could always stay here if you like."

"Thanks, Reggie. We'll see... I still don't know how long I'll have to be in Rio."

"You're going to leave?" Reginaldo worriedly asked.

"Maybe," Marcos admitted. "Don't worry. Soon you'll be settled in and on your own and you won't even need me anymore."

"I wouldn't say that," Reginaldo frowned.

"Here, let's get a look at you as king," Marcos said, taking the crown in his hands and placing it upon Reginaldo's head. "It's perfect," he chuckled.

"Then why are you laughing?"

"I don't know," he shrugged. "I've never seen anyone wearing a crown up close like this. Except during Carnival."

"It's not very comfortable, in case you were wondering," Reginaldo informed him as he wriggled beneath the crown's weight.

"It doesn't look too comfortable," the other admitted.

"How do other kings stand it?"

"I don't think they wear them around much these days," Marcos guessed.

"Does that mean I won't have to either?" the king asked.

"I guess not."

"Marcos, will the museum remain closed?"

"I think so, otherwise it would disturb you too much."

"That doesn't seem fair. Seems like I'm the one disturbing things."

"There was some talk of putting you up at the Copacabana Palace, you know, the famous hotel."

"That sounds fine."

"Well, the Senator decided it would seem too much like a joke, which is something we've got to avoid with this whole king business."

"I'm sure some would find putting a king in a museum rather poignant as well," Reginaldo laughed. "Which is not to say I'm ungrateful. What are those papers?" he asked, noticing the packet of documents at Marcos' side.

"Ah yes, let's see... hmm... some documents the Senator sent over." A smile spread across his face as he read: "Daily Tasks of His Royal Highness?"

"Say what?"

"Looks like an old list of daily activities for King Pedro the Second," Marcos explained. Affecting an official tone of voice, he began to read: "His Imperial Majesty should regularly wake at 7 o'clock and, after having done His *toilette*, should kneel while giving grace to God in prayer."

The two exchanged a look of doubt.

"At 8 o'clock," Marcos continued, "His Majesty shall partake of a small lunch in the presence of a physician, who shall examine His food to insure that it is savory and that it contains sufficient protein..."

"Ooh, how nice," Reginaldo reflected.

"...And to prevent His Majesty from eating too much."

"Ouch, now that will be difficult. What else?"

"Let's see... blah, blah, blah... Hmm," the young man stopped.

"What is it?" Reginaldo wondered.

"It remains forbidden," Marcos started reading again, "for any servant to converse with the Emperor, unless otherwise summoned. Further, it remains forbidden for any Negro to dally in His Majesty's quarters, requiring instead that each should enter strictly upon unavoidable occasions."

The two men paused.

"Well," Marcos said, finally breaking the silence, "I really should go see that lady about the apartment. You'll be okay here by yourself?"

"I'm not a child, Marcos. I can chat with Bebel a bit, stroll through the exhibits. Fulfill my daily tasks," Reginaldo added, picking up the papers left on his desk.

"Ok, well, I won't be long," Marcos assured him with a slight wave goodbye. "Oh," he added, stopping at the door. "It's probably best to stay inside for a while. At least until I get back. You know, to avoid the crowds outside."

"Sure," the king nodded.

When Marcos had gone, Reginaldo grabbed the crown and put it back on his head.

"I suppose one could get used to the feel of it," he pondered aloud.

It then occurred to him that this was the first time he'd been truly alone since finding out he was king. He'd hardly had time to digest the news when, already, here he was in the city of Rio de Janeiro, inside the former royal palace receiving instructions designed to ensure the safety and comfort of a king. And, to – literally - top it all off, he was wearing a crown! Yet, as he swiveled one hundred and eighty degrees in his chair to gaze out the window, his thoughts kept wandering back to Cruzília. Thanks to Isabel, his home and garden would be well cared for, but what about things at the supermarket? Would the other staff know what products went where and the logic behind their placement? Ideally, Reginaldo believed, one should be able to walk into any supermarket on this great big earth and know exactly where the item you're looking for should be. There were two schools of thought, really. First, there were those who arranged products according to their end use, placing, for example, the snack chips with the sodas since, after all, the two will most likely be consumed in concert. Then there were those more analytical types that arranged items according to composition and location in the nutritional pyramid. Reginaldo proudly belonged to the latter. To which school of thought did his *Mercado da Serra* colleagues subscribe? It suddenly occurred to Reginaldo that he had forgotten to ask.

"Oh, dear," he worried aloud.

If an aide were to enter at this moment to seek the king's council, he or she would only see, over the back of the seat, the top of Reginaldo's head with the crown resting there, quite crooked, amongst these thoughts of home.

IX

Excerpt from Sir William Taylor's *A Life in Brazil* (1819)

The timid traveller may begin to feel quite anxious in this city, for Rio de Janeiro seems to never sit still, each and all caught in a constant state of motion. Even those establishments that one would expect to find settled, such as markets and commercial stalls, ambulate continuously about the streets in search of buyers. Furthermore, many stationary vendors are not quite stable, for they erect their façades at a different corner each new day, Therefore, when out to purchase meats, vegetables, or fruits, one cannot rely on the past, but is rather obliged to tour the city until he happens upon the appropriate stall.

Currently there reside in Rio de Janeiro nearly 40,000 inhabitants, which I have here divided into the following classes:

1000 members of the Court

1000 employed in public offices

1000 who draw support from lands or maritime commerce

700 priests

500 lawyers

200 medical men

40 established merchants

2000 informal retailers

4000 clerks, apprentices, and commercial servants

1250 mechanics

100 vintners

300 fishermen

1000 soldiers

1000 sailors

1000 free Negroes

12000 slaves

4000 female heads of household (widows)

This city, while charming, was but so recently little more than a colonial port and its narrow streets seem ill-fashioned to contain such a growing, and itinerant, population. The deleterious results can already be observed, for waste, an unavoidable consequence of all society, courses publicly through a shallow trench down the center of the street.

To conclude today's entry, I will add that I find this colony of Brazil one of the most truly curious of the New World, as if the Portuguese have taken advantage of their exile to create their own Paris in the tropics. Here in the capital, many of the weekly newspapers are published in French; plays are performed in French; romances, poetry, all published in French by the recently created Portuguese Royal Printing Press. The monarchy seem to have forgotten that it was a Frenchman who forced it here in the first place.

I do not find such genuflection surprising, however, for this society is generally disposed towards imitation - to a degree where they ignore their own true delicacies. One in particular that comes to mind is a bean stew, which the people call fejoata, I believe. Quite possibly it is the addition of tripe and other remaining bits of swine they find unpleasant, but the fact that it is a food of the African slave undoubtedly adds to their distaste. This is a shame, for we foreigners take less scruple in maintaining appearances and many among us have sneaked a taste and it is truly quite delightful!

"Flavia?" Gustavo whispered, staring up into the early morning sky as the two lie inside sleeping bags across the street from the museum – or palace, rather.

"Yeah?" she replied.

"You awake?"

"I just responded to your question, didn't I?"

"Who'd you vote for? Did you vote for the king?" Gustavo asked.

"We weren't voting for the king," Flavia corrected him, "we were deciding on a form of government. And, no, I didn't."

"No? What'd you vote for?"

"I voted null," she confessed.

"Null? But why? Why not vote for an actual choice?"

"What's the point, Gus? You think it really makes a difference whether we get this guy or any other from an array of idiots that are slimy enough to get the nomination?"

"I guess not. I'm just a little surprised. I had you pegged as the civic-minded type."

"King, president, prime minister... they're synonyms, Gus, for leech. If only it were just your blood they were after," Flavia laughed to herself. "What was that?" she suddenly said, lifting her head.

"I didn't hear anything."

"Could be somebody leaving the palace."

"At this hour?" Gustavo asked, lifting his arm and glancing up at the wristwatch that told him it was just before six-thirty. "Probably wait staff. I'm gonna grab some breakfast, you want anything?"

"No, I'm fine. Hurry back, though. You never know when they might try to leave."

"Gotcha."

Reginaldo Santos didn't know much about his ancestors, perhaps they were royalty just like the government said. Either way, he thought, one thing is certain: somewhere up in the family tree there's a farmer. Strange occupation for a royal, sure, but it was the only way of explaining his life-long habit of waking up just as the first rays of sunlight topped the horizon. The early morning hours were precious to him, the most productive of the day, although he consumed rather than produce, spending a majority of this time planted in his favorite chair reading and enjoying several consecutive cups of thick black coffee. But he awoke this morning hundreds of miles away from his beloved books, and the kitchen staff brewed what was more like tea than real coffee. So, he made up his mind to go in search of both.

The coffee he found immediately. It wasn't difficult, for, after all, this is Brazil. But back at the palace they insisted on serving an imported American brand of java, believing that a monarch should cultivate more worldly tastes. If they only knew that, meanwhile, the rest of the world was spending millions on the Brazilian coffee the palace judged inadequate. Here at this tiny coffee stand they didn't spend millions, but they did offer the strong domestic brew that Reginaldo loved. The only problem was that they served it in these tiny little plastic cups that barely fit between the thumb and index finger. Reginaldo pondered this situation carefully before finally deciding what was to blame.

"The heat?" Gustavo asked.

"Sure, think about it," Reginaldo said, pleading his case to this jury of one. "Who could stand to drink a full-sized mug of coffee in this sweltering heat? Where I'm from this is hardly a problem, we can drink coffee like normal people, but here in the tropics one must resort to taking theirs in a thimble," he laughed.

"Guess I never thought about it that way."

After throwing back five or six thimbles of this dark, sweet coffee - an amount which didn't fail to catch the eye of the old man behind the counter - Reginaldo decided he'd best be on his way before the day's heat and humidity set in.

"Well, it's been a pleasure," Reginaldo told his interlocutor.

"Same here," Gustavo said. The young man had meant to ask the stranger where he was from, but now the portly fellow was already turning to leave. Probably from Portugal, Gustavo guessed, due to the comment about the tropics and the accent that was strange, yet familiar.

As Reginaldo turned his attention to fulfilling his second mission – the desire to leaf through a book or two – he realized that he had left the palace without a city map. Rio de Janeiro was a mighty big place to navigate without some sense of direction, and with all these hills it was easy to get yourself turned around and confused. As Reginaldo pondered his options, a municipal bus came barreling down the street and, as if steered by the hands of fate, came to a stop just inches from his feet as its double doors swung briskly open. Reginaldo was about to ask the driver a question when a surge of passengers came towards the exit, obliging him to step back and to the side. Once the exodus had abated, he stepped back into the doorway and asked: "Where you headed?"

"Back into downtown," the driver sighed impatiently.

"Could you tell me if there's a library back that way?" Reginaldo asked the man.

"Mighty big library," the driver confirmed. "But you don't need me to get there. It's just a couple of blocks that way," he added with a jerk of his head. Corner of *Rio Branco* and ... well, near Floriano Square."

"Oh, thanks! You see I'm new in town and -" Reginaldo paused, seeing the less-than-riveted look in the man's expression. "I'm sorry," the king apologized. "You probably have places to be, people to pick up. Well, thanks again."

Walking into the heart of downtown, Reginaldo could witness up-close, as never before in his life, a mass of traffic that alternated between racing headlong to who-knows-where, and prolonged moments of a slow, viscous slog. Modern buildings towered above older, more ornate, structures, although both generations seemingly destined to the same decay. And, finally, the king pondered a hurried populace that moved back and forth amongst it all. Most prominent among this mass was a tireless army of street vendors who lined the sidewalks, hocking an infinite array of miniscule knick-knacks manufactured in neighboring Paraguay and far-away China: watches, flashlights, radios, cassette players, videogames, glow-in-the-dark jewelry - batteries never included, but don't panic, they sell those, too - sunglasses, umbrellas, sandals, paper-thin tank-top T-shirts that read Copacabana across the front, beach towels, sarongs, and football jerseys of city, state, and national teams. The realization that Cruzília had none of these things was really quite pleasing. Suddenly, those old colonial churches Reginaldo had always complained about didn't seem in such bad shape, after all. Maybe the municipal library was big enough already without that Special Collections wing. And, really, building a big fancy museum along the plaza might attract too many tourists and quickly clog Cruzília's narrow little streets.

When Reginaldo finally reached the *Praça Floriano* he found himself at the center of that mass, caught in a vortex of darting businesspersons and other fast-moving pedestrians. To escape, he headed towards the first place that caught his eye: an historic building, quite possibly a museum for the entrance was lined with banners announcing a visiting exhibit of some sort. Unlike his new home, this place was fully functional, and the signs seemed to advertise a less contemporary collection that was more to his taste. Reginaldo could not believe his luck when he realized that the exhibit was showcasing a series of paintings from the nineteenth century, specifically the years of the Braganza monarchy.

Did they know I was coming? he wondered to himself, for the coincidence really was difficult to believe. But, then again, he argued, with the historic change in government, an exhibit of this nature made perfect sense. Once inside the *Museu Nacional de Belas Artes*, Reginaldo approached the front desk for information.

"Hi, I understand there's an exhibit of paintings from the uh...," he stuttered. "From when there was a king."

"The Imperial Period?" the employee smiled.

"Uh huh."

"'The first one' I guess we have to say, now. If at first you don't succeed, try try again," the employee laughed.

Reginaldo stared back blankly.

"Down this corridor to your right," she finally said, pointing. "Just follow the signs."

Reginaldo did just as she said, following the signs and a red velvet rope to a wing of the museum that was divided into several large rooms where carefully spaced paintings lined the walls. After browsing through several of them, he paused before a large portrait of a young boy dressed in military uniform.

"Now, who could this youngster be?" he wondered aloud.

A beautiful gold medallion was fastened snugly at the boy's neck, overlapping a blue sash that ran diagonally across his chest. One hand rested firmly upon a cutlass, while the other was entwined in the weave of his belt. In the background one could just discern the outlines of a throne and an insignia thereupon that read "P II."

"Pedro the Second," Reginaldo guessed.

Reginaldo continued to move about the room, lost in... well, admiration would be too strong of a word to use, for what he felt more closely resembled simple appreciation, the realization that this business of a king down here in the tropics was really quite novel, never mind the fact that he was said king. He stopped before a painting that drove the point home, for would such an absurdity, he thought, ever been possible if Rio de Janeiro had not hosted a wayward monarchy? The scene was a perfect mixture of savagery and civilization, which some have claimed captures this country quite well. In the work, the emperor sits upon his throne beneath a concrete dome as trumpeters herald the young nation's independence. Along the horizon behind him, a magnificent chain of mountains hovers above fields of lush vegetation. His Royal Highness is not alone among the palms, for an army of soldiers, citizens, and slaves clamor restlessly at his feet. Native American warriors also kneel at the steps to this mighty throne, joining an infantry that surrounds the platform on all but one side, an area left open so that the waves of the Atlantic Ocean may lap gently against its steps. To the left, a boat loaded with coffee and sugarcane has drifted ashore, while a cornucopia spills the fruits of this land at the monarch's feet.

A black mother and child can also be seen, displaying a loyalty that rivals that of the soldiers. The woman wields an axe in one hand with a rifle in the other, which she rests upon her shoulder. Even the tiny child at her feet has joined the spectacle, carrying a sickle nearly his same size, which could easily become an equally, or even more, imposing weapon than those the soldiers carry. In fact, this assembled mass seems so agitated and well-armed that is quite easy to interpret this scene from an entirely different perspective. That is, to imagine that, instead of celebrating the monarchy, they have come to forcefully remove it from their shores. But one shouldn't read too much into these things, Reginaldo cautioned himself. After all, it's only a painting, not real life.

Carta Régia, 08 de março de 1993, Rio de Janeiro

Dear Isabel,

Have you ever noticed on a map how the city of Rio de Janeiro hangs there crooked from the coast, fooling its inhabitants who, while believing they're traveling East, are actually heading South, and when traveling South are actually turning back West into the heart of Brazil? How can one trust a city that won't even tell you just where you're going? Even with their maps and compasses, the city was still able to fool the interminable stream of travelers that so often sought safe harbor in its bay. These foreigners believed they had stumbled upon an earthly paradise sculpted by Mother Nature herself – and one sculpted with pleasure and even abandon, as She combined every shape and form imaginable to create its landscape of mountains and rivers.

The only sensible conclusion I can draw from the disparity between their impressions and mine is that these explorers had the pleasure of approaching Rio by sea, while Marcos and I were unfortunately forced to approach the place over land, from the Northwest corner to be exact, passing through such an infinite array of slums that they cannot be measured by distance, but instead by time, for we must have driven hours before I saw a house with a garden, or a child with shoes. You must be wondering why such surprise when a child without shoes is so common back in Cruzília. At home we have good earth for them to walk upon while in the outskirts of this city it is different. Here they run and play atop a jagged layer of discarded appliance parts and a dusting of trash that rustles like fallen leaves whenever a strong wind works up the courage to enter and flush out the streets. And, speaking of children, we must have arrived in the midst of an academic holiday for here in the city I have never in my life seen so many young ones out on the street during school hours. In fact, now that I think about it, their absence could be school-related for perhaps the money they earn selling bubblegum and candy is destined to cover the expenses of some extra-curricular activity, their class' production of Macbeth, *or* Henry IV *for example. I now feel sad at having, just minutes ago, refused to purchase some sweets from an adorable, if not a bit pushy, young boy. "I'll take a dollar's worth," I'll reply the next time I happen to see one of these roving, entrepreneurially-minded thespians again.*

Yours Truly,

Reggie

LEAVING THE MUSEUM, Reginaldo sauntered across the crowded plaza towards another, equally imposing, historic building: the National Library. As he lifted his foot to place it on the first of twenty-odd steps leading to the entrance, Reginaldo noticed a street vendor stationed some thirty meters away and decided he could use a snack before setting about his studies.

"Can I get a hot dog?" Reginaldo asked, approaching the man while digging a few bills from his pocket.

"Sorry, Cap'ain, all I got's sandwiches," the man replied.

"Really?"

"'Fraid so."

"I'll take a turkey sandwich, then," Reginaldo sighed. "If you have it, that is."

"Turkey sandwich coming right up!" the vendor confirmed.

"You don't like hot dogs?" Reginaldo asked, taking his pre-wrapped sandwich from the man.

"Ain't a question of like, Cap'ain, just a law of economics," the vendor replied. "Cost a lot of money to keep them dogs warm all day, like the customers like 'em."

"Right," Reginaldo agreed.

"So, how 'bout something to drink?"

"Lemonade?" Reginaldo mumbled with his mouth full.

"Well now I don't got lemonade," the man apologized, "but how 'bout a Shangoh?"

"A what?"

"Shangoh," he repeated. "It's what all the kids ask for these days. Gives you energy, I hear."

"Is it cold?"

"Is it cold?" the man laughed. "Now cold I can do. Is it cold," the vendor chuckled again to himself. "Much easier to keep something cold, thanks to styra foam. Take beer for instance."

"No thanks," the king interrupted.

"What's that?"

"I don't drink beer."

"No, I mean take beer as an example of styra foam's keeping something cold," the vendor explained.

"Oh, I see."

"Bottle of beer can sit in the sun for hours out there on the beach and still be cool - as long as you've got it inside the styra foam. But try to keep a dog warm even in this heat... impossible," the man sighed.

"Interesting," the king nodded.

"Trust me, if I could invent some material to keep things as warm as I can cold, I'd be a millionaire. Lot more money in hot foods, that's for sure, Cap'ain."

"Name's Reggie," the king said, taking his drink.

"Well, hello there Cap'ain Reggie," the man replied as he extended his arm for a handshake. "Oh, sorry," he apologized, seeing that Reginaldo no longer had a free hand to offer in return. "Folks call me Jefferson."

"Have you been vending for long, Jefferson?"

"Been almost ten years."

"Wow, ten years!" Reginaldo repeated between bites.

"Yep, ten years and they's still hounding me," Jefferson complained as he stepped back into the shade of a statue honoring composer Carlos Gomes. Removing his cap, he slowly wiped the sweat from his brow.

"Hounding you?" Reginaldo asked, surprised. "Who?"

"Cops, of course," Jefferson sighed, shaking his head. "Things been fine for a long time and now they come round telling us we gotta clear the streets, that we're blocking traffic, junking up the place. All because of some king," he added.

"King?" Reginaldo asked.

"Yep. I guess you heard we gotta king now, right?"

"Uh huh," Reginaldo mumbled.

"Can't keep a President round for two weeks before he go dying on us or stealing our money," Jefferson laughed, "so now they gonna give a king a try, like a king somehow diff'rent."

"Right," Reginaldo agreed.

"Well, don't let my yappin' make the Cap'ain late for work," Jefferson said, motioning towards the library.

"Late for work?" Reginaldo wondered, following Jefferson's

movement. "Right, the library. I guess I'd best be off. It was a pleasure, Jefferson."

"Pleasure's all mine," the vendor nodded before wiping his brow again and replacing his cap.

As he entered the National Library, Reginaldo was stopped in his tracks by the enormity and magnificence of the place. "Holy Jesus Mary and Joseph," he thought to himself before quickly seeking the Lord's forgiveness for the blasphemy. The heavenly father would have to let it slide this one time, for Reginaldo had never seen such a setting designed solely for books, those who love books, and the well-being of both. Long tables equipped with individual lamps under which to read, several couches and chairs put together to form a sort of reader's nook off to the side. It was as close to paradise as he had ever been. And the smell... the aroma of so many yellowed pages, which for him might as well have been petals of the most rare flower.

Once again, members of the Braganza dynasty had appeared to welcome their heir. There at the doorway stood statues of Pedro one and two, the father in marble, the son made of plaster. Reginaldo was unaware as to whether or not the selection of material was meant to convey some sort of political and historical commentary on the toughness of each emperor. Either way, they both loomed magnificently over this bastion that protected within its walls the treasures of both Portuguese and Brazilian culture. It was old Dom João who, as he fled from Napoleon, had prescience enough to take with him Portugal's *Real Bibliotheca d'Ajuda*. The collection lived up to its name, for it helped out considerably by planting the seed that would eventually, with the help of private donors, become Brazil's National Library. Dom João was generous, but the man was no fool. So when Brazil declared its independence from Portugal, the king made sure that the new country would appreciate the treasures he had given her by charging a handsome sum for the privilege of storing his books. And what books they were: first editions from Venice, Milan, Rome, Amsterdam, Nuremberg, Paris, Madrid, and, of course, Lisbon; Fust and Schoeffer's Latin Bible, printed in 1462 on parchment in two large volumes; a 1797 edition of Cervantes'

Don Quixote, one of only seven copies; Holy Bibles in Spanish, Hebrew, Latin and Greek; a 1572, first edition, of Camões' *Os Lusíadas*, and other maps, Jesuit manuscripts, original drawings and coins.

Having finally taken it all in, Reginaldo got his wits about him and headed for the Information Desk to meet the Beatrice that would be his guide, the Ariadne that would lead him through this labyrinth. On his way, the king suddenly realized that he saw no books upon the shelves, nor any shelves for that matter.

"Good morning," he said cheerily to the young woman behind the counter.

"Good morning, sir," Milena replied.

"You wouldn't happen to know where all the books are, would you?"

"We store them away from the public for their own safety – the safety of the books, that is."

"I see," Reginaldo smiled.

"But all you need to do is find the call number in the catalog and I can retrieve the titles for you," she explained. "What were you looking for, exactly?"

"Oh, History books I suppose."

"Eastern, Western, or World History?"

"Wow, uh... the Americas, ours."

"Brazilian history?" she asked.

"Yes. I've just come from across the way," the king pointed, glancing back towards the museum. "Have anything on the monarchy?"

"Lots. How about I bring out a few of the best introductory materials for starters?"

"That sounds great."

Soon thereafter, his arms piled high with books, Reginaldo

made his way to a far corner section of the mammoth library and took a seat at one of the tables. After stacking the books neatly in front of him, the letters on the spine still legible, he removed from his pocket the last bit of sandwich and resumed his lunch, making sure that no one was looking before each bite. The titles alone were enough to fascinate him: *The American Emperor, The Emperor's Beard, An Empire in Sandals, A King in the Tropics, Amazon Throne, Tropical Versailles*. How could he have ever guessed that the court's relocation to Rio - one seemingly arbitrary historical act, a simple change of address - would generate so much interest and leave behind a paper trail so long? Historians are a funny lot, Reginaldo laughed to himself. Finishing his sandwich, Reginaldo licked his fingers clean and grabbed a book from the stack. At last, his second mission of the day now completed, the king began to read.

X

THE GOVERNESS KNELT down to bring the nine year old's face gently into her hands, but stopped just short of such tenderness, as all adults did, and instead ceremoniously bowed before the tiny monarch.

"Pedro," the Regent began, "this is Dona Mariana, your new governess."

Mr. Vieira had interrupted the play of little Pedro and his sisters, Januaria and Francisca, to introduce this middle-aged woman now entrusted with their upbringing. Barely a week had passed since Pedro the First left the palace in the early morning hours, sending from his ship a letter explaining to the young children that he and their stepmother must set sail immediately for Portugal. With merely a farewell peck on the cheek as they slept, the king left behind these little ones still dressed in mourning black from the death of their mother; an attire all too appropriate, coincidentally, for neither would they again see their father alive.

As usual, through death and desertion, the children carried on with their studies. Januaria read quietly, while Francisca examined a globe that she spun around quite recklessly, stopping its motion with her index finger as she pointed to the myriad islands that formed the Portuguese Empire. And little Pedro, now the Emperor of one of its larger slices – Brazil - was busy tracing the letters of the title he had inherited overnight from his father; *Your Royal Highness, Your Royal Highness, Your Royal Highness, Pedro* the paper in front of him monotonously read.

It wasn't the boy's sallow complexion that caused the governess' initial reluctance, but rather the formality she knew must always be observed in his presence. Still, while the princesses seemed healthy enough, in Dona Mariana's estimation, the emperor's sickly countenance did remind her of the dubious lineage that branched out behind these children; one that, perhaps, did not branch out widely enough. Was this stagnant gene pool, a commonplace in so many royal families, to blame for the history of melancholy and insanity that plagued the House of Braganza?

Surely it wouldn't help matters, the governess thought to herself, but she prayed the more violent fits would not appear until after her service was completed.

"Besides looking after you and the princesses," the Regent told the emperor, "Dona Mariana will be your instructor for French and the piano."

"Oh, he looks just like his mother, God rest her soul," the governess commented in regard to Pedro.

"I hope that means he'll take after her and not his father," Vieira chuckled to himself. "The father was too difficult to keep up with, especially between the hours of -"

"Say no more, sir, please... the children," Dona Mariana whispered to Vieira, cutting short his barb.

Poor child, it was the truth; your father was a handful. Leopoldina was a saint for having put up with him for as long as she did. In the end, they claimed she died of influenza, but many suspected that she had actually died of loneliness. And, by all appearances, it was solitude she had bequeathed to her children.

"Well, Pedro, young ladies, Dona Mariana. I'll leave you four alone to get acquainted," Vieira told them. "Remember, the tutor arrives in half an hour," he added, glancing down at his timepiece.

"Thank you, Mr. Vieira, we shan't miss his appointment," Dona Mariana assured the Regent as he left the room. "Well now," the governess cheerily exhaled, clasping her hands behind her back and leaning in closer towards the children. "Where should we begin?"

"WITH THE DECLARATION of Independence," Pedro answered, seated behind a tiny desk.

"Very well," the tutor agreed as he paced back and forth collecting his thoughts. The professor was still a young man, but already a rather humorless pedant, and he showed little patience with this, his most prestigious, student. It was true that little Pedro struggled in the areas of Natural Science and Law, but History was a subject they both visibly enjoyed.

"Your father was in the state of São Paulo when the mail arrived from Portugal," the tutor finally began, becoming quite serious. "Court officers carried the papers over hill and dale from Rio and found the emperor on a deserted country trail beside the River Ipiranga."

"They took the mail to him all the way out to São Paulo?" little Pedro interrupted.

"Well, they wouldn't have usually done it, but the news was especially important," the tutor explained. "May I continue?" he asked, after little Pedro had paused to contemplate his response.

"How did they know it was so important?"

"How did who know?"

"The letter carrier. Did he open it?"

"No, a courier would not open royal correspondence."

"Then how did he know it was so important that he'd have to go all the way out to São Paulo?" the boy pressed on.

"Any and all correspondence from the king's father would have been sufficiently important to trouble a mere mail courier," the tutor scoffed. "Can we go on?"

"Fine," the boy agreed.

"He was on horseback," the tutor continued, reciting a story whose wording rarely varied, "accompanied by a regiment of his bravest men when they hailed the leader and handed him the packet of mail. Along with more orders, insults, and repressive laws, there contained also an ultimatum: a new government had been appointed for Brazil. Pedro the First would have to return to Lisbon within thirty days. Disgusted, your father spit upon the paper in his hands, before crumbling the letter and throwing it aside. Then, he ripped the Portuguese insignia from his uniform, unsheathed his sword and spurred his steed forward up a nearby hill. Reaching the top, the king's horse reared as he turned to face his followers, and waving his sword defiantly in the air he shouted: 'Independence or death.' 'Independence or death', the officers quickly responded, knowing in their hearts that they were now forever separated from Portugal, even if it meant war and bloodshed."

Little Pedro peeked his head into the main hallway, looking left and then right to verify that the path to the servant's entrance was clear. All was indeed quiet, but he held his breath all the same as he tip-toed through the halls, deciding that the cessation of all possible bodily functions would improve his hearing in case someone were to take a step, open a door, or call his name. Ducking out a side door and stepping onto the lawn, Pedro took a deep breath knowing he was safe, but did not slacken his pace. Seconds later, he burst through the rickety door of the servant's cabin, out of breath once again.

"Pedrinho?" the man inside asked, surprised.

"Hide me, Rafa," Pedro panted, peeking back from whence he

came through a crack in the door. The emperor had reached the cabin of Rafael, a former soldier and slave who had served beside the king, little Pedro's father. In exchange for his military service, Rafael had been freed from both slavery and further combat, and given a home on the grounds behind the royal family's residence in the district of São Cristóvão, where he served as a sentry.

"Hide you?" Rafael asked the boy. "From who?"

"From that awful lady."

"Now what lady's that?"

"The governess," Pedro explained.

"Oh, I see," Rafael sighed, "the new gove'ness. Is she that bad?"

"As bad as all the others, I guess, with her stupid French and piano lessons," the boy complained, leaving his post at the door, and coming towards Rafael.

"Right, French lessons again."

"It's so stupid, we live in Brazil," Pedro argued. "Why do I have to know French?"

"Ceremonies, I s'ppose," the old man shrugged.

"I'm sick of ceremonies," the emperor whined. "Every day there's a trip through town, and every night we have dinner with a bunch of old people I don't even know. They won't let you wear the same thing for both, and changing clothes means you have to take a bath, you know!" he pointed out to Rafael. "Do all kings have to take so many baths?" Pedro wondered.

"I s'ppose," Rafael sighed. "'though I can't tell you for certain since I never lived around any other kings."

"I wish I could run away," the boy smiled. "You know, go and live on a deserted island - just like in the adventure books!" he shouted.

A chuckle from Rafael interrupted the boy's daydream.

"What's so funny?" Pedro asked, indignant.

"A king living on a deserted island?" Rafael laughed. "All by hisself?"

"What's so funny about that?" little Pedro demanded.

"A king all by hisself? What's a king if he hadn't got nobody around for him to rule over? You young'n's sure are funny sometimes."

Frustrated by his inability to form a response, Pedro decided to change the subject.

"Tell me a story, Rafa."

"A story? Hadn't you s'pposed to be with the gove'ness?"

"Come on, real quick. Please..." the boy begged him.

"Quick," Rafael insisted. "Then you best get on back to the house 'fore they come looking for you."

"I'll go back right after the story," Pedro assured him.

"Well, alright then. Now, what kind of story?"

"About papa."

"About papa, eh?"

"From the days when you rode together in the army," Pedro decided.

"Alright, then. Let's see..."

As Rafael searched his repertoire of Pedro's favorites, the boy dragged a few tattered pillows onto the floor and curled up at his side to listen. His upturned glance let the old man know it was all right to proceed.

"Your father was in the state of São Paulo," Rafael began, "when a man on horseback rode up to the royal company that was waiting there on a country trail beside the River Ipiranga. The man was carrying a big bundle of letters. 'From Portugal' he explained."

What were they waiting beside the river for?" little Pedro interrupted.

"Well, you see they was waiting," Rafael reluctantly began, "while your father took care of some pers'nal bus'ness there by the river."

"Hmmm." Pedro thought he understood.

"And after they hailed him several times and didn't hear a response, the king's top officer took the packet of mail from the courier and decided to pers'nally deliver this most important message that come all the way from Portugal. He found your papa some twenty meters away, squatting on down in a dense thicket of underbrush with his body cov'red from the neck down, out of sight. The officer was willing to wait, but the king insisted that he read the news to him out loud. After all, it was sent from the mother country and the messenger had gone to all that trouble to find His Majesty in the backwoods of São Paulo. So the officer read; wouldn't you know it, another sour note from Portugal with more demands. Only, this time, it contained an ultimata: A new gove'nment had been all arranged for Brazil and your papa would have to hop aboard a boat for Lisbon right then, or give back his crown! When he heard these words, your papa screamed out in disgus' and let loose a near endless stream of obscenities, which I'm not at liberty to repeat. Then, he turned his face to the heavens with calls to the Lord for sweet peace and freedom as a scream ripped through the air: 'Independence or death,' the king shouted. 'Independence or death,' the officer laughed, knowing that the king's potty break was over and they could fin'lly get going on their journey."

Leaving the books he had removed from the shelves still on the table, Reginaldo rushed hurriedly out the front door and down the library steps, crossed the street, and entered the *Museu Nacional de Belas Artes*. Inside the same exhibit, Reginaldo moved from painting to painting as if looking for something. A museum employee noticed Reginaldo's agitation and approached him.

"May I help you, sir?" the employee asked.

"Where's Rafael?" Reginaldo questioned him without removing his eyes from their search.

"Excuse me?"

"Rafael, Pedro the Second's..." Reginaldo began, but stopped short, for he wasn't sure how to describe the relationship between the two. "The king's friend," he finally decided.

"I'm not familiar with this subject," the employee apologized.

"Don't you have any pictures of a former slave who looked after Pedro?" Reginaldo wondered, turning towards the man.

"I'm aware of only one work, by Debret," the employee explained, "of Pedro as an infant with a black nurse-maid..."

"Maybe that's it," Reginaldo suggested, grabbing hold of the man's shoulders. "Where?" he eagerly demanded.

"But the nurse is female," the employee told him, "most likely a slave girl who looked after the infant. And, unfortunately," he reluctantly added, afraid he might further upset Reginaldo, "we don't have that work here."

"No other paintings that might show Rafael?"

"I'm afraid not, sir. I've never seen a portrait of Pedro the Second with a slave. Just the one I mentioned and it's unclear if the child in that painting is actually little Pedro."

Reginaldo sighed in frustration, finally releasing his grip from the poor man's shoulders.

"I'm sorry, sir," the employee again apologized, adjusting his ruffled blazer. As the man slowly wandered away, Reginaldo was left alone inside the exhibit, silent as he stared somewhat accusingly at the portrait of young Pedro in his military uniform.

XI

"Bebel, have you seen the king?" Marcos asked, coming to a

stop between her desk and Reginaldo's office.

"No, sir," the governess answered. "He isn't with the tutor?"

"No," Vieira sighed, "the tutor says he sent him back to you for his lessons in French. Apparently the rascal has gotten lost somewhere between here and there."

Vieira was right; for the first time in his life Pedro was lost. And it felt wonderful. Instead of returning to the main house after leaving Rafael's cabin, the boy had headed towards the street, leaving his jacket and sash in a nearby bush so that he wouldn't be recognized in public. Trying to recall the route he had often travelled to the City Palace, Pedro walked for nearly an hour before he finally saw the lamps of downtown Rio. Evening was approaching, and the day's commerce was slowly coming to a close. The French boutiques, the Portuguese markets, the English auction houses, the taverns, grocers, factories, distilleries, moneylenders, sweatshops, and dealers of slaves and silver had all closed their doors. The crowds had drifted from the shops and instead began to gather around the theaters and salons. And there was none more popular, or magnificent, than the Theatro de São Pedro de Alcântara.

Since the arrival of the Portuguese court, the São Pedro had become the veritable bastion of the dramatic arts, not simply for Rio, but for the entire country. It was perhaps the only stage in Brazil where one could see tragedy as well as comedy, opera as well as vaudeville, performed by the most reputable companies from France and Portugal. Pedro stood there, transfixed, as he gazed up at the building that rose nearly six stories tall above the street, its majesty easily rivaling that of the City Palace. The building's fourteen large paned-windows across its façade and the atrium that sheltered its entrance lent the theater a welcoming and convivial air, which formed an ironic reminder of the difficulty most patrons experienced when they tried to secure a seat inside.

"You wanna go in?" a voice suddenly addressed the young emperor. Lost in his appreciation of the structure, Pedro hadn't noticed the boy's approach. The two now stood, side by side, admiring the grand theater. "Hey?" the boy said, this time poking the emperor in his side.

"Excuse me?" Pedro asked, stepping back with surprise.

"I said do you wanna go in?" the other repeated. As Pedro pondered the question, he took advantage of the distance his step back had created to quickly look the boy over. He must have been his same age, and although he was very light-skinned, Pedro judged him to be a Negro, mainly due to his clothing. His pants seemed much too small, for they fell just below the knee, and despite the heat he donned a brown vest, perhaps to conceal his tattered and ill-fitted shirt. When he noticed that the boy wore no shoes, Pedro decided that he was, in fact, a Negro and guessed that he might even be someone's slave.

"Go in?" Pedro finally echoed.

"You been looking at that place a mighty long time, like maybe you was thinking of going in. You know a secret way?" the boy anxiously asked.

"A secret way? Why do we need a secret way?" Pedro wondered.

"Unless you got some money, a secret way's the only way we getting in," he explained. "You got some money?"

"Money?"

"Yeah, money."

"Well, I don't carry money," the emperor matter-of-factly told him.

"Hee hee," the boy laughed. "That's a good way of putting it. I don't usually carry much money neither," he smiled, jovially slapping Pedro across the shoulders and sending the frail child a couple of steps forward. "Well, looks like we ain't getting in," he concluded.

"But the building is named in my honor," the emperor wanted to argue, forgetting that there was a Saint Peter of considerable import who had come along before him. However, remembering that he must maintain his disguise, Pedro held his tongue.

"Unless..." the boy suddenly murmured, his face breaking out into a smile.

"Unless what?" Pedro wondered, noting his excitement.

"Unless you don't mind walking down the road a ways. See, I know about a secret way in another place," he explained. "You int'rested?"

"What kind of place?"

"Another theater. But it ain't nearly this big," he admitted, glancing towards the formidable São Pedro. "That ain't a problem, is it?"

"I guess not," Pedro shrugged.

"Alright. Let's go, then," he decided, motioning for the emperor to follow along behind him. "Oh, by the way," he said, stopping suddenly and turning back around. "I'm Jacob."

"I'm Pedro," the emperor admitted, already forgetting his intention to conceal his identity.

"Pedro," the boy repeated. "Well, alright, Pedro. Follow me," Jacob winked, as they resumed their course.

Mrs. Castro sat quietly inside the parlor, busily knitting a cap for a baby that ten years of marriage had failed to produce. As she stared at the closed door that separated her from the slave girl at work in the kitchen, she began to speculate if perhaps Clara weren't sabotaging her attempts to become pregnant. What was she really up to there in the other room? Suddenly, it occurred to Mrs. Castro that allowing the girl to prepare their meals unattended was really quite reckless. Perhaps Clara had slipped some foreign root into the soup that attacked her mistress' reproductive mechanisms; an herb and an incomprehensible chant from this voodoo magic that all the Negroes practiced around the city.

"Clara?" Mrs. Castro called, suddenly feeling the need to look upon the slave girl to assure herself that, beyond the door, Clara wasn't busy pouring spiders' legs and insect shells into the broth.

"Yes ma'am?" Clara asked, wiping her hands on her apron as she pushed open the door.

"I was wondering how supper was coming along," the mistress said to her.

"Jus' fine, my lady," Clara nodded in response.

"Almost ready, I trust?"

"Almost," Clara agreed.

A pause followed in which the two women stared into each other's eyes.

"Alright, that's fine," Mrs. Castro finally decided, sending Clara back to work.

If it were not herbs she was dumping into the broth, perhaps the slave girl had resorted to casting a more direct spell, one that required nothing more than a glance at the victim and a prayer to Ogun, Oxum, Oxumarê, or any of these other asssonant gods and goddesses. That stare had been awfully sustained, bordering on subordinate. With such musings, Mrs. Castro continued to accuse some nebulous mystical power for her inability to conceive when, in fact, the culprit was all too biological. It wasn't any sinister glance from Clara that caused her mistress' ovaries to dry up, but rather her master's attraction to another sort of evil eye beneath the hem that consumed the life-giving waters of the Castro well.

"Clara?" the mistress again called out.

"Yes ma'am?" the young woman answered, quickly returning to the door.

"What's taking so long?" Mrs. Castro suspiciously asked.

"Well, I can't seem to find Jacob —"

"I sent Jacob to run some errands," Mrs. Castro interrupted. "So you'll have to make do without his help tonight."

"Yes ma'am."

"And careful how you look at me, you hear?" the mistress warned.

"Yes ma'am," Clara nodded.

"Well, off you go," Mrs. Castro ordered, waving Clara back into the kitchen, as she returned to her knitting.

At last, Pedro and Jacob reached the theater district of the *Rua da Vala*, where the sound of loud, rollicking pianos spilled forth from the many salons and clubs that lined the narrow street on each side. In the Rio de Janeiro of the 1840s, waltzes were reserved for the parlors of the nicer homes, *lundus* for the slaves' quarters, while in the city's bars and nightclubs polka reigned supreme; the samba still en route from Africa.

"Here, this way," Jacob whispered as they ducked in between buildings.

"Alcazar Lyrique," Pedro read as they walked past the entrance to the small theater.

Peering through a side window that no one had cared enough to conceal, the two boys looked in, surreptitiously, onto the illicit world of adults. Pedro barely recognized the instrument he had studied for so many years; no one had ever made the piano do the things it was now doing. Accompanying these musical acrobatics was a woman who was also doing things Pedro had never seen before.

"Can she walk around like that?" Pedro asked, referring to the actress' ivory breasts that were all too visible beneath the diaphanous veil of her lingerie. "Isn't that prohibited?"

"It's alright," Jacob assured him. "She's from France. That's how all the ladies dress over there."

"Right," the emperor nodded.

"You stay here," the boy told him, leaving his place at the window.

"Wait!" Pedro worried. "Don't leave me here all alone," he begged.

"I'll be right back," Jacob assured his friend.

Reluctantly, Pedro stayed behind and again turned his attention to the scene taking place inside the theater. Suddenly, an actor entered from stage left and took hold of the woman's hand.

"Naömi," he wept, dropping to one knee.

"Mon cher," she sighed in response, pressing his head into the tiny alcove between her waist and bosom.

Before any similar scene, an audience would have been moved to tears by such tenderness, but this crowd slowly began to snicker. Their reaction confused young Pedro, until he realized who the man in uniform was intended to represent.

"Mon Pierre," the woman again sighed. "Pour quoi pars-tu?"

"Pierre?" the boy repeated to himself, recognizing the moniker his French tutors had always used to address him. "Father?" he whispered.

"I must leave you, mon amour," the actor breathed into the black lace of the woman's fallen camisole. "My country needs me. I must return to rebuild our magnificent Europe," he said, taking his head from her belly and looking up into her teary eyes.

The actress responded, but Pedro was unable to understand her words. Frustrated, he cursed himself for not having paid more attention to his lessons in French.

"I will," the man assured the woman. "I will send for you as soon as possible." Then, leaving his position on bended knee, he stood up and walked out across the stage towards the audience. "Take care of this Brazil after I'm gone," he sighed, seemingly lost in soliloquy. "Teach her to speak with the tenderness of your native tongue, show her men the seductions of your body, and instruct her women to continue such enchantments after you've gone. Teach her people to cherish the words of Corneille, Racine, and Rotrou, as on so many an afternoon you and I have," he smiled, turning to face her once again.

The woman muttered something between her tears that little Pedro was again unable to understand. Then, the two lovers met in a heated embrace as the stage lights dimmed. When at last they were brought back up again, the man had disappeared and was replaced by a line of topless female dancers, their hair and makeup not unlike those of the original Naömi, who was now stretched seductively across the top of the piano. Lighting a cigarette that dangled precariously from its holder, the king's lover crossed and uncrossed her legs in mid-air, revealing a matching set of garters and stockings - but not much more - beneath her camisole.

Suddenly, the piano exploded into song, sending the line of women into motion as they began to dance. Naömi, for her part, remained recumbent, puffing steadily away on her cigarette. Then, she began to sing:

When your beau says he's got to go

Don't say a thing

He's every inch a king

(just remember to hide the ring!) the female chorus added.

When that old ship's horn begins to blow

Don't say a thing

He's every inch a king

(and thank heavens you're not the queen!) the chorus again sang.

Royalty was on the wane,

But now it seems erect again! (oh!)

"What'd I miss?" Jacob asked, returning to his place beside

Pedro.

"Nothing good," he told him. "Just a lot of kissing and dancing."

"Yeah," Jacob sighed. "There's always a lot of that. Here, have some," he offered, holding out something that looked to the emperor like a bamboo stick.

"What is it?" Pedro asked, taking the object in his hands and turning it around.

"What is it?" Jacob laughed. "Haven't you never seen sugar cane before?"

"Of course I have," the emperor lied. "I just couldn't see it clearly here in the dark." Pedro looked down at the stalk, trying to decipher just what it was that one did with unprocessed sugar cane.

"Look," Jacob said, after some twenty seconds of silence. "If you don't want none I'll take it back."

"You take some first," Pedro decided. "It's your cane, after all."

"Fine," the boy agreed, "but the first bite's always the best." Jacob twisted the stalk and sunk his teeth into it as the sweet juice came pouring out of his mouth and down his chin.

"Ai," they both giggled. Jacob wiped his face with his one hand and offered the punctured cane to Pedro with the other.

"Your turn," he told his friend.

Pedro closed his eyes, half afraid he would injure himself, and bit into the gash that Jacob had made. Again, the boys laughed as the juice sprayed in every direction. The sweetness of the cane was the most delicious sensation Pedro had ever experienced. And had the emperor ever laughed this way before, to the point where his stomach almost hurt? Never. In fact, the palace physician would have actively sought to avoid such abdominal stress. A shame, really, for it was such a nice pain to feel your sides ache with laughter.

Suddenly, a disturbance inside the theater caught the boys'

attention.

"What's going on?" Pedro asked his friend.

"I don't know," Jacob told him.

"How come the people are leaving?" the emperor nervously observed.

Then, someone inside the theater shouted: "Police!"

"The police?" Pedro cried.

"Again?" Jacob answered.

"Again? This has happened before?"

"Oh yeah," the other said, dismissing Pedro's concern. "They show up ev'ry once in a while."

"You've got to get me out of here," Pedro told him, looking left towards the street and right towards who-knows-where.

"Don't worry," Jacob assured him, "they never go after us kids."

"You don't understand," the emperor said, standing up and again looking around for an escape. "No one can know I was here. You've got to help me," he pleaded with Jacob.

"Alright, alright, calm down. We'll think of something."

Inside, the screams grew louder as the policemen began chasing the half-naked actresses off the stage. All along the Rua da Vala strip, the mayhem grew as word spread that the royal police had arrived to enforce the court's strict codes of decency.

Suddenly, as the boys peaked around the edge of the theater, they felt a hand grab each of their collars.

"Show's over boys," a policeman laughed as he dragged them into the street. Jacob shouted out, but Pedro was much too scared to scream. He simply looked over at his friend with a muted plea for help. Jacob must have understood, for he quickly freed himself from the officer, stepped back, and planted his most forceful kick ever into the man's shin. The policeman bellowed in pain, releasing

Pedro's collar and grabbing hold of his ailing limb.

"Now!" Jacob screamed. "Now, Pedro, go!"

The emperor disappeared down the street, running as fast as he could. So scared was he that he forgot to even once look back to check on the fate of, or to thank, his new friend.

XII

Excerpt from Mrs. Charles Kingston's *Letters from the island of Teneriffe, Brazil, the Cape of Good Hope, and the East Indies* (1821).

... and while in this wretched city I found solace in the thought of pursuing the society I left behind; on this occasion in the form of theatre. After several visits, however, I have decided to quit these outings for the experience falls ever shorter of my already meager expectations. I refer not only to the performances themselves and to the dismal quality of the actors, but also to the audiences' comportment during, what should be, despite its quality, a solemn and erudite experience. Even at the distinguished São Pedro, one is likely to hear guffaws from the assembled crowd at the most inappropriate of moments and, worse!, to sense the aroma and spray of saliva as it travels from uncouth mouths, as if one were lounging on the docks of the Guanabara.

Modesty prevents me from imagining what atmosphere must pervade the less-sophisticated establishments; bawdy dance halls that do not merit their designation as theatres. It is well recognized that most bachelors exit the São Pedro and descend into the Rua da Vala district, the quarter of town that, deserted by day, awakens only after dusk. At least there these bachelors' behavior will be more in keeping with that which appears on stage.

This brings me to what is, as a woman, a subject of much

concern. That is, the fate of females in this country. For those who perform in the Vala district, I cannot concern myself, for such damage already done leaves little hope for salvation. The fortunes of those still modest, however, we must seek to preserve.

At present, it is not uncommon to observe the most distinguished of ladies rear their heads back only to deliver forth a patch of saliva that would challenge the most prodigious example our drunkards back in London could offer. Furthermore, these Southern ladies possess little scruple for where and when they satisfy their most mundane of urges, relieving an itch in all manner of locations with no regard for the hand they may be seconds away from offering in greeting. I must be growing accustomed to their ways for I find my expectations have been steadily lowered, now pleased by she who first removes her glove before setting about this most private of tasks. And now you understand my sadness at being lost in a country with so many females, but nary a lady to be found!

Exiting the library, Reginaldo noticed a bus arrive at the stop with a placard in the window that read: COPACABANA. How could he have forgotten? He was now a resident of the very city that boasted such a well-known landmark, a beach whose fame reached around the world. And the bus had pulled up right here in front of him, as if challenging him to hop aboard and experience its wonders. Surely one could not let such an opportunity just pass by, unheeded, so Reginaldo decided to accept this tiny detour before heading back to the palace.

After some twenty or thirty minutes of winding through city streets, he caught a glimpse of the sun setting over the buildings and mountains behind the beach and decided to get off for a better view. Stepping down from the bus, Reginaldo was met by a battalion of roller-bladers and joggers that whizzed past him in all directions. He considered jumping back onto the bus for his own protection, but soon realized that the attack could easily be avoided by stepping out of the designated bike path. Indeed, the pace of the sidewalk suited him much better, and he walked along Copacabana Beach for nearly an hour.

As darkness approached, Reginaldo noticed up ahead the flashing neon lights of a long strip of nightclubs and restaurants. Out along the opposite sidewalk, various women talked amongst themselves, while others leaned through car windows to chat with men in imported cars backed up along the *Avenida Atlântica*. Finding an empty bench from which to view this spectacle, Reginaldo decided to sit down and write to Isabel back in Cruzília. Pulling a collection of postcards from a plastic grocery bag, he splayed them out in his hand and chose one that pictured the lights of Copacabana Beach.

"Perfect," he decided, as he looked around to verify the similarity between the card and his present location. Then, with the pen's cap held between his teeth, he wrote:

Carta Régia, 15 de março de 1993, Rio de Janeiro

Isabel, you may have noticed from the above dateline that today is the celebrated Ides of March, and I feel that I, like Brutus, have betrayed a beloved Caesar. What I mean is that I fear my previous judgment of Rio may have been too harsh for now it is night and the city has made it through the afternoon heat to awaken full of splendor. Now dark, the lights from the houses on the hillside sparkle as if the city had slowly ascended into the heavens and come to rest between the stars. Down here on earth, there is another sort of sparkle to be found, this one emanating from the flashing neon signs along Copacabana Beach (see front of card) and from the jewelry that dangles from the ears, necks, and arms of this city's fairer sex. (continued on next card)... Reginaldo scribbled, as he pulled another postcard from his stash.

Rest assured that I am proceeding with great caution through these areas, for it is well known that the women of the tropics make less scruple of granting personal favors than those of the more temperate areas of this world. One might safely conclude that the warmth and leisure of the Tropics leaves them especially inclined to licentiousness. I, however, can neither confirm nor deny these impressions. But let me close by reminding you, Isabel, to count your blessings for having had the good fortune to be born where a winter chill keeps us humble!

Yours truly,

Reggie

When Reginaldo finished writing, he put away his materials and suddenly realized he was quite famished, not surprising for it was nearly eight o'clock. He rose from the bench and headed towards the intersection, crossing over to the other side of the *Avenida Atlântica* in hopes of finding a bite to eat. Strolling along he passed by a nightclub with a sign that caught his eye for obvious reasons: Palacio dos Prazeres.

"The Pleasure Palace," Reginaldo laughed, reflecting on how, before becoming king, he had never noticed the many references to royalty in our everyday lives. There were the laudatory adjectives such as majestic and palatial, or something could be of regal proportion, and then the even more mundane designations of king-sized and queen-sized, which identified an object as being above average. But the uses were not always positive, for someone could create a royal mess, or royally screw things up, or be a royal pain. Seeing Reginaldo stopped out in front of the club, lost in such thoughts, a woman called out to him in broken English:

"Good Night, Sir! You like show of woman? Beautiful Brazilian girls, especially for you..."

"Excuse me?" Reginaldo asked, confused.

Before he had time to even think about quickening his pace, the woman had glued herself to Reginaldo's side and was already leading him inside the club.

"Ma'am. Excuse me, ma'am," he stammered, trying to wriggle

from her grasp.

"Come, the show is now begin."

As he entered, his protests were drowned out when music began to play. The other patrons were mostly men seated at tables lit only by a single candle glowing red inside a glass bowl. They soon interrupted their conversations and gave their full attention to the stage. There, a woman dressed as Carmen Miranda emerged from the shadows, but without Carmen's customary tutti-frutti hat. Instead, she was sexualized as the real Carmen was, perhaps, never allowed to be: the dress tighter and smaller, the hemline much higher, and the look in her eyes downright naughty.

How would you like to spend a weekend in Havana?

The music, too, had abandoned its former playfulness and was now a siren's song meant to tempt this room of modern day sailors. Hesitant to take a seat alone at one of the tables, Reginaldo headed for the more inconspicuous sanctuary of the bar, which was located near the back of the club.

"What can I get for you tonight, sir?" the bartender asked as Reginaldo approached.

"What can you get for me?" he wondered. "Oh, a drink?"

"It is a bar," the man pointed out.

"Right," Reginaldo agreed. "I'll take a lemonade, then. Thanks."

"A caipirinha you mean?"

"No, just a lemonade," the king said.

"Just lemon, water, and sugar? No alcohol?" the bartender again verified.

"That's right," Reginaldo smiled, turning back towards the stage. Before long, the number was already coming to an end as the crowd stood and applauded; there were even some whistles from a dedicated few. The singer curtsied graciously and darted back behind a red curtain. Reginaldo sat sideways on his stool and scanned the club. There was nothing particularly palatial about it, just another dimly lit room with low ceilings, a tiny stage, dance floor, and casino-grade carpet. Then, by way of a small set of stairs set off to the side of the stage, he noticed the woman reappear. Greeting a few men along the way, she approached the bar and pulled up a stool beside the king. Reginaldo cursed his luck.

"Hi there, how are you?" she asked him.

"Just fine, thanks," Reginaldo replied, quickly looking away, but not before noticing her change of outfit. She had shed the Carmen costume and now wore a strapless blue dress that hugged her body tightly until just above the knee, at which point it flared out gradually to finally stop at the top of her high heels. Her hair had been freed from its wrap and now hung in a loose curl to where it barely brushed the sculpted bones of her clavicle. And although she was now seated, Reginaldo imagined that, nose-to-nose, she would prove to be quite tall. Giving him a good looking over, as we've just done to her, she grabbed a cigarette from a pack lying on the bar top and again spoke:

"Don't recall seeing you here before, although the face is familiar," she noted.

"I'm not from around here," Reginaldo explained.

"On vacation?"

"More or less."

"Ooh, a man of mystery," she laughed as she lit her cigarette. "Just how I like 'em," she added, exhaling a large cumulous cloud of smoke in the king's direction.

"And you?" Reginaldo ventured.

"I'm also shrouded in mystery," she winked back at him.

"No, I meant, are you from around here?"

"I've been around here so long," she sighed, "I've forgotten just where I'm from. That's a lie," she suddenly added. "No one should ever forget where they're from," she warned, pointing the cigarette directly at him. "And the name's Marcela," she smiled, offering up her hand for Reginaldo to kiss. "Marcela Seville, a pleasure."

"I'm Reggie," he told her, reluctantly kissing her hand. "So," he bravely continued, "you a fan of Carmen?"

"Sure," Marcela nodded. "We also do some American stuff: jazz, soul, and classic HoMotown hits. You know Diana Ross, The Temptations ... just as long as it's recognizable to the gringos. It's the compromise the management and I came up with after I refused to do one more slutty version of The Girl from Ipanema," she smiled. "Evening, Dante."

"Good evening, dear," the bartender responded, as he approached their end of the bar to deliver Reginaldo's drink. "The usual?" he asked her.

"No," Marcela began, looking now at Reginaldo. "No, I think I'd like to try something a little different tonight. A strawberry daiquiri," she finally decided, turning back to the bartender. "And make it a virgin, if you would, honey," she added. "A girl can always dream, right?" she joked with a shrug of the shoulders and another wink of her eye for Reginaldo.

A bead of perspiration began to fall across the king's temple.

PACING BACK AND forth inside the palace, Marcos looked down at his watch yet again, then headed into Reginaldo's office to use the telephone. Flipping through his tiny notebook, at last he found the page he was looking for, which read:

MONARCHY ?!?

NOT TEIXEIRA

THEN WHO?

REGINALDO SANTOS

CONJUNTO BELA VISTA, 147

CRUZILIA (MG)

(LOTS OF...)PORK RIBS & "WHIPPED" POTATOES

ISABEL (34) 256-1808

He dialed the number beside Isabel's name.

"Hello, Isabel?" he asked. "It's me, Marcos. No, everything's not fine. It's Reggie. He went out this morning and still isn't back. I'm starting to get worried."

"Hmm...," Isabel sighed.

"I would call the police," Marcos added, "but that would alert the press, and I really don't want the media involved in this."

"Right, I understand."

"So, I don't know what to do. Any ideas?"

"And the library's probably closed already, right?"

"The library?" Marcos asked. He was perplexed by her question, but thought it best to jot down LIBRARY? in his notepad anyway.

"And he doesn't really have a job," Isabel noted. "Well, besides being king. Maybe he's just out site-seeing?" she suggested.

"Yeah, probably so, but it's already past eight o'clock. And he's not familiar with the city," Marcos pointed out, the anxiety in his voice coming across quite clearly over the telephone.

"Ok...ok... take it easy..."

"Isabel, is there any way you could come to Rio?" he asked.

"What for?"

"I know I hardly know him, but I can tell Reggie's been out of sorts these days, without his friends and all."

"I was afraid this might happen. Tell you what," she decided. "Let me check the bus schedules and I'll call you back."

"Fantastic. Wait, what about Reggie? What about tonight?"

"He's a big boy, he'll be ok," she tried to assure him.

"Ah... I don't know Isabel," Marcos sighed. "This city is dangerous. I just hope no one's out there taking advantage of Reggie's innocent nature."

"Another drink?" Marcela suggested to Reginaldo, the two now seated at a booth in a rather dark corner of the nightclub.

"Sure," he agreed.

Marcela motioned to the server, then turned back to the conversation.

"King, you say?" she verified. "So maybe that's why the face is familiar."

"You'd have been the first to recognize me," Reginaldo admitted.

"Does that mean you don't always wander around the city like this, bar-hopping and what-not?"

"No, usually I'm fairly well-behaved," he joked. "But I couldn't stand it any longer locked up inside that palace. It's my first time in Rio, I want to see the city, meet people. Besides," he confided to her, "the coffee's no good there."

"I'll take another daiquiri – virgin!" Marcela said to the waiter when he arrived, "and my friend here will have another ...?"

"Lemonade," the king smiled.

"Lemonade?" the other two asked in unison.

"That's right. A lemonade."

"Ok," Marcela shrugged, sending the waiter on his way. "So, what's this about the coffee? They treating you like some kind of prisoner, bad coffee and all?" she laughed.

"No, not really. It's just that my friend Marcos is pretty busy these days, he doesn't have much time for site-seeing," Reginaldo explained. "And I haven't said anything about the coffee so as not to offend anyone. They're all trying so hard to please me."

"Well, I'm not sure I can help you on the coffee front, but whenever you'd like to get out of that palace for a while and see the city, you let me know, alright? It's a deal?"

"It's a deal," Reginaldo agreed. "And you?"

"And me, what?" she asked.

"You just work... here?" Reginaldo stammered, casting a glance around the nightclub.

"Here is a lot of work, I'll have Your Majesty know."

"I just —"

"You think I just get up there and shake my ass and that's all?" she interrupted him.

"No..." he shrugged in response.

"I arrange all the musical numbers — mine and the other girls'," she continued to explain, "and I do most of the costume shopping. I'm involved in every part of the show."

"And you're never... afraid?"

"Afraid of what?" Marcela laughed. "Of breaking a heel?"

"It's just that I thought there might be some danger involved in working with... men," he said after a pause.

"Mr. Reggie the King... understand this: I am not a whore," she told him. "And the other girls... no one here has sex for money. Sure," Marcela shrugged, "several have their boyfriends, but, prostitutes we are not."

"I'm sorry, I didn't mean to..."

"That's ok, Reggie," she interrupted him. "I understand."

Another uncomfortable pause followed her pardon, but fortunately the drinks arrived to distract them.

"So, how do you like Rio so far?" Marcela asked after the waiter had gone.

"I'm getting used to it. Is it always so hot?"

"Pretty much. Lose the cardigan, it might help," she added, glancing down at his outfit.

"I imagine you must enjoy living here."

"Oh, I love it," she assured him. "It's really the only place where I can practice my profession. The only place in Brazil, at least. My life is totally different here in Rio," she concluded as she lifted the drink to her lips.

"So you weren't born here?"

"Nope. Would you believe I'm from the South?" she asked him, an eyebrow raised as she stirred her daiquiri.

"Sure, why not?" Reginaldo shrugged.

"Well, usually people are surprised to meet a dark-skinned person from the South," Marcela explained. "They always associate the region with blond hair, blue-eyed European immigrants. Kind of like yourself," she added, noticing his light features.

"It's true, you don't look German."

"Spanish descent, actually. Well, besides African, obviously," she laughed. "My parents came to Brazil from Uruguay. A great-grandmother on my father's side was Spanish. Seville is an homage to her," Marcela explained. "Is it an homage even when it's paid to a woman?" she asked the king.

"Good question. Shouldn't it be femmage instead?" he suggested.

"And why is there no such thing as an homme fatal?" Marcela wondered. "You see, king, how the cards of this world are stacked against a girl?" she laughed.

"I guess homme fatal would be redundant," Reginaldo suggested.

"Ooh, that's a good one," she sighed.

Just then, a man approached the table: "Five minutes, Marcela."

"Well, if Your Highness will excuse me," she said, rising to leave. "It's back to work for me. We'll talk more later, ok?"

"Sure, of course... I'll be right here," Reginaldo assured her.

"Perfect," Marcela smiled as she leaned down to place a kiss upon the king's forehead.

XIII

"Oh, for heaven's sake," Vieira scoffed as the young lady stepped forward and bowed, accepting the king's hand and kissing it gently. "Others must touch their lips to that hand after you've gone."

"Vieira!" Pedro exclaimed, surprised by the regent's treatment of the young woman who had come to petition the crown.

"Your Majesty, this woman has come to request a favor she knows she does not deserve," Vieira explained. "Young lady, you have shamed the father that brought you to this land seeking a better life," the Regent told her. "And you have some nerve coming here before — "

"Please, let her speak," Pedro ordered.

Glancing towards Vieira and seeing that he would not again interrupt, the woman began: "Your Majesty, I am called Teresa de Jesus." Pedro immediately recognized a strong Spanish accent to her speech. "De Jesus," she repeated, "though my father believes me unworthy of that name. He calls me a prosti — "

"You will control your tongue while in the presence of His Royal Highness!" Vieira thundered.

"Vieira," Pedro sighed. "Please continue," he said to the now terrified young lady.

"My father thinks me indecent and requests my leave. I have done nothing indecent, Your Majesty, I swear!"

"You will not swear in the presence of His —"

"Please, Vieira!" the emperor again interrupted. "Now, Miss," he continued in a soft, entreating voice. "Why does your father believe you have damaged his honor?"

"She doesn't keep decent hours," Vieira offered before the young woman had a chance to respond.

"He watches over me the entire day," she explained. "He has the neighbors keep watch while he is gone. After he sleeps, the night is the only freedom I have."

"Freedom to distribute your favors? Dark corners for dark habits, Miss!" Vieira condemned.

"It's not true, Your Highness. I have committed no sin. Not against my honor, not against my family's," the girl offered in her defense.

"Very well. And what favors did you have to request from the crown?" Pedro asked the young woman.

"That you might speak to my father, convince him I have done no wrong. I hope this will prevent him from sending me away." As she spoke, the girl looked directly into the eyes of the young monarch and for a moment she could have sworn it was as if their two souls met, as if her petition had been felt as well as heard. After all, were they not the same age? One might imagine them peers in any normal situation. Sweethearts, even. Perhaps such intimacy was not simply her imagination, for Pedro soon looked away, seemingly frightened by the connection and its intensity.

"You shall have your response in the coming days," Vieira dryly announced, breaking the silence.

"Thank you, Your Highness," the girl whispered as she was led away to make room for the next petitioner. Pedro, with his head still lowered, did not respond.

THE NEXT MORNING, Pedro entered Vieira's office as he was poring over various papers, mechanically scribbling his signature and stamping them with the royal seal. Sensing a presence at the door, the Regent lifted his head. Pedro remained silent for a moment before Vieira finally asked: "Yes, Your Majesty?"

"The woman who was here yesterday to petition," he timidly began, "who'd had the argument with her father..."

"Yes..."

"What will happen to her?"

"Her case has already been dealt with, Your Majesty. She's been deported."

"Deported?" Pedro reacted with surprise.

"The action was taken in accordance with her father's wishes," Vieira reported dryly, returning to his work.

"Isn't deportation a might extreme in this case?" the boy asked, approaching the desk.

"As in any domestic conflict, the court is hesitant to contradict the will of the father," the Regent explained.

Although resigned to losing such legal arguments with Vieira, Pedro couldn't help but seek details of the young woman's fate.

"Deported to where?" he finally asked, fearful of the Regent's answer.

"Down into the River Plate region. Let those fools deal with her imprudence," Vieira laughed.

"The River Plate?!"

"With all due respect, Your Majesty," Vieira said, once again looking up from his work and growing increasingly impatient. "I think the young woman should feel fortunate she wasn't sent to the West Indies, where her kind really belongs."

"I just feel —"

"Assemblyman Castro!" Vieira called out over Pedro's shoulder, interrupting the boy's protests. "Won't you come in?"

"I won't be intruding?" the Assemblyman politely asked.

"Of course not," the Regent assured him. "His Majesty and I

were just finishing up here. Isn't that correct, Your Highness?"

"That is correct," Pedro sighed, seeing that the two men were waiting for his reply. "I've got other business to see to, so I'd best be off," the young man lied.

"Don't let me keep you, Your Highness," Vieira said, throwing an arm around the boy's shoulders and leading him to the door. "We'll talk later," he said condescendingly, patting him on the back.

"Good day, Your Majesty," Castro bowed as Pedro was ushered out of the room. Closing the door behind his charge, the Regent leaned back and closed his eyes in exasperation.

"Sometimes, Joaquim," he sighed, looking over at Castro. "I think I'm the governess around here."

"Oh really? How so?"

"If you haven't noticed... please, have a seat," Vieira interrupted himself, motioning towards the chair in front of his desk. "If you haven't noticed, the emperor is still a child. Only fourteen," he pointed out. "Neither of us has any children, but now I can honestly claim to know what it's like to fight off their whims. If only it were sweets or toys he was after!" Vieira lamented.

"What sort of whims?" Castro wondered.

"Oh, it's these damn petitions he's taken an interest in," Vieira explained. "It's my fault, I suppose, since I'm the one who suggested we reinstate the ceremony. I thought it would enhance his stature as it did for his grandfather."

"I believe it has," Castro noted. "The boy is well-liked."

"I agree, he has become quite popular. But it's gone to his head, Joaquim. He believes himself qualified to rule in nearly every matter, with absolutely no regard for the law."

"But he accepts your decisions?" Castro verified.

"Like I said, he's just a child. I think he recognizes deep down that he doesn't know enough to contradict me."

"Have you considered anticipating his Majority?" Castro dared to ask.

"I complain about the boy's immaturity and you suggest he's fit to be king?" Vieira laughed.

"Prince, king," Castro said, waving his arm about. "Either way you're caring for the boy. Isn't it more advantageous to you if at least he's a king?"

"I'm not so sure."

"You said it yourself, the boy is not interested in politics -"

"Except for the petitions," Vieira corrected him.

"Sure, there's this matter of the petitions," Castro laughed. "But he hasn't shown an interest in policy, correct?"

"Correct," Vieira admitted.

"Let him have his silly petitions, then," the Assemblyman declared, now becoming quite animated. "So much the better! You, and the Assembly of course," he was quick to add, "will shape the policies and the boy will give his signature to that which you recommend. Vieira," Castro smiled, "Pedro's assuming Majority would benefit us all."

"Anticipating majority?" Vieira worried, still finding the idea rather brazen. "Would the country accept it?"

"Of course. You said it yourself, the boy has become quite popular. The people adore this monarch that was born right here in Rio. He's their little Brazilian," Castro laughed.

"And you've got the numbers in the Assembly for its passage?"

"We can get them," Castro nodded.

"Then go ahead," Vieira sighed. "Introduce the measure."

"Fantastic!" the Assemblyman announced with a smile. "The legislation's already been drafted, and I will go out of my way to personally bring it up for a vote before the entire chamber," he explained as he rose to leave.

"Will it take long?" Vieira wondered.

"The voting?" Castro asked, turning back around.

"No, its implementation."

"No, it shouldn't take long at all. But Vieira," the Assemblyman added before leaving.

"Yes?"

"We'll do our part, but you'll still need to do yours."

"How do you mean?" Vieira wondered.

"You'll still need to take this boy and fashion him into a king," Castro advised the Regent, doffing his hat as if to wish him good luck with the challenge ahead.

XIV

The following morning, Marcos lay sleeping on the living room sofa inside the palace when the clanging of silverware began to slowly work its way into his unsettled dreams. Opening his eyes, he realized that the sounds were coming from the small room where he and Reginaldo usually take their breakfast.

"Reggie!" he cried upon entering the room. "I've been worried sick. Where in the hell have you been?"

"I —"

"I was afraid to call the police and create a media circus," Marcos continued, interrupting Reginaldo's reply. "Then I called Isabel, who was also worried. To calm me down she's agreed to come to Rio... I fell asleep on the —"

"Isabel's coming?" Reginaldo asked.

"She arrives this evening. But what about you, Reggie?! You didn't bother leaving a note with Bebel to let us know where you were? Where were you anyway?"

Before Reginaldo had a chance to respond, Marcela burst through the door.

"Heavens, you two always shout so early in the morning? And I thought I was the drama queen," she laughed.

Marcos quickly turned to Reginaldo, looking for an explanation.

"Marcos," he timidly began, "this is my friend Marcela. Marcela, this is Marcos."

"A pleasure," Marcela smiled, offering her hand for Marcos to kiss.

"Nice to meet you," Marcos said dryly, shaking, instead, the proffered hand.

"Oh come on, Marcos, there's no need to be shy," Reginaldo told him. "She doesn't bite."

"Not this early in the morning, at least," Marcela added, the two sharing a laugh at the young man's expense. "You'll have to pardon me, Marcos," she apologized, "it's just that I'm a bit overwhelmed this morning," she said, pretending to fan herself. "I've never woken up in a palace before. The dream of every little girl, right?"

Although Marcos felt the desire to ask just when Marcela might have been a little girl, he resisted.

"Coffee, Marcela?" Reginaldo offered with a poorly disguised grimace.

"Oooh, right. The coffee," she remembered from the previous night's conversation. "Not yet, sweetie. First, I wanted to see if by some strange chance you boys had any nail polish remover in this palace of yours."

"I'm pretty sure Bebel has some," Reginaldo suggested. "She seems to touch up every hour. Ask the staff down below to show you her desk, it should be in one of the drawers."

"Now, I don't want to go invading someone's privacy."

"Don't worry," Marcos scoffed, "there are no top secret files tucked between the tabloids."

"Well, if you insist..."

After Marcela had exited the room, Marcos again looked to Reginaldo for an explanation for her presence.

"I know Marcos: 'there dallied a Negro in His Majesty's quarters,' I've already committed an imperial no-no," Reginaldo joked.

"It's not that, Reggie —"

"Then let me explain that she's just a friend," Reginaldo assured him. "We met last night at the club —"

"Club? What club?" Marcos worriedly asked, pulling out a chair and sitting down at the table.

"The Pleasure Palace in Copacabana," Reginaldo admitted, blushing. "But it's not what you think," he quickly added.

"Regardless of what I think, Reggie, Isabel and I were really worried about you."

"You were?"

"Yes," Marcos admitted.

"You're right," Reginaldo finally conceded. "I shouldn't have worried you two with my escapades. Accept my apologies?"

"Of course." After a pause, which Reginaldo seized in order to spread a goodly amount of guava jelly onto his crumpet, Marcos continued: "So, what's up with this Monica?"

"It's Marcela," Reginaldo corrected him between bites.

"Right, right... Marcela. 'She' is a what?" Marcos asked, making a gesture in the air of placing quotes around the word.

"What do you mean 'she'?" Reginaldo asked, mimicking the same gesture.

"Reggie," Marcos laughed, "you haven't noticed that this Marcela is really more of a Marcelo?"

"Just what are you trying to say, Marcos?"

"Like the majority of 'women' along the Copacabana strip," Marcos began, lowering his voice to a whisper, "Marcela is a transvestite... a man dressed as a —"

"Marcos!" Reginaldo shot back indignantly, though still whispering. "I won't have you talking this way about a friend of mine. Maybe she's not as pretty as the girls you go out with, but she's working very hard to follow her dream in this city and she deserves our respect."

"I'm not calling her ugly, or trying to put her down," Marcos argued. "I'm just trying to tell you that she's a —"

Again, Marcela burst into the room, a bottle of clear liquid and a collection of cotton balls in hand.

"Whispering, gentlemen? Well, I guess the only thing a girl hates more is not being whispered about," she winked.

"So, you found some?" Reginaldo asked, seeing the tiny bottle in Marcela's hand.

"What, nail polish remover? No, but I made do with what I had in my purse," she smiled. "*Stolichnaya* should do the trick, don't you think? Vodka," she explained to the men after receiving two equally blank stares.

Marcos turned to the king with yet another disconcerted look.

"Marcela," Reginaldo said to her, becoming more serious. "I think Marcos is a little worried by your presence here in the palace."

"Is this true, Marcos?" Marcela asked in an injured tone of voice. "Why?" she wondered, drawing up a chair next to his at the table.

"Look, it's nothing personal," Marcos lied, "it's just that we have to be extremely careful with the king's activities — what he does, who he's seen with. A ... mysterious woman," he stammered, tripping over the correct adjective or noun we'll never know, "or any one at all inside the palace will certainly attract the media's attention. Haven't you seen those vultures camped outside?"

"I understand completely, Marcos," she agreed, nodding her head. "You can rest assured that I will do everything I can to avoid even the tiniest hint of scandal. I won't call any attention to myself while I'm here. Oh, shit!" she suddenly cried. "One second —"

Marcela jumped up and darted out of the room, leaving Reginaldo and Marcos to look to one another, shrugging their shoulders in confusion. Seconds later, Marcela popped back through the door.

"Sorry about that," she coyly smiled. "Probably best to go ahead and grab my laundry from the terrace," she explained, holding up a red lace brassiere.

"A bikini?" the Mayor asked, inspecting a tiny representative of the item's lower half.

"I wish, sir."

Hovering above the Mayor's desk, Police Chief Viana was busily arranging a selection of boxes, loudly removing sheets of tissue paper, and displaying the items upon the tabletop.

"It's known as a G-string," the Police Chief explained, "although the kids have taken to calling it 'dental floss' because of this little —"

"I understand, Viana," the Mayor cut in. "No need to enter into details."

"Well, as you can see, then, this suit makes the already miniscule bikini seem like a diaper."

"Viana," the Mayor sighed, "I assume this fashion show has some purpose?"

"Indeed it does, sir. You see, I got to thinking about what you said the other day about how Rio should project an image worthy of an empire."

"Yes..."

"Well, it struck me that we should begin by enforcing a certain level of decorum in our dress and behavior."

"Right..." the Mayor tentatively agreed.

"Especially in our dress," Viana continued, "since I feel that's the area where we've really let things go."

"Get to the point, Viana. What have you done?"

"I've asked all of my men on beach patrol to crack down - no pun intended, sir - on the use of the G-string bikini and other revealing apparel. You're familiar with the *maillot*, sir?" Viana asked, removing another item from among the piles of tissue paper.

"I believe so."

"It's a one piece unit," the Chief explained, extending an arm beneath the suit in order to properly display the item to the Mayor. "Not only does the rear portion cover nearly twice as much surface area," he continued, turning the bathing suit over, "it also secures and hides the waist and belly-button, creating a nicely controlled profile from bust to thigh," Viana concluded, sucking in his paunch and turning to his right to demonstrate the advantages of the larger suit.

"When you say 'crack down'," the Mayor squinted, "just what are we talking about here?"

"My officers calmly approach the offending individual and ask her to kindly cover her indecently exposed areas," the Police Chief explained.

"Viana, it's a beach. These girls are just trying to get a nice tan."

"But that's just it, sir," Viana excitedly replied, "these young women are leaving the beaches and entering restaurants and other public spaces without first covering themselves properly. And when they do add clothing," the Chief laughed, "it's something ridiculous like a T-shirt, as if that could conceal their buttocks!"

"Well, Viana," the Mayor sighed as he began to rub his eyes in exasperation. "You're going to ruin the lives of thousands of teenage boys throughout the city, but I guess we can handle that. Just keep the enforcement discreet, agreed?" he said, looking up again at the Chief.

"Of course, sir."

"And Viana..."

"Yes, sir?"

"Don't forget this," the Mayor said, holding out to him, loosely grasped between his thumb and index finger, the now illicit G-string bikini bottom.

Marcela Seville might have been Marcelo, Miguel, or even Sebastian back in wherever it was she came from, but in Rio de Janeiro, along the Copacabana strip between the Avenida Princesa Isabel and the Rua Francisco Otaviano, none of that mattered. Rio's ten million inhabitants had provided the anonymity she was searching for; its enormity the great equalizer. And living and working along the strip she had come to feel that, not only was she no longer her provincial self, she was no longer even Brazilian. Ironic since, to so many foreigners, she represented Brazil incarnate, flesh and blood, satin and rouge. At times she truly understood Carmen Miranda's identity crisis in far away Los Angeles and decided that, after all, aren't we all a bit like the girl with the tutti frutti hat.

"Marcos, you're sure you don't mind?" she asked as the two prepared to leave the palace.

"Not at all. I'm headed to Ipanema so your apartment's on the way," he assured her. Yet, what seemed like a previously scheduled trip across town was actually a determined attempt to get Marcela out of the palace as quickly, and as inconspicuously, as possible. "Just one thing," Marcos added, glancing down at her outfit. "You don't have anything else to put on, do you?"

"What? Am I all wrinkled?" she worried, checking her dress.

"No, it's not that. It's just... you know. The reporters out front," he reminded her.

"Oh, right."

"And the hair?" he added.

"What about the hair?"

"It's probably real, right? Not a wig?" he confirmed.

"Ok, I didn't mind the dress comment," she told him, "but now you're just trying to get slapped."

"I'm sorry," he sighed, "but how in the hell are we gonna get out of here without being seen?"

"Alright, calm down. I'm thinking..."

"You're right, let's think," Marcos agreed, but kept his eyes trained on Marcela.

"God dammit," she said after a pause, shaking her head. "I can't believe I'm going to do this."

"Do what?" Marcos anxiously wondered.

"You got a maid that works here?"

"Here at the palace? Uh huh."

"Is she about my size?" Marcela sighed, passing a hand over her figure.

"More or less," Marcos guessed. "Not as tall," he pointed out.

"Will I fit in her dress?"

"I think so," he nodded, finally realizing Marcela's plan. "And there's got to be an extra outfit somewhere around here. Stay here, and I'll go look. But wait," he said, suddenly stopping. "Do you really think this will work?"

"You ever seen someone look twice at the help?" she cynically asked.

Upon returning to Brasília, the newish, but now perhaps the

former capital of Brazil, the Senator began a series of visits along the *Avenida das Nações*, the city's embassy row, to assure the representatives of these powerful nations that, despite the rather strange and unexpected shift in its form of government, Brazil was still a safe bet for foreign investment. Now, at two o'clock in the afternoon, Antonio Cruz waits in the lobby of the American Embassy, his most dreaded, and therefore his last, stop of the day.

Not long after the Senator's arrival was announced by telephone to the staff upstairs, a bright-eyed young man - obviously an American, Cruz laughed to himself - walked into the lobby, flashing his embassy badge at every checkpoint.

"Senator Cruz?" he politely asked, recognizing the lawmaker from both newspapers and television. "If you'll follow me, I'll take you directly to the Ambassador," he said, motioning towards the entryway that was guarded by two soldiers.

"Thank you," Cruz nodded.

The Honorable Senator had met the Distinguished Ambassador on several occasions before today; at the diplomat's swearing in, and at holiday dinners hosted by the embassy. They had even met to discuss legislation. And while these latter meetings had often grown quite tense, today's *tête-à-tête* could prove to be the most nerve-racking of all. Cruz had taken a class in American History during college, so he knew that the colonies fought a bloody war to free themselves from the British Crown. The Ambassador would surely look suspiciously upon Brazil's reversion to monarchy.

"Senator Cruz," the Ambassador smiled as the lawmaker entered his office. "Please, have a seat."

"Thank you, Ambassador." After having studied the language in high school, and a year abroad in Baton Rouge, Louisiana in the early seventies, the Senator's English was really quite good. And the subsequent annual trips to Miami kept it sharp. "I'm happy you agreed to see me," he told the American.

"Of course," the Ambassador nodded. "Actually," he continued,

"I was looking forward to speaking with you as well."

"About the referendum?" the Senator guessed.

"Exactly."

"That is why I have come," Cruz explained. "I want to assure your country that this transition will be smooth. No changes in Brazil's trade policy, no fiscal monkey business," he added, throwing in the monkey business bit he had learned back in Louisiana. That's how it is with a foreign language, you learn something solid and cling to it for safety.

"That sounds great," the Ambassador conceded. "But Mr. Cruz," he added before pausing. "Monarchy?"

"That's correct," the Senator nodded.

"A king?" the Ambassador again asked.

"The people have spoken," Cruz shrugged, grinning with embarrassment.

"But a monarchy, Senator? This isn't the nineteenth century. For heaven's sake, we're only a decade away from the twenty-first."

"Given Brazil's history, we thought the option should be included on the ballot. We didn't expect the voters to actually choose it," the Senator lied.

"That's quite a gamble to take. And you lost," the Ambassador pointed out.

"With all due respect, we do not see it that way."

"Unfortunately, Senator, others might. This change to a monarchy might strike some investors as, well, how should I put it?" the Ambassador asked himself. "Silly," he concluded. "If the Ford Company is considering a new location for one of its plants, they're more likely to pick a place that has a stable democracy, a leader they can trust. You know this."

"I do," the Senator nodded. "And I know that this outcome might scare away some who would like to spend their money in

Brazil, so I'm here to guarantee you that Brazil is stable, our economy friendly to investment."

"And this new king won't want to change any of the country's economic policies? Can you guarantee investors that?"

"This king won't be causing any monkey business with the economy," the Senator sought to assure him. "He can't do anything without our approval, and Congress is committed to low tariffs."

"Deregulation? Even privatization of some of the state-run industries?" the Ambassador suggested.

"Deregulation, yes. We are still discussing privatization."

"Well, Senator," the American sighed. "Let's hope Congress' actions can allay investors' worries."

"I think we can," Cruz smiled as he stood to shake the Ambassador's hand before leaving.

"Ok, come on. Help me get this thing off," Marcela said, tugging at the buttons of the servant's black and white dress while seated in the passenger seat of Marcos' car. "Jesus Christ, what material do they make this stuff out of, anyway? Some kind of burlap and polyester blend? And look at this," she said to him, holding up the dainty cap that accompanied the outfit. "You should be ashamed of yourself for making another human being wear this shit," she told him. "I want you to burn this dress when you get back to the palace, you hear me? And if you ever tell anyone that it was actually on my body..."

"You got it," Marcos laughed.

"You think I'm kidding, don't you? I'm not joking," she swore to him. "Damn, I'm gonna swipe some dresses from the club so that at least these poor women can clean in style," she said, shaking her head.

"Hey, come on," Marcos stopped her. "We don't need any more women running around the palace in turquoise lamé," he reminded her, glancing down at the previous night's dress she held in her lap.

"Ok, try not to stop for a while," she requested. "I'm gonna change."

"You're going to change in the car?"

"Yeah," she shrugged. "It won't take but a second."

"Sure, but... here in the car?"

"I'm wearing underwear," she assured him. "Besides, the top is up," she argued. "No one will see. That is... as long as you keep your eyes on the road and don't peek," she added with a wink and a smile.

"Ha ha ha," Marcos sarcastically responded.

Then, without further warning, Marcela jerked her hips forward towards the dashboard as she pulled the dress past her torso and over her head.

"Oh, my God, what a relief!" she cried once the dress was removed. "Damn, that burlap made me all hot," she complained, flapping her arms up and down in an attempt to cool off. "I'm sorry, honey, but I need some air," she told him, flipping the air-conditioning on to full speed as she turned the vents to blow directly onto her underarms and neck.

"Hey, easy with the AC," Marcos worried.

"Let's go topless," Marcela suddenly suggested.

"Excuse me?"

"You know, let's open this baby up," she said, tapping on the car's retractable roof.

"That's fine, but the dress?" he reminded her.

"Oh right," Marcela remembered, glancing at the pile of lamé still in her lap. "But then can we put the top down?"

Finally fully clothed and off the media's radar, Marcos agreed to open the convertible's top to let in the wind and sun. Still, Marcela was dissatisfied. Something was missing.

"You mind if we go along the beach?" she asked.

"I guess not," he agreed.

"Ahhh that's it," she sighed, closing her eyes and taking a deep breath when at last they pulled onto the Avenida Atlantica. "Ever notice how you can taste the ocean before you can even see it?"

"I'm not much of a beach person myself," Marcos confessed. "I like to look at it, like this, from a distance, but I hardly ever go into the water."

"I don't really go into the water either," Marcela admitted, "but I do like to feel the hot sand between my toes, the sun beating down on my face... boys all around wearing Speedos," she added with her customary wink.

"I'll admit the beer tastes better at the beach," Marcos quickly said, bringing the conversation back to a safer topic.

"Oh, yeah, without a doubt," Marcela seconded. "I think it has something to do with the salt coming off the sea. It's like nature's own bowl of beer nuts coming across the sands," she reflected, betraying the amount of her time spent in bars and nightclubs. "Hey, speaking of which," she suddenly said, leaning forward. "Can you pull over so I can grab a drink? I'm dying of thirst."

"But we're in the middle of traffic," Marcos worried, looking at the cars all around him.

"Please, please, please," Marcela whined. "Just real quick? Ooh, yeah, right over there," she said, pointing to a vacant parking space.

With no small amount of honking and profanity from fellow drivers, Marcos managed to guide the car across traffic and into the space.

"Thanks hon'," Marcela smiled, jumping out. "Be right back," she added, blowing him a kiss.

Marcela darted across the street and headed towards a cabana-like kiosk positioned along the beach.

"One coconut water please," she announced, offering to the boy behind the counter a single bank note held firmly between her index and middle finger. "And garnished with an umbrella if you don't mind, dear."

While waiting, Marcela surveyed the crowd gathered along Copacabana Beach and noticed a small disturbance among the sunbathers. While she was away, Marcos took the opportunity to rest his eyes, rotating his head in an attempt to relieve the stress that had accumulated in his neck last night on the tiny couch.

"What do you think is going on over there?" Marcela asked the young man when he returned with her drink.

"Cops been hassling the girls about their bikinis, making them put on shorts as they come off the beach," the attendant explained.

"Their bikinis?"

"I even seen one cop passing out those sarang things," he added.

"Sarongs?" Marcela verified, correcting the pronunciation.

"Uh huh."

"Good Lord, what has gotten into this city?" she wondered aloud. "Hope they don't go after Speedos next," she winked to the boy, grabbing the coconut and heading back to the car.

As Marcos continued to rest his eyes, the sudden sound of tires screeching along the pavement jerked him to attention, as a car skid to a stop just short of Marcela.

"What the...!?"

Marcela and the occupants of the car — also a convertible – were busy trading curses when Marcos suddenly noticed that it was Juliana behind the wheel, Tatiana at her side.

"Oh my god...," he murmured.

"Marcos?!" Juliana screamed, finally noticing him.

"Juli... momô!" he said in shock.

"What the...!" both Juliana and Tatiana gasped, looking back at Marcela, still outside the car. In this section of Copacabana, a young, upper-middle class chap in the company of a transvestite meant only one thing.

"Babe, I can explain!" Marcos shouted, his eyes darting between Marcela and the convertible. "She's a friend of the ki—"

Juliana had already stomped on the accelerator, the peeling of tires drowning out the rest of his explanation.

"Just wait here!" Marcos yelled to Marcela before pulling the car into traffic after his loved one. He sped to where he was almost beside her when, fortunately, the light turned red at the next intersection.

"Juliana, I can explain!" he shouted across to her car. The young woman continued to stare straight ahead. "Tatiana, tell her that that woman's a friend of the king."

"He said she's a friend of the –"

"I heard him!" Juliana interrupted her friend.

"She's not what she looks like," he continued, "she's a singer! Very talented, the king assures me."

Tatiana shrugged, as if to say that communication was useless at this point, so Marcos gave up his pursuit, turning right at the corner and circling back around the block. Leaning against a signpost, Marcela waited where he had left her, calmly smoking a cigarette and enjoying her coconut water through a straw, the tiny umbrella tucked gently behind her ear.

"So," she said to Marcos, taking a drag on her Hollywood cigarette. "Who was it that nearly killed me?"

"Marcela," he sighed, as she stepped back into the car. "Weren't you watching the traffic?"

"Sorry, I got distracted. So who was it?"

"My girlfriend," he told her. "Or ex-girlfriend, maybe, after this little incident. She lives in São Paulo, I don't know what she's doing here," he added, murmuring to himself.

"Ahm. The girlfriend, I see," Marcela nodded. "And only one block," she added, shaking her head.

"How's that?"

"You only drove one block after her," Marcela explained, taking a drag on her cigarette. "For true love a person will search the four corners of this world," she told him.

In response, Marcos shot back his best sarcastic smile. "What was I supposed to do, leave you to walk home?"

"Oh please," Marcela scoffed, "she would've stopped on the next block. She just wanted to feel sought after. You know, make you men work for it a bit."

"You don't know Juliana. She's pretty stubborn, and I know she wouldn't have given up so easily. Look, forget it," he told her. "I'll give her a call later to explain —" Marcos stopped, his thought left incomplete.

"To explain what?" Marcela asked, turning to him. "Explain... me?" she correctly guessed.

"I'm sorry, Marcela. I didn't mean to offend. It's just that I'm a bit tired today and not in a very good mood."

"That's quite alright, Marcos. You haven't offended me. A beautiful, elegant woman," she said, motioning to herself, "in the company of a taken man such as yourself — it's a predicament that always needs some explaining. But," Marcela added, turning towards him with both her right eyebrow and index finger raised, "could it be that you don't love this girl as much as you think?"

"What's that supposed to mean?"

"Why are you with her if she's so stubborn, jealous, bitchy — "

"I only said stubborn."

"So you did, sorry. But, anyway... one block?" Marcela repeated.

"I stopped out of consideration for you."

"Oh, stop with this for you business," she interrupted. "This isn't about me, it's about you and that hussy. So tell me: Why are you with her?" she asked in a voice dripping with amateur psychology.

"Look, Marcela. Juliana and I..."

"Yes..."

"We've known each other since childhood," he said after a pause. "We've grown up together, our families are old friends, her father's my boss for Christ's sake! It's like we're living the same life, always meant to be together."

Leaning over to pinch Marcos' cheek, Marcela smiled. "You still haven't mentioned lu-ove," she said, dragging out the last word as if a musical note. "You know, Marcos," she began in a tone of mock severity, "I noticed the blue of your socks doesn't quite match the blue of your suit—"

"What? Yes they do," he argued.

"You're right, they do and that's my point."

"What point?"

"Look at you," she laughed, "you're a walking, talking, organize-your-day, your week, your life black leather-bound daily planner with removable clear bookmark for easy reference. But I bet you've got a tie that matches this car, no? Some sweet red thing that hangs there in the back of the closet to remind you that, when he wants to, Marcos can let it all hang out with the best of 'em."

"Marcela, are you trying to offend me on purpose?" he wondered.

"I'm not trying to offend you, hon'. I'm just asking you if that girlfriend has anything to do with the 'break this glass in case of emergency' safety valve you've got tucked away inside."

"Safety valve?"

"Ask yourself, Marcos. Is she your matching pair of blue socks?"

"Huh?"

"'Cos maybe if you got rid of the blue socks, you could also do without the fancy red tie," Marcela concluded.

Marcos shrugged his shoulders, not quite knowing how to respond to Marcela's cryptic analogy.

"Ok, I'll stop bugging," she promised him.

"Blue socks?" he repeated.

"Forget it," she told him. "I'll stay out of your business. After all, what the hell do I know?" she admitted. "I just met you."

"Right," Marcos nodded.

"So? Shall we?" she suggested, motioning towards the road ahead.

"Sure," Marcos sighed as he pulled back into traffic.

"The prohibition of the G-string certainly has its merit," Viana said to himself as he exited City Hall, but he couldn't help think that there still remained more fundamental reforms to be made, something that would really make the Mayor sit up and take notice. And the city, too, for that matter. His attempt to reconstruct the city from its beginnings had been too ambitious, he decided. It wasn't necessary to probe so far back into history, since his task was much more limited. What would it take to turn Rio back into an empire? That was all he needed.

Viana stopped in the midst of this question and repeated to himself: "back into an empire." That's it! Why was he racking his brain so when, after all, hadn't the city already undergone a comparable transformation after the arrival of the Portuguese court some two hundred years ago? Viana didn't expect to be able to reproduce every change – some were surely no longer necessary – but at least he could borrow some ideas.

But from where? he wondered. Photographs from the era? Perhaps. But what Viana really needed was that very ingredient that is so valuable to those in his profession: witnesses.

Well, if it's old, he thought, it's bound to be stored somewhere in a museum, or in the library. Yes, he congratulated himself, in the National Library! They hang onto everything over there.

Then, turning towards his patrol car, Viana suddenly stopped.

No, he thought. I should immerse myself in a world as close as possible to that of the Portuguese court. Forget the patrol car, Viana declared. I'll walk to the library! Besides, he admitted, it helps me think. So, forsaking his wheels, Viana spun around on his heels until he faced downtown, pressed his cap firmly down upon his head, and was off on foot to see if any witnesses back in 1808 had bothered to write any of this stuff down.

XV

"SO, WHO'S HUNGRY?" Reginaldo smiled, leaning over Marcos' shoulder as the foursome drove along in the convertible. Marcos, of course, was at the wheel, with the newly arrived Isabel in the passenger seat, Reginaldo and Marcela in back.

"Ah, it's too early for dinner," Marcela argued.

"How about some karaoke first?" Isabel suggested.

"Karaoke?" Marcos worried. "Again?"

"I remember you liking it just fine back in Cruzília," she reminded him.

"C'mon, Marcos," Reginaldo goaded him. "The audience is begging for an encore. Perhaps Marcela knows of a place?"

"With karaoke? 'Fraid not, king. How about something a little more Brazilian? You know, a little flavor of Rio," she suggested.

"We are not taking Isabel to some strip club," Reginaldo told her.

"I meant music," Marcela said. "A little old style samba, for example? The kind you rarely find anymore."

"Sounds great," Isabel agreed.

"I don't know how to samba," Reginaldo complained. "In general, I'm not very good on my feet."

"Why did I have a feeling you weren't?" Marcela joked, glancing down at Reginaldo's less than athletic middle. "Don't worry, most people just sit there and listen anyway. And drink lots of beer," she added with a wink.

"I could use a beer," Marcos chimed in.

"Isabel?"

"Let's do it."

"Reggie..."

"Sure," he shrugged.

"So," Marcos asked, looking back to Marcela through the rear view mirror. "Where to?"

TO THE LIBRARY, Viana reminded himself as he meandered on foot through the streets of downtown Rio. As we've seen, upon entering the National Library and coming face to face with its catalog of a near-infinite array of books, journals, and other sources of information, a person can feel quite overwhelmed. But when confronted with this situation, Police Chief Viana, being a man of reason and procedure, headed straight to the Information Desk for tips.

"Oh, good afternoon officer," Milena said, noticing the man in uniform approach her. "Can I help you?"

"I'm looking for witnesses," Viana said without thinking, still lost at sea in his earlier brainstorm.

"Witnesses? Has there been some sort of incident?" she worried.

"Oh no, I'm sorry," Viana apologized, recognizing his mistake.

"What I mean is that I'm looking for some sort of historical record of what the city might have been like in the early 1800s."

"I see," Milena nodded.

"Can you recommend a history book or two?"

"The 1800s, you say. Well," she stopped to think. "Are you interested in any historical event in particular, a political movement, the Uruguayan War?"

"I suppose the arrival of the Portuguese court would be that event," Viana guessed.

"Oh," Milena said with a recognition that pleased the Chief. "They've just been recently returned. I'll only be a second."

After turning the convertible around and heading back to the northern side of the city, the four friends found themselves in an increasingly abandoned part of Rio, a side of the *cidade maravilhosa* rarely shown to tourists. Marcos noticed the change and began to get fidgety.

"Maybe we should put the top up?" he wondered aloud.

"We'll suffocate without the breeze," Marcela argued.

"I've got AC, if you'll recall?" he reminded her.

"Perhaps Marcos is right," Reginaldo decided. "We could be targets for attack in such a flashy car."

"If something were to happen to the king..." Marcos worried.

"Oh, for Christ's sake, I'll throw myself in front of the bullet if it comes to that," Marcela laughed. "Just drive fast and go through the red lights, we're almost there."

"Go through the red lights?" Reginaldo interrogated her. "You are trying to get us killed!"

Minutes later, the car turned onto a dimly lit street lined with older, elaborately designed houses and shops that had long since fallen into decay. Marcos parked the car on the street, pulled up the convertible's top, and checked several times to make sure all the doors were locked. The four followed the sound of music and light streaming from an isolated doorway, seemingly the only sign of life in the neighborhood. Climbing a fragile flight of wooden stairs, they entered the bar and took a seat.

"Order me a beer as cold as a seal's ass, will you? I'll be right back," Marcos grumbled, dropping his keys and phone onto the table.

"What's eating him?" Isabel asked the others.

"Love troubles," Marcela guessed. "So, what's everyone want to drink?"

Marcela looked about the restaurant for a waiter, when suddenly Marcos' phone began to ring. The three looked at each other.

"Shouldn't we answer?" Isabel suggested.

"I'll get it," Marcela volunteered. "I think I know who it might be. Hello?" she breathed in an erotic, throaty whisper. "She hung up," she announced to the others, amused.

Marcela and Reginaldo laughed to themselves.

"That's cruel, the poor thing..."

"You're right, Isa," Marcela agreed. "I'll leave her in peace. So, where's that waiter?"

Again, the telephone rang.

"The little vixen!" Marcela cried.

Marcela answered the phone again, this time in her normal voice: "Hello, Marcos' portable," she politely spoke. "Ah, no. He's indisposed at the moment. Care to leave a message? Veronica," she repeated, looking at the others with eyebrows raised. "Veronica from Brasília. And he's got your number? Ok, you're welcome, *tchau*. Ahoy," she said, hanging up the phone. "Looks like our little sailor's got a girl in every port of call."

"THE LINE'S STILL busy," Tatiana told her friend, shaking her head. "We'll try again in a few minutes."

"Forget it," Juliana declared, seated before a vanity mirror and combing brusquely through her long, brown hair. Across town she, Tatiana and another friend were preparing their clothes, hair, and make-up for a night out.

"It's not like he's seeing this floozy behind your back," Tatiana tried to console her. "You heard him; she's a friend of the king."

"Either way, I don't really care. He's been very distant lately and I'd rather not think about him for a while. Tonight I just wanna go out and have some fun. After all, we're on vacation, right?"

"Fine," Tatiana agreed.

"Andrea," Juliana said, turning to the other friend. "Does your father drink?"

"Alcohol? Sure," she nodded.

"Do you know where he keeps the liquor? You know, the hard stuff?" Juliana asked her.

"I have an idea," she said. "I'm sure we could find it."

They did find it, something clear that smelled a lot like rubbing alcohol, stored in a lower kitchen cabinet.

"Jesus, how old is this stuff?" Tatiana winced as she went back for another whiff.

"I don't know," Andrea shrugged. "You think it's gone bad?"

"I think it started out bad."

"Here, let me see it," Juliana said. "This'll do," she decided, sampling a drop from the mouth of the bottle. "Shot glasses?" she asked Andrea.

"Uh..."

"Never mind, we'll use these," Juliana decided, removing three champagne glasses from another cabinet. "Ok, girls, gather 'round the table. In a circle, just like in the Westerns," she said, pointing to the chairs the other two should occupy to properly complete the scene.

Having filled their glasses more than halfway, the three young women exchanged looks between themselves like gamblers preparing to foil an unsuspecting novice. As they threw back the shot in unison, Juliana let out a triumphant scream while the other girls covered their mouths to block the burning liquid that refused to go down. And, just as in the Wild West, this first shot proved to be only one of many.

With the obvious increase in activity that rainy morning, the residents of Lisbon could tell something strange was afoot. Traffic in the streets was unusually dense, as carriages hurried back and forth between the harbor and the city's center. People in the streets interrupted their errands and watched the commotion with a confused fascination. Occasionally, one would call out to a tilbury driver, trying to pry the tiniest hint from the servant's lips of what his bosses were up to, moving about so frantically and with such haste. And towards the harbor. Why? It wasn't long before the townspeople caught wind of what was going on when they finally heard that the king and his court, along with some fifteen thousand nobles, had decided to call upon the nation's history of maritime success for yet one more miracle: to lift the Portuguese Empire from the perilous grasp of General Napoleon and escort her safely to the shores of its American colony, Brazil.

Meanwhile, the procession of carriages continued. Inside, entire families sat praying with their household belongings following close behind, items stuffed hastily into trunks for the transatlantic journey. And the onlookers, apparently neither royal nor noble, were left wondering, what about us? They rushed to the harbor to see if there might remain an empty seat for them and their loved ones, but there was none. The fleet of seven ships was already full. Their fear quickly turned to anger as they cursed the king as a coward for fleeing his native Portugal, attacking the passing carriages with spit and stone.

Dom João received word of their concern and decided he would have to speak to calm their fears and anger. He stepped out onto the bow of his ship, the *Principe Real*, and addressed the sopping wet crowd down below that had, by now, completely surrounded the harbor.

"My dear people," he nervously smiled as he looked from face to drenched face. "Our separation is merely temporary, a safeguard against this military threat that cannot be avoided. With the court's removal, or rather, relocation," he corrected himself, "Napoleon and his troops will have no need to threaten our ports, our city, nor our country, for we take with us our kingdom's most valuable treasures. The General will leave Lusitania a frustrated tyrant, and be forced to seek his fortunes in more distant lands."

The king's words were persuasive, for the crowd's anger slowly began to dissipate. In its place, a tinge of sadness washed across the faces of the assembled townspeople, a change Dom João did not fail to notice.

"Do not mourn my departure," he urged them, "but rather dream of the day when we as a kingdom will be reunited on Portuguese shores. For you may trust my word that, soon, I will be back!" the king bravely cried. However, many in the crowd failed to hear the last word pronounced, for another scream had suddenly rung out and successfully competed with his.

"The Queen Mother?" the crowd mumbled to themselves, recognizing the blood-curdling cry of the old bitty, a shriek of which only the insane are capable. "The Queen Mother is off as well?" they wondered aloud, looking over to the second ship, *A Rainha*.

The king, noticing the people's distraction, decided to make his call once again.

"Trust in me," he began, raising his right arm, "for I will be —"

Then, another shout interrupted the renewed declaration. This one, however, from a third ship docked out in the harbor. A wave of smiles broke across this sea of faces as all came to the same happy conclusion: Carlota, too! She would also be gone! Had she begun arguing with a lover before the ship had even left the harbor? How many noblemen was the king escorting to Brazil who had already made him a cuckold many times over here in Portugal? The people's sadness now turned to pity. Not for themselves, but for their monarch who would most likely never escape his troubles, no matter how far he sailed. Finally, the lead ship fired its farewell shot, which was echoed by salvos from the remaining six, and then they were off.

On March 8, 1808, the fleet entered Rio's Guanabara Bay and the American colony ceased to be just another jewel in the crown of the Portuguese empire. Suddenly, Brazil was the crown! And tiny Portugal, abandoned, left to its dire fate at the hands of Napoleon's thugs. Police Chief Viana was suddenly overcome with pity, an emotion he never thought himself capable of in relation to Europe. How could a person living in the so-called Third World feel sorry for someone in the First?

"Sir?" one of the librarians whispered, interrupting Viana's thought. "Sir, the library's about to close."

"Close? Already?" Viana wondered, looking at his watch and realizing that it was already eight o'clock. Good Lord, he'd spent all afternoon rummaging through these old books. His wife must be worried sick. He hadn't called, which he usually has the courtesy to do when he knows he won't make it in time for dinner. She wasn't a jealous woman, but how would he explain his arriving home so late? At the library reading all afternoon and into the evening? He wouldn't believe it himself. And his wife knew he was no bookworm, to put it gently.

"And to make matters worse," Viana moaned to himself, as he gathered his materials, "I didn't even come up with any recommendations for the Mayor."

"So, anyone wanna walk along the beach?" Isabel asked the others, as the four lingered over a table of empty plates and scattered silverware. The group had moved from the samba bar and they were now seated at a patio restaurant that overlooks the hotels and other buildings lining the arc of Ipanema Beach.

"You young'ns go on ahead," Marcela told them. "We old folks need time to digest."

"Shall we?" Marcos suggested to Isabel.

The two exited the patio and descended a flight of steps toward the beach. Reaching the sand, Isabel kicked off her sandals and ran toward the water, leaving Marcos the difficult task of trying to keep up in street shoes.

"It's so sad!" she called out, turning in circles as she looked to the sky. Then, suddenly feeling the water on her feet, she let out a playful scream. "Oh, it's so cold!"

"I tried to warn you," Marcos reminded her.

"The ocean is so beautiful, even at night," she added, leaning down to dip her hands in the water.

"So why's it sad?" he asked.

"Say what?"

"Didn't you say it was sad?"

"Oh, the sky," she explained, looking up. "You can't see any stars. That's what you city people are missing, you know," she told him. "You may be able to find a lot of things here, but never a sky as starry as in the country."

"Guess I never thought much about it," Marcos shrugged, following her gaze upward.

"No?" she confirmed. "So you've never heard about the origin of the stars?"

"Origin of the —"

Before Marcos could finish, Isabel had taken him by the hand and plopped down upon the sand, obliging him to do the same. The two, now lying on their backs, looked up to the heavens.

"Once upon a time," she began, "there was a beautiful young girl, called Day, who was much beloved by all the beings on

Earth. But lately Day had become quite sad — a change that all noticed. After much time had passed, and Day remained melancholy, the Forest Mother went to speak with the young girl. 'Why are you sad, my lovely Day, when you offer so much to this Earth? Your light, your heat, your very presence pleases us all.' 'Because I do not possess that which all others have down below,' the young girl responded. 'A love of my own,' she revealed. Despite the further kind words offered to her by the Forest Mother and others, Day remained sad. Finally, the Forest Mother made a decision, saying 'Day, you shall have that which you do not possess. Day brings heat, so I grant you the coolness of shade; Day's light tires the eyes, so I offer you the respite that darkness provides. Your love is called Night and soon it shall arrive.' Day became so very happy, but also quite anxious waiting for her love. Several hours having already passed, and tired of waiting, Day decided to head out in search of her love who had yet to arrive. She started out West, and traveled for miles and miles, when she suddenly caught a glimpse of the shade the Forest Mother had spoken of. Excited, she moved quickly to reach her promised love, but each time Day got close, Night would withdraw further and further away. Meanwhile, on the other side of the world, Night also wandered in search of his love. And every time he spied the emerging rays of dawn, he would approach quickly, yet never able to reach Day. And to this day the two lovers wander the Earth, each searching for the other, but never able to meet."

"And the stars?" Marcos wondered.

"Kisses," Isabel explained. "Tiny drops of light Day leaves scattered across the heavens so Night will know that she hasn't forgotten him. And this is why it's so cruel for cities to steal the stars from the sky. Night will think that Day no longer cares."

"That's nice," Marcos acknowledged. "Is it a Native American legend?"

"More or less."

"One that your father used to tell you?"

Isabel rose suddenly, leaning on her elbow.

"How do you know about my father?" she asked him.

Marcos also lifted himself up and looked to Isabel.

"Reggie told me," he admitted.

"He told you about my father?"

"About your family... about you."

"So you know that he died when I was a child?" Isabel asked, lying back down on the sand.

"Yes, I do," Marcos nodded. "Listen," he said, "are you angry with me?"

"That's one of the reasons Reggie and I are so close," she continued, ignoring Marcos' question. "We know what it is to lose a parent. You feel as if you've been somehow cut in half. And, as if that weren't hard enough, you realize one day that you're slowly losing the memory of them as well. For Reggie, losing his mother must have been made worse, since he never even knew his father."

Marcos remained silent; the silence of one who has known little tragedy in life and realizes his sympathy will ring hollow.

"I'm sorry, Marcos," Isabel apologized. "I must be depressing the hell out of you."

"No, I'm fine. It's nice hearing you talk about your family, your life... the stars."

"What about you?" she asked, sitting up. "Uncover for us this mystery that is Marcos Antonio."

"Mystery, eh?"

"I would say so. I mean, we know you're from São Paulo, that you work for your senator there, but other than that...a big X, the unknown."

"The unknown... I agree," he laughed.

"How's that?"

"I don't know, I just feel kind of out of it these days," he admitted to her. "I haven't even been in Rio for two weeks and already my life in São Paulo seems like ancient history, a past life."

"Nostalgia, perhaps?" Isabel suggested.

"For the city?"

"For someone?"

"Honestly?"

"Naturally."

"No," he confessed.

"What about that girl that called earlier?"

"What girl?" Marcos wondered.

"From Brasília... uh... Veronica?"

"Veronica called?" he asked, surprised.

"At the bar. Sorry, we forgot to mention it."

"That's fine, but Veronica is just a friend from college. There's somebody else," he admitted. "Another friend, in São Paulo."

"A female friend?"

Marcos shrugged his shoulders.

"I'll take that as a 'yes'," Isabel concluded.

"Since we're speaking frankly... yes, a girlfriend. And not just one of those summer flings. We've been together for three years already."

"Wow."

"Well, three years officially," he clarified. "We've been friends since grade school."

"It does sound serious. So, what made you ask Reggie about me?"

"I don't know. Curiosity, I guess."

"I also saw you looking at me back at the bar. A taken man such as yourself shouldn't go around checking women out and asking questions about them," Isabel playfully chided him.

"Taken man? That's the second time today someone's called me that," he nervously laughed.

"Well," Isabel shrugged. "Three years."

"A question for you," Marcos said after a pause.

"Shoot."

"At the end of your life, thinking back on all that you accomplished, things you saw, emotions lived... wouldn't you feel a certain bitterness if you discovered that you married and spent your whole life with someone mainly because you shared the same zip code?"

"I see that my little story did depress you," Isabel smiled.

"No, seriously, wouldn't you feel somehow cheated to learn that it was just simple proximity that brought you together and not some higher power?" Marcos pressed. "I guess," he added without waiting for a response, "I guess I'm just afraid of looking back upon my life with regret."

"That's practically unavoidable," Isabel predicted. "There'll always be something we wish we'd done differently, or not done at all."

Something done differently. Marcos turned the phrase over in his mind as he recalled his earlier conversation with Marcela. If he were a walking, talking, organize-your-day, your week, your life black leather-bound daily planner with removable clear bookmark for easy reference kind of guy, like she claimed, what was he doing sitting next to a beautiful girl on a beach in Rio de Janeiro on a weekday night? He didn't need to rely on a flashy red sports car and matching tie in order to let loose with the best of them. He could be unpredictable, dammit. For example, who would imagine that he might just now curl his arm around this young girl's waist, draw her body closer and move in for a kiss?

"I'm sorry, Isabel," he apologized, quickly withdrawing from her.

"It's ok," she calmed him.

"No really, I'm sorry," he said, embarrassed. "I'm not myself today."

"I don't know, Marcos," she sighed, leaning forward and wrapping her arms around her knees as she stared into an invisible sea. "Maybe you are."

One might say, if privy to his habits and daily routine, that the Chief of Police is also not himself this balmy Brazilian evening. After leaving the library, Viana stopped at a public telephone, called his wife, and explained where he'd been and what he'd been up to for the past several hours. She, too, had lost track of time, for a few friends had stopped by and were still laughing about old times in the Viana living room. The Chief was not anxious to round out that circle, so he proposed that he stop off for a beer while out, and promised that he wouldn't be long. After hanging up, he turned West, which was actually North, and meandered through the nearby Floriano Square, passing by more than a few open-air cafés in which he could have ordered a beer on tap, fried bacalhau, or any array of sun-dried meats. Instead, he found himself carried farther afield, into the crowded streets of the once-colonial outpost. Perhaps only a philosopher preoccupied with the past, as Viana had lately become, could appreciate these early examples of urban planning; relics that had escaped the fever of urban renewal in which their kind was paved over and then expanded to boulevard proportions, such as the nearby Avenida Rio Branco, the Beira Mar, and avenues Presidente Wilson and Kubitschek. Such grandiose thoroughfares were often rewarded with the names of grandiose men, but why had these smaller streets never been bestowed an equal honor? An honor, we point out, to both named and namesake, for wouldn't Viana find the comparison between himself and this stretch of curvy road quite flattering? Something about it remained so humble, and yet noble, having been spared a boulevard's hubris.

You see, it wasn't just that Viana, as a result of abandoning his patrol car, had become a man who moves about on foot. No, it was far more serious; the Chief had become an absolute *flâneur* – one who extracts real enjoyment from strolling the streets and turns said stroll into an art. When – and why – had the term pedestrian donned its pejorative cloak? Deep down, Viana knew he was, in part, responsible for this unsavory view of public spaces. Law enforcement's relationship with the street was not always so cozy. Public spaces drew in the public, and this led to crowds, and crowds led to mischief. Therefore, you attack the source of the problem. Viana recognized the logic behind the argument, but he was beginning to lose sight of the sense.

Meanwhile, several miles away – but seemingly centuries from the epoch in which Viana found himself immersed – the sound of thumping techno music bellowed out of a bright yellow building where cars waited, lined up in order to valet park. Inside the Bar Mostarda, Juliana, Tatiana and other friends were talking loudly as a young man — one of the friends — arrived at the table carrying three drinks which he distributed to the others.

"*Caipiroskas* for the ladies," he announced.

As the young man leaned over the table to hand one of the girls her vodka and lime cocktail, Juliana gave his buttocks a forceful slap.

"So whaddya say, Renato?" she slurred. "Let's see you shake that ass."

"Jesus Christ, Juliana!" Tatiana scolded her.

Renato looked to the others with a reassuring glance and gentle nodding of the head.

"All right, Juliana. Shall we?" he asked, motioning towards the dance floor.

"What's gotten into her?" a friend asked, seeing Juliana so shaky on her feet.

"Drowning her sorrows," Tatiana explained.

If Juliana's eyes had been able to focus for more than a few seconds, over Renato's shoulder she would have seen Gustavo, Milena and Flavia seated there at a corner table in the back.

"Flavia, maybe you can explain this to me," Milena guessed. "Is Rio going to become the capital of the country again?"

"No one knows, really. I hope to find out during the coronation, when we finally get to interview the king."

"And we'll finally get a good look at him," Milena remarked. "Why so much secrecy?"

"That's exactly what we've been trying to figure out," Flavia told her.

"They say the Mayor's going to block off the streets downtown for an official parade and all kinds of hoopla."

"You bet," Flavia confirmed. "He's the one hoping this city becomes the capital again, so he wants to create a real spectacle," she explained.

"Hold up," Gustavo cut in. "Is the ceremony tomorrow or Saturday?"

"Saturday," Flavia answered. "Why?"

"Damn! There's a beach volleyball tournament on Saturday."

"You and your intellectual hobbies," Flavia laughed.

"Volleyball tournament?" Milena asked, surprised. "Won't they cancel it because of the coronation?"

"Cancel it?" Gustavo responded, shocked that one could even consider such a thing. "No way. This tourney's been planned for months."

"Will anyone show up?" Milena wondered.

"To the beach? On a Saturday? Are you kidding?" Gustavo laughed. "Question is, who's gonna go to some ceremony downtown on the weekend when they could be at the beach?"

"He's got a point," Flavia admitted. "It's cool, Gus," she told him. "Go to your tourney, enjoy the beach. I don't need you to film the ceremony."

"No?"

"Nope."

"Flavia's kind of nice when she drinks," Gustavo said to Milena with a wink and a smile.

Back at the patio restaurant, Marcela nursed a Mai Tai, while Reginaldo sat across from her rather quiet and pensive.

"Hey King, what you thinking about?" she asked him.

"The press conference."

"Right, your debut... the coronation. Tomorrow?"

"Day after."

"Have you already prepared a speech?"

"I think Marcos has put something together," he mumbled. "It's just that I'm a little nervous about speaking in public."

"Do what I do," Marcela suggested. "Just imagine the entire audience in their undies, since — after all — I'm dancing around in mine!" The comment succeeded in wrenching a smile from an otherwise gloomy Reginaldo. "So why's Marcos writing your speech?" she wondered. "It's your coronation, you don't have anything to say? Don't want to talk a little about yourself, where you come from... your impressions of Rio?"

"The heat, for example?" he suggested.

"For the love of God," Marcela warned him, "you are not going to get up there and talk about your stupid obsession with the heat."

"But, haven't you ever thought about it Marcela? Heat is a real sociological danger. The places that are the hottest are also those that suffer most in this world."

"Oh God, here we go..." she sighed.

"For example," Reginaldo said, sitting up and pulling his empty plate closer to him. "Here in Brazil," he began, taking his gnawed pork chop bone and arranging it on the plate so that it mimicked the Brazilian coastline. "Here in Brazil..."

"That's Brazil?" Marcela laughed.

"Bear with me," he pleaded with her. "It's just for the purposes of this demonstration."

"How appropriate, scraps not fit for a dog," she scoffed.

"As I was saying, here in Brazil there's abject poverty in the Northeast," Reginaldo began again, pointing to the top corner of the larger portion of bone that splayed slightly to the right, "but the poverty slowly diminishes as you work your way to the South," he continued, running his index finger down the bone, "until you arrive in the southern states where it's cold — it even snows — and where – coincidentally? I ask you – they enjoy a quality of life almost equal to Europe's. In the United States the phenomenon is the same. Only that, over there, it's the opposite," he explained, turning the bone one hundred and eighty degrees. "Their South is more messed up while the Northeast — New York, Washington, Boston — is an example of progress and ingenuity the whole world tries to emulate," Reginaldo concluded, leaning back in his chair as if to rest his case.

"So, in this theory of yours, what exactly do you think the heat does?" Marcela asked. "Melt their – wait! our - brain cells?"

"No, Marcela. I'm not sure, but it seems that the cold stimulates people's ingenuity and drives them to build homes, make clothes and machines that will keep them from freezing to death. Necessity is, after all, the mother of invention," Reginaldo smiled, quoting the old saying. "In the Tropics, with no danger of cold and such natural abundance all around, we lack a similar stimulus to get out there and develop. And so we're left to wallow in poverty."

"Interesting theory," Marcela commented, unimpressed. Shaking her head, she added: "And it doesn't strike you as just a tiny bit curious that these same underdeveloped tropics were the places that suffered the most from colonization? From men," she continued, picking up the stubs of Reginaldo's half-eaten carrots, "who built up sugar plantations in our Northeast," she said, marching the carrots across the plate and tromping over the bone-shaped Brazil, "cotton fields in their South with intricate systems of human slavery and all the brutality that came with it? It seems to me that it's not the heat you should worry about, but rather the Europeans," she concluded, snapping a bite from the carrot.

Reginaldo mumbled something beneath his breath in response.

"So, Reggie," Marcela wondered, "is there anything you do like about the city?"

"Of course," he assured her, but could not disguise the pause he was forced to take in order to think.

"Well?" Marcela asked, pulling out a smoke. "I'm waiting," she slurred as she lit the cigarette held between her lips.

"The lights of the city, for example. They really are beautiful," he said, looking up into the hills that surround them.

"Those lights?" she verified, pointing her cigarette above his head. "You think those lights are beautiful?"

"Don't you?" he asked her. "Look at them," he said, turning around. "It looks as though someone planted gigantic Christmas trees all throughout the city. What are they, anyway? Houses?"

"You really don't know, do you?" Marcela asked, releasing a large plume of smoke in his direction.

"I guess not," Reginaldo shrugged.

"They're *favelas*, Reggie. Slums, shantytowns, cardboard cities, call them what you like."

"Slums?" he asked. "But I already saw the slums," he told her.

"What do you mean you already saw the slums?" she wondered.

"On the outside of town," he explained. "When Marcos and I drove in."

"Well, king," she laughed, "we've got plenty to go around! I thought you'd been around the city already."

"I have. I guess I never noticed."

"Yeah, well, you wouldn't be the first who's ignored them," Marcela noted.

"But..." he stuttered. "They're so beautiful at night. And the views of the city the residents must enjoy..."

"I'm guessing it doesn't make up for the lack of running water."

"No, of course not."

"Well, it's getting late," Marcela said, slightly annoyed as she glanced down at a non-existent watch. "Shall we gather the kids and go?"

"Sure," Reginaldo agreed, but his thoughts were elsewhere.

Hardly a word was uttered during the short ride back to Marcela's place in Copacabana. Marcos had left the top down on his convertible so that the four friends could enjoy the feel of the evening air in their face and hair as they circled the beautiful Lagoa de Rodrigo Freitas. This intrusion of the outside world was the perfect excuse to ignore the tension that simmered inside the automobile. We can safely assume that Marcos found it difficult to introduce a suitably neutral topic of conversation after that first stolen, clumsy kiss. Isabel, perhaps unwilling to help, remained quiet as well. Only Marcela's silence was one of peace as she enjoyed the night air. And Reginaldo?

Shantytowns? he thought, still smarting from his conversation with Marcela. Favelas? he kept asking himself, as if repeating the word would help clarify its existence, would resolve the contradiction between apparent beauty and bitter reality. As Reginaldo looked up into the night sky, he found himself staring at Christ the Redeemer, interrogating the enormous statue that loomed there in the background above the lake and the rest of the city. It's unfortunate, Redeemer, that Your eyes and limbs are made of concrete, for perhaps, if otherwise, You might have noticed the misery churning beneath You and lent a hand. Instead, above the fray You remain, facing East towards the bay, effectively turning your back upon the poorer northern half of the city, and welcoming with outstretched arms the wealthy who only love You for Your beaches. Reginaldo imagined those holy arms reaching towards the sky as The Redeemer fell victim to one of the myriad petty assaults that plague this city. Unlike the street children who merely tug upon Your robes in their perennial plea for alms, these bandits from the hillside are only taking from You by force what they feel, as Your children, they deserve. Uneasy, Reginaldo closed his eyes and tried his best to enjoy the ride.

The next morning, Reginaldo found himself once again drawn to the museum. This time, he stood before a large painting whose title plaque read: "Coronation of the Emperor Dom Pedro II." At the center of the canvas a Cardinal of the Catholic Church could be seen placing a crown upon the head of a young boy that kneels at his feet, the child's knees resting upon a pillow. Backing slowly away, other priests who flank the Cardinal came into view amid a sea of faces belonging to the spectators that watched the event from all sides. Feeling the edge of a viewing bench touch his legs, Reginaldo let himself fall back onto the couch, his gaze unbroken. Noticing Reginaldo's fascination with the piece, a museum employee approached, coming to a stop behind him on the other side of the bench.

"1842," the man said.

"Excuse me?" Reginaldo asked, surprised.

"The painting was done by François René Moreaux in 1842, not more than a year after Pedro the Second was made king."

"He looks so tiny," Reginaldo noted.

"He was only fifteen."

"I know, but in the middle of that crowd he looks even smaller than I had imagined."

"He was rather timid and withdrawn," the employee explained, "preferred the quiet of his studies to the hustle and bustle of the court. Yes, just fifteen," he continued after a pause. "Hard to imagine even an extroverted young man taking on such a burden at that age. He must have felt quite overwhelmed..."

"Afraid," Reginaldo suggested.

"Terrified."

"Yes..."

There was a pause.

"Well, enjoy the exhibit," the employee said as he stepped away, leaving Reginaldo alone with the painting.

PART THREE

XVI

A twenty-one gun salute announced to the city of Rio de Janeiro that the young emperor was on his way from the residence at São Cristóvão to the City Palace. The procession was led by a series of cavalry regiments, aligned according to rank, while behind them there followed a near equal number of horse-drawn carriages that transported various officers of the Court, the children's tutors, and other royal attendants. These were placed according to an unwritten rank, their importance determined by their proximity to the crown, represented concretely in the order in which they fanned out from the king. Three vehicles rounded out the parade, winding slowly behind the others in single file. Mr. Vieira was seated in the first coach, followed by the Princesses Januaria and Francisca in the second vehicle. And, finally, the Emperor himself, alone in a silver-spangled coach drawn by, not one, but eight of Brazil's finest thoroughbreds. From within its green, velvet-lined interior, Pedro waived to the crowd, which grew ever larger as they neared the Palace Square and the Imperial Chapel.

Hours earlier, after his robes, medals, and other garments had been placed upon him by a coterie of servants and royal handlers, Pedro had remained in the dressing room. And, though just steps away from the full length mirror, the young man's stare seemed to meet no object outside his own mind.

"How fortunate you're still here," Vieira's voice broke in, causing Pedro to turn. "Yes, take a long look at those faces above you," he went on, mistaking the aim of the young man's gaze, referring instead to an array of portraits that lined the walls of the room. Pictured there were the royals who had come before young Pedro: Afonso Henriques the Conqueror, Henry the Navigator, the Lost King Sebastian, spiffy titles that seemed to contain in just a few words an entire history of brave deeds and accomplishments.

"As you can see, Pedro, these robes are not meant to be worn by just any man. History beckons and she requires nothing less than greatness. You are yet a young man, but if Your Highness sets about your studies with more diligence there is nothing to prevent you from following in the steps of your father, and his father before him, and so on."

Pedro nodded, still somewhat remote.

"But you must approach this position with more sobriety," Vieira continued to counsel. "These diversions into the banalities of procedure – these petitions, for example – are not worthy of your time."

"But it was you that - "

"I suggested you perform the ceremony, not the paperwork," Vieira argued. "A petty mind does a petty king make, and Time will honor no such man. Are we understood?"

Pedro again nodded.

"So come, let us take this moment to begin anew," the king's aide proposed, grasping Pedro at the shoulders and turning the young man towards him. "Just look at you," he beamed. "I feel a parent's pride run through me as if I myself were your father. But, alas, you're no longer a boy to be fawned upon. Today, Pedro, you become a king."

When at last the entourage arrived, the cavalry formed a perimeter so wide that it nearly filled the entire Palace Square, leaving the citizens of Rio to peer over military heads, or rush to the upper floors of their houses, if they wanted a look at the carriages that came to a stop beneath the palace verandah. Finally, the Emperor stepped into the doorway of his coach and bowed graciously before his subjects. He was dressed in military attire, with a gold medallion fastened snugly at his neck, overlapping a blue sash that ran across his chest. One hand rested firmly upon a cutlass, while the other was entwined in the weave of his belt. Both medal and cutlass shone brightly in the mid-day sun as Pedro lifted his hand to wave to the crowd. Amid the joyous dancing, cacophonous bells, and jubilant gunshots, it is unlikely that anyone at all heard the jeers and complaints of anticipating the king's rule, but we may confidently imagine that such warnings were voiced. After all, the emperor was just a child, and to bend the law to one's whim was to temp the wrath of fate.

"A disaster waiting to happen," Viana grumbled aloud to himself.

The Police Chief was well aware of the risks involved when a large gathering of people came together. He knew, of course, that it was impossible to call off the coronation, but, really, couldn't the Mayor see that he was creating the exact climate for civil disturbance that he had asked Viana to try so hard to avoid?

No use fretting, he thought to himself. The show must go on. And it was at moments like this that Viana realized the Mayor cared more about the spectacle than for the safety of the public. What could you expect? The Mayor didn't understand, like Viana, the beautiful enigma that is law enforcement. Despite this discrepancy, the Police Chief followed the Mayor's order to keep the downtown streets clear of unwanted traffic and solicitors, which wasn't difficult for this part of town was usually quite deserted on the weekends. The majority of his officers had been placed at the entrances to the hilltop shanties to ensure that no roving bands of juvenile delinquents and other riff-raff would get the idea in their heads to come marching down the mountain in protest and subsequently divert the media's attention away from the coronation. This was, easily, the Mayor's worst nightmare. Viana had tried to convince him that most of the city would be out along the beaches today, especially with the volleyball tournament going on, and so perhaps they should keep their usual cadre of officers there to protect the sunbathers. If you were a roving band of thugs, Viana argued, wouldn't you hit the beach on Saturday? Even rabble need a holiday. But the Mayor was adamant: secure downtown at all costs. To make matters worse, the 4th annual "Miss Bum-Bum Rio" contest was to be held today during the volleyball tournament's intermission. Once every three hundred and sixty five days, the city's finest rear-ends would gather to shake their stuff for the fans and other assembled pervs at the Ipanema Beach event, until only one fanny was judged worthy to wear the Miss Bum-Bum Rio crown. It was an orgy of beer, sweat, and sunscreen that was enough to make any decent person long nostalgically for the days of gladiators and lions' dens.

There'll be more dental floss at that event than in a dentist's medicine cabinet, the Chief of Police thought to himself, as he again mourned the fact that his officers would not be there to enforce his recent policy on bikini use.

As Viana continued his musings, a modest procession of a half dozen luxury cars started to make its way through the streets of downtown Rio towards a large stage located in the center of the downtown plaza. At the end of the line was Reginaldo, sitting on the top of the back seat of Marcos' car, waving to the people on the streets and to the paltry crowd that had assembled. The sight of a balding, overweight man straddling a convertible like some teen-aged festival queen was hardly enough to distract the majority of citizens out running their errands from farmer's market to supermarket, even had they known this figure was their king. Fortunately, since the end of the military dictatorship, government parades were so rarely relevant to one's life. Most were happy just knowing this entourage was passing them by. Only worry if they stop, folks would think to themselves, for the wounds of tyranny are slow to heal.

When this procession did, at last, come to a stop, Reginaldo, the Mayor, and other officials exited their vehicles and took the stage, coming to rest in a row of chairs located behind a podium.

In his living room at home, the mood was anxious as the Senator and his wife watched the ceremonies on television.

"Juliana doesn't want to watch?" the Senator asked his wife. "It is Marcos' handiwork after all."

"She hasn't left that room since she got back from Rio," Melba told him.

"No? How come?"

"Sick, I guess."

"Same thing she always catches after a trip to Rio, I suppose?" the Senator smirked, referring to the souvenir hangover his daughter usually brought back from the coastal city. Melba gave her husband a censuring glare and turned back towards the television.

The Mayor, approaching the podium, nodded to the crowd that had gathered before the stage, but saved his smile for the television audience at home.

"Today all of Brazil," he beamed, "and all the world, for that matter, can agree that Rio de Janeiro is truly a capital city. We are again ready to burst onto the world's stage and prove our overwhelming potential, both at home and abroad."

On the tiny television set in her apartment, Marcela watched the coronation while, in the background, two friends practiced dance steps for that night's show.

"Oh boy," she said to them, "just look at the gleam in those beady little eyes. This man is loving all the attention."

Gustavo, in the middle of a row of bleachers watching the highly anticipated beach volleyball tournament, cupped a hand over one ear as he tried to better hear the coronation ceremony on a hand-held radio.

"And so," the Mayor continued, "it is with immense pleasure and pride that I present to the Brazilian people our new king, His Majesty Reginaldo the First!"

The crowd responded with a light applause that fell well short of matching the Mayor's excitement. Reginaldo stood and approached the podium, visibly nervous. Beside him, perched atop a pedestal, a crown rested upon a small, red velvet pillow.

"What in the hell is he wearing?" Marcela giggled, referring to the thick garnet robes Reginaldo had donned for the occasion. It looked as though the king's men had raided a consignment costume shop on the eve of carnival, when all the decent outfits had long ago been rented out. And, knowing his disdain for the heat, Marcela shuttered to think of what little clothing the king must be wearing beneath that musty cloak. Flavia, seated in the front row of journalists, may have thought the same as she glimpsed a pair of flip-flop sandals beneath his robes.

"Thank... Uh, thank you, Mayor," Reginaldo stammered, "but really you can just call me Reggie."

The crowd chuckled, which put Reginaldo a little more at ease. There was a short pause as all became quiet, waiting.

"Well, they've prepared a speech for me today," Reginaldo began, "but I haven't read it yet and I don't think I will. I prefer to speak to the people, not as a politician, but as a friend. Someone you might strike up a conversation with in a bar, for example."

Again, the sound of laughter was heard from the crowd. The officials gathered on stage began to murmur amongst themselves, glancing nervously towards Marcos who would quickly look away in response.

"Since this referendum vote," Reginaldo continued, "and in the two weeks that have passed, while you all have gained a king, I have gained a history — a sketch of my past that I had not known before. For this I thank, first of all, you – my fellow countrymen – for choosing to entertain a monarchy and, second, the Lord above for granting me such good fortune. And while I don't want to appear ungrateful, I feel obliged to comment upon what I have seen since arriving here in Rio."

Hearing this, Marcela placed a hand over her eyes and silently prayed: "Oh God, please don't let him complain about the heat."

Inside the offices of the Supreme Court, Veronica was also watching the ceremony on television between breaks in her perennial perusal of legislative documents. Hearing these last comments from Reginaldo, she abandoned her reading and approached the TV, pulling up a chair and turning up the volume.

"Since leaving my hometown and arriving in Rio," Reginaldo continued, "I have met many wonderful people, made many new friends."

Isabel, seated to the left of the stage, glanced toward Marcos, but her smile was greeted with a worried look from the young man.

"I've had my first samba lesson, and even sampled a caipiroska. Yet, I have noticed an unsettling reality," Reginaldo remarked, abruptly changing his tone. "One in which individuals do not recognize their fellow citizens as part of themselves, as their other halves, you might say."

At this comment, members of the audience felt obliged to look to their neighbors seated around them, as if to remedy this lack of recognition to which the king referred.

"We do not see," Reginaldo continued, "that the welfare of others is so much a part of our own well-being. That we cannot be truly complete as individuals while our other, less fortunate halves go hungry, or otherwise suffer. In our streets I have seen among us some gorged to the full with dishes of every sort while these other halves plead like beggars at their doors, emaciated with hunger and poverty."

The audience now began to talk loudly amongst themselves, for the tone of the king's speech was definitely not what they had expected.

"And I can't help but find it strange," Reginaldo went on, "that these poverty-stricken halves should suffer such injustice in silence," he said, raising his voice. "We should be amazed that they do not come down from the hills and take these others by the throat or set fire to their houses."

This sent the officials on stage into a near frenzy, while the audience also grew more and more restless. Amid the confusion, a reporter close to the stage shouted a question:

"Does this mean Your Highness would not support a proposal to make Rio the capital of Brazil?"

"I don't know, I'm not familiar with this proposal," Reginaldo admitted.

Sensing that something had to be done, the Mayor jumped up and ran to speak with the leader of the small military band that had been commissioned for the event. Flavia took advantage of the confusion as well and shouted:

"Just what are your proposals, Your Majesty?"

"Proposals? Well, I -"

The military band began to play, interrupting Reginaldo's response, while at the same time Marcos' mobile phone began to ring. The Mayor approached the podium, grabbed the crown from its pillow and handed it to Reginaldo.

"Here, take your damn crown," he growled over the feedback caused by his muffling of the microphone.

"I really didn't mean to offend, I was just -"

Before Reginaldo could finish his apology, he was led away by security guards. Following these events by radio, Gustavo got up from his seat and started exiting the bleachers.

"Where're you going?" a friend called after him.

"I've gotta make a phone call," he explained, turning back around.

"But the bum-bum contest is about to begin. You don't wanna miss that."

"It won't take long. I'll be right back," Gustavo assured him.

"Get me a beer while you're down there?" the friend smiled, holding up his empty plastic cup.

Back at the ceremony, the military band continued to play as the audience began to disperse. Along the steps leading to the stage, a line of journalists had formed to interview the public officials as they exited.

"Two asses were crowned today," the Mayor cried angrily, referring, of course, to the contest and the coronation. "The citizens of Rio don't deserve this kind of treatment," he added. "If the king isn't happy with our city, ship him off to Brasília!"

"We at Amnesty International," a man with a French accent told another interviewer, "interpret this reference to half-men — the half of man being the child — as a clear denunciation of the treatment of street kids throughout the city."

Bounding down the stage steps, head lowered to avoid reporters, Marcos nearly ran right into Isabel.

"Hey!" she shouted, extending an arm to catch him as he blew past.

"Where's Reggie?" he greeted her.

"I don't know."

"Jesus, this guy's a handful."

"Hey, take it easy," Isabel said, trying to calm him.

"Take it easy?" Marcos growled. "The king of Brazil, who I'm supposed to be advising, has just told the entire country that the poor should burn down the houses of the rich! And you tell me to take it easy?!"

"They didn't let him finish."

"Thank God!" he cried. "Look, Isabel, I don't really want to see him right now. Tell him that I need to return to São Paulo for a few days. Can you guys take care of him while I'm gone?"

"Take care of him?" she wondered. "He's not a child, Marcos."

"I'm not so sure of that right now. Look, at least see that he makes it back safely to the palace."

"Yeah fine, no problem," Isabel assured him. "When are you coming back?"

"I don't know," Marcos sharply replied as he started to walk away.

"I can't say that I'll still be here when you get back," she called out to him.

Marcos stopped and turned back towards her.

"Look, Isabel," he began, coming closer. "I like you very much. Really. But things are kind of crazy right now and I'm not sure if this...," he paused. "If us... I just don't know if it's worth it to wait around for me," he finally blurted out.

"Worth it?" Isabel repeated.

"I should go," he sighed. "Take care of Reggie. I'll try to call from São Paulo."

Before Isabel could say anything more, Marcos was pulling away, blowing back a kiss before he turned.

"Worth it?" Isabel murmured again to herself.

Then, already some distance away, Marcos whirled abruptly back around and shouted to her: "And for the love of God, take the limo, not the bus!"

"Very entertaining. Better than that volleyball match, I bet," Flavia remarked, speaking from a broadcast booth near the stage.

"Sure was," Gustavo answered, standing at a pay phone. "Sure you don't need my help?"

"Yeah, I'm fine. Nothing more to see here, really. If you want, stop by the office later. I'm headed there now to look up some things."

"The office?" he wondered. "But it's Saturday."

"Sure, but things are starting to get interesting," she smiled.

"I wanna be prepared."

EYEGLASSES AGAIN PERCHED at the end of her nose, Veronica had turned off the television and resumed her work when a telephone at the other end of the office began to ring.

"Hello?"

"Good afternoon," the voice at the other end said. "My name is Flavia Mores, I'm a reporter with the Tele-Journal in Rio."

"Yes, how can I help you?"

"And you are..."

"My name is Veronica, I'm an aide to Judge Barbosa."

"Barbosa... He was the one that disqualified the Portuguese heir, right?"

"That's correct," Veronica dryly replied. "It was Judge Barbosa that informed the Senate of the unconstitutionality of a foreign-born heir."

"Veronica, I need to learn more about the powers of the king, just how the relationship between he and the congress is going to work, that kind of thing. You wouldn't happen to be able to help me with that, would you?"

Later that evening, Reginaldo, Isabel, and Marcela gathered around their usual table inside The Pleasure Palace. Seated with them were two of Marcela's friends, fellow dancers Luzia and Claudia, who, oddly enough, were wearing white button-up shirts, suspenders and loosely knotted neckties.

"It's about time a politician spoke the truth around here," Luzia declared. "Sure is," Claudia agreed. "Great speech, Reggie!"

"Thank you, ladies. Me, a politician?" he whispered to Isabel.

"You know, what I don't understand," Marcela began, "is why

every tourist to Rio is shocked to see the poor pressed up against the homes of the rich. I guess they prefer them hidden away, out of view from their sensitive first-world eyes. Well, I hope we haven't ruined your vacation as well, Reggie."

"Ruined my..." Reginaldo stammered. "I thought I was saying what you wanted to hear," he explained to her.

"What I wanted to hear?" she wondered. "I didn't ask to hear a thing. Forget it, I can't sit here and argue with you all night. Luzia, Claudia, let's go."

The three performers rose from the table and made their way backstage, leaving Reginaldo and Isabel alone with their lemonades.

"Reggie," Isabel said, placing a hand on his.

"Marcela always takes things the wrong way," he complained.

"I think I'm going to head back home," she told him.

"To the palace?"

"No, back to Cruzília."

"Back to Cruzília?" he asked, heartbroken. "When?"

"Tomorrow."

"So soon?" Reginaldo moaned.

"Yeah, well, I miss Mom already. And what about your garden?" she added, smiling. "Who's gonna take care of the plants and flowers with me off gallivanting in Rio?"

"I understand," he reluctantly agreed. "The city does wear upon one. Thanks for coming, though. It helped with my homesickness."

"Of course, Reggie," Isabel smiled. "Say, you think they have a telephone here I could use?" she asked, looking around the club.

"At the bar, I believe. Ask for Dante," he told her.

As Isabel headed towards the bar, the lights inside the club began to dim and all looked to the stage. Slowly, the thick red curtain opened and Marcela appeared wearing an elegant red evening dress, while Luzia and Claudia, in addition to the suspenders and necktie, now wore top hats as well with mustaches drawn in above their lips. They sat at two small tables on stage, and as Marcela sauntered between them, she sang:

Tonight I cried, I cried

A sight too pitiful for the stage...

"Does daddy know you're here?" Juliana asked, pulling Marcos quickly from the hallway and into her bedroom.

"No, your mother let me in," he told her.

"He's upset, he wants to talk with you," she said as she began to pace back and forth.

"But I'm here to talk to you."

"About that floozy?" she wondered.

"She's a friend of the king's, Juliana. I was just giving her a ride home."

"What in the hell is the king doing with that tramp? And why does he have to drag you into it?"

"I offered to -"

"Oh, I see," Juliana laughed.

"She needed-"

"Oh, she was needy, was she?"

"Look," Marcos explained, "I didn't come here to talk about Marcela."

"Marcela is it?"

"Juliana, I didn't -"

"So what did you come here for?" she asked, coming to a stop directly in front of him.

"To talk about us, to apologize," Marcos told her.

"Apologize for what? You just said she's a friend of the king's and nothing more. What should you have to apologize for?"

"For my..." Marcos stumbled, "for my being distracted lately. I know I haven't been there for you these last few weeks."

"Well, you're right about that," she admitted.

"But you know it's because I've been busy with work, right?"

"You're blaming Daddy?"

"What?! No, not at all. I'm just saying that it's not because of you, or us, that I've been this way."

... locked myself in the dressing room

chased an upper with a downer

and a mouthful of gin ...

"I accept your apology, if that's what this is," Juliana said after a pause. "But don't think we're back to normal just like that," she added, snapping her fingers.

"Of course..."

"'Cos we're not."

"Right."

"I'm still angry with you."

"As you should be."

Suddenly, Marcos' mobile began to ring. As he prepared to answer, Juliana flashed him a defiant look.

"It might be Reggie," he argued. "What if it's important?"

Juliana's challenge did not waver.

"You're right," Marcos agreed. "It's probably nothing, and if it isn't, well, it will just have to wait," he concluded with false conviction.

Isabel returned the receiver to its cradle and remained seated for a moment at the bar.

I cursed the passage of so many years

tried, in vain, to paint away the tears

and dressed myself in too many jewels

as have done before me, oh so many fools

Meanwhile, Juliana betrayed the beginnings of a smile as Marcos glanced back worriedly to the phone that had finally stopped ringing.

XVII

Not more than two weeks had passed since Clara and her friend Benedita started bringing their wash to the public fountain located at the center of the Palace Square. For years they had washed their household's linens in the fountain at the *Campo de Sant'ana*, for it was a much shorter walk and, besides, many other slaves would also gather there so the two women could visit with friends while they worked. But why the slaves had decided to claim as their meeting place the very square in which the pillory was erected was a mystery to Clara. Who could relax and talk to another when the whole time that whipping post burned in the corner of your eye like a sore?

And that was when you were lucky enough to find it unoccupied, which wasn't always the case. At other times you'd see every slave in the square gathered quietly in a circle around the post, just behind the prison guards who held the four or five captives who were next in line. At the guards' feet, a selection of whips and belts would be laid out on the ground from which the foreman could choose. Most were little more than long ropes with wooden handles, but others were rather sophisticated. These often had longer handles, perhaps affording the wielder a more secure grip, and instead of bearing one simple, long whip, they branched out into four or five smaller ones, which could strike the recipient at several spots with only one swing of the arm.

The foreman and his victim would be at the center of this crowd, the offending slave tied to the pillory at five different points along his overstretched body. First, a knot made around his wrists, which were raised and tied together at the opposite side of the post. A second rope bound his waist, and a third wrapped tightly around the lower edge of his naked buttocks, pulling the flesh taut so that the impact of the whip could be more painfully felt. The last two ropes would be tied around the prisoner's knees and calves, just above and just below the trousers that had been yanked to his ankles. And for the length of time that it took to inflict one hundred lashes, a witnessing slave nearby was supposed to remain detached enough to carry on with chores and conversation? Clara wondered. How could one see and hear such a thing without abandoning body and mind right there in that square and ascending to somewhere, anywhere, far away from what was mistakenly called humanity? So Clara convinced Benedita to walk the extra distance to the Palace Square where one might forget for an hour or two that he or she was another's property.

And, besides, the fountain at the Palace Square was much larger. It stretched out lengthwise from the main portico of the palace for nearly fifty meters, and was about a half-meter deep. On an average day, close to one hundred washerwomen would gather around its cement border to visit with each other while they worked. Looking around, one would believe they had been transported back to Africa, the sea of black faces so dense and so complete. Except for Clara, of course, who had always lived in Brazil and, therefore, knew no other land.

"Ben'dita," Clara said one day, suddenly stopping her work. "You ever notice that line of folks coming from the palace?" she asked her friend, pointing to an area just south of the building.

"Petitioners," Benedita explained, as if everyone already knew.

"Petitioners?" Clara echoed. "Petitioners for what?"

"Favors, I s'ppose. Folks in need of help from the king."

"How come they's black folks in that line?" Clara wondered, seeing one or two in line amongst the Whites. "I guess they's freepersons," she concluded.

"Could be," Benedita agreed, "but I hear they even let slaves kiss the king's hand if they want."

"Slaves kissing the king's hand?" Clara responded with surprise. "Why the king going to want a bunch of black folks kissing on him?" she laughed.

"Ev'rybody got to do it, girl," Benedita told her friend. "It's part of the petitioning."

"So what happens after you slobber all over the man's hand? How do you make your petition?"

"You just ask him," Benedita explained. "Just ask him while you're there."

"Ask who? The king?"

"Uh huh."

"How do you know all this?" Clara interrogated her friend. "You ever made a petition before?"

"Not me person'lly. Some of my kinfolk," she explained.

"And what happened?"

"I told you what happened, girl. They walked in and kissed his hand -"

"No," Clara interrupted her. "I mean what came of the petition?"

"Oh, I don't know," her friend shrugged. "Had something to

do with goats. I think they got it all straightened out 'fore too long."

Satisfied with Benedita's answers, Clara finally stopped her questioning and went back to her work, soaking the clothes in the water and slapping them dry on the hard rocks that formed the fountain's border. Imagine, she thought to herself as she worked. A person could just walk up and speak directly to the king. Not only a person, but even a slave, she reminded herself, glancing again towards the line of petitioners that stretched around the palace. Sure you had to kiss his hand, but wasn't that worth the opportunity of having your voice heard? And that's not just a manner of speaking, for the king would literally hear your voice. And Clara would hear his. She laughed to herself imagining the king passing by in his tilbury one day and her overhearing some important order given to an aide. Clara would look up from her work and chuckle knowingly to herself. "I know that voice," she would say. "That's the voice of the king."

When Clara finished her work, she gathered up the damp linens, said goodbye to Benedita, and started off on her walk back to the Castro home. She walked for several blocks along the *Rua do Ouvidor*, then turned North up the *Rua da Quitanda*. It was on that stretch of road that Clara saw what she had hoped to avoid. She cursed herself, knowing she should have taken another way home, but the Quitanda was the quickest route and, after talking so long with Benedita, she was already late getting back to the house.

Up ahead, the group of slaves had been directed to stop in front of a store window as the trader talked with the merchant inside, trying to convince the man that he needed an extra couple of hands around his shop. Clara quickly crossed to the other side of the street, but found herself stopping to look back at the men who were bound together by a single chain that ran from one neck to another with less than one meter between each cuff. But they weren't all men. At the head of the line stood a boy of perhaps fifteen, a child no older than her Jacob, Clara guessed. The younger ones were always placed at the front, for it was just good business savvy to show the public one's most healthy specimen, the very finest of what a dealer had to offer. Seeing that the shop owner was still reluctant to buy, the trader ordered the slaves to jump about, dancing and engaging in other forms of exercise to exhibit their physical strength and agility. The words and music that must have been, in a faraway place, a song of joy, now bled unenthusiastically from their mouths. The steps their feet and legs performed, together with the incredible blackness of their skin, led Clara to believe that they had just arrived to Brazil, perhaps aboard one of the many ships that so often entered Rio's harbor; vessels from far-away places like Guinea, Angola, and other proud kingdoms of West Africa. From the Bay of Benin to the Bay of Guanabara, their journey was far from over when they entered this harbor. With eyes still squinting as they adjusted to the sunlight and their first ever view of the Americas, the slaves were brought up from the holds of the ships and bound together, as these in front of Clara were, and transferred into smaller boats, which would carry them ashore at Valongo Beach. At Valongo, the newly arrived Africans would wait inside giant warehouses until they were either displayed at market, or paraded about the city. If a slave didn't sell in Rio, this journey would continue as he was carted off to the mines farther inland, or perhaps to the burgeoning coffee plantations of São Paulo, or even as far south as Rio Grande do Sul.

As she hurried past the Valongo slave market, Clara saw others waiting outside along the walls of the warehouse. They were not yet being exhibited to any buyer, but were instead bracing for a fate they could scarcely imagine. Or perhaps they knew. Perhaps they were able to communicate despite the confusion of African languages, some captives speaking Yoruba, others Hausa, Kikongo, KiMbundu, Fulani, Lingala, Lunda, Otchimbundu, Swahili, and Arabic. As if knowing that words were destined to fail them, they took to illustrating their thoughts with charcoal on the walls of the giant warehouse. Clara stopped to watch as an older man, bound accordingly to the last buckle of the chain, reached out above the heads of the other future slaves and began to sketch his message, not with words that would most likely go unheeded, but with images that might linger. Moving sharply downwards, as if stabbing the body of an enemy, his hand traced the first of what would be the caravel's three straight and unbending masts that, despite their strength, seemed barely able to secure the bloated and fraying sails that struggled against the wind. Beneath, the hull bowed in upon itself from the pressure that pulled at the ship's base from all sides, remaining afloat from Luanda to Rio de Janeiro by sheer miracle or curse. What message was the drawing intended to pass on? Clara wondered. It could not possibly serve as a warning, she decided, since any slave who saw it would already know all too well of these ships and what they carried and where their cargo was headed. Why had the old man bothered to put charcoal to brick, then? Clara scoffed, seemingly belittling his work. To remember? she asked herself. No, Clara, to remind, the man's gaze argued in response.

"Clara, is that you?" Assemblyman Castro yelled downstairs when he heard the back door close. "Clara?"

He's upstairs, she thought. If he needs me, why doesn't he just come on down? Clara asked herself. But she knew the answer.

"Clara, could you come upstairs for a moment?" he again called.

Without responding she slowly crossed the length of the parlor and made her way towards the stairs. As she took the first step, Clara lifted her head and heard splashing as the Assemblyman checked the warmth of his bath water. That singular, unmistakable sound haunted her for the next twelve steps. At the top of the stairs she turned down the hall towards the master bedroom, walking with that distinctive gait that results from a mixture of haste and hesitation, between the fear of making one's master wait and the hope that one will never arrive.

"What took you so long?" he asked as he stood naked before her, just outside the entrance to the bathroom.

"I... I saw a friend at the fountain," she stammered.

"What took you so long to climb the stairs, I mean."

"Oh, well I -"

"Come, Clara," he interrupted, motioning for her to enter the room. "I need help with my bath," he explained. "Grab the cloth from the hook and start with my back," he told her, sighing as he entered the tub. "Still nice and warm," he smiled.

Clara did as she was told. She took the cloth from where it hung on the wall and approached the tub, coming to rest on her knees directly behind the Assemblyman.

At least he's in the water now, she thought, for it spared her the shame of having to look directly upon his nakedness.

"That's good," he sighed as she touched the cloth to his pale white skin. "Get the shoulders, too," he reminded her.

Clara ran her hand from one shoulder to the other with a feigned tenderness that sought to hide her disgust.

"With a little more force, Clara," the Assemblyman told her. "I won't break," he laughed.

Again, Clara passed the washcloth along his shoulders and down between his shoulder blades as her master relaxed his neck and eased his head back to where it almost touched hers.

"The upper arm, too," he requested, extending his right arm out from the tub, obliging Clara to leave her place behind him. Shuffling on her knees to the right, she faced his profile now, but did everything she could to keep from looking directly at him.

"The chest, Clara. Scrub my chest as well," he then told her.

Clara leaned in towards him in order to reach across his chest, quickly turning her head to the left and looking down at the tiles so as to avoid those eyes that now sought hers.

"So modest for a Negro," he laughed. "Almost coy."

"Yes, sir," she mumbled in response.

Suddenly, she felt the Assemblyman's fingers wrap tightly around her wrist, the grip nearly dampening the flow of blood through her veins with its force. Then, with this hold upon her, Castro slowly pulled Clara closer to him as he guided her hand down his chest, then his belly, and finally into the water.

"Don't look away, Clara," he whispered into the ear that was now touching his face. However, the Assemblyman didn't pull back to allow her to turn her head, but rather kept his cheek pressed firmly against hers so that she couldn't help but hear as he began to breathe more deeply. Clara stared hard at the wall, afraid to close her eyes for fear of the images that might appear in her head, and it took her entire will to sever that hand from the rest of her body as long as it touched his. The wash cloth had by now slipped from Clara's hand and was floating away across the water, propelled along the tiny waves caused by the motion beneath.

"I've found a buyer for Jacob," Castro said to her coldly, as if speaking to a colleague of matters of little mutual interest. He had since released her hand and these words were the first after several minutes of silence in which she swore he napped.

"A what?" Clara whispered, still kneeling on the bathroom floor.

"A man who's interested in purchasing Jacob. He's nearing sixteen, Clara, and a boy at the height of his abilities shouldn't be lazing about here with no real work to do," Castro explained, rising from the tub and holding out his arm for a towel. Clara rose to fulfill the unspoken request as the Assemblyman continued: "A Negro in his physical condition is needed out on the plantations, instead of underworked here in the city and likely to get mixed up in all sorts of mischief. It's for his own good —"

"For his own good?" Clara interrupted him. "For his own good to take him away from his mama and the only place he's ever called home?"

"Clara," the Assemblyman warned her.

"For his own good to send him out to break his back in the sun?"

"Clara," Castro repeated.

"No more heart than to sell his own blood," she continued, but was cut short by a hard slap to the side of the face, which sent her falling again to the bathroom floor. Clara landed hard on the palms of her hands, her arms bent beneath her, her forehead just inches from the cold, wet tile.

"I'm sorry, Clara," the Assemblyman whispered to her, but did not kneel to help her up. "I'm sorry, but you've no right to question how I run this house. Now, come on, get up. Your mistress will soon be home," he reminded her. "She'll want to know about supper."

XVIII

Excerpt from the personal letters of William Atkins, author of *A voyage to Guinea, Brasil, and the West-Indies; in His Majesty's ships the Swalow and Weymouth; giving a genuine account of the islands and settlements thereupon found; describing the colour, diet, languages, habits, manners, customs, and religions of the respective natives and inhabitants, with remarks on the gold, ivory, and slave-trade* (1849).

I thought I might begin this missive with a declaration those back home may find quite remarkable, and therefore read more voraciously of my travels: In this year, eighteen hundred forty-nine, Rio de Janeiro is quite possibly the largest African city in the world. The statement's absurdity does not escape its author, yet one must often trust in a witness knowing very well that the strangeness of such marvels will distort and obscure his testimony.

You will have even less reason to place credence in my words if you recall that in a previous dispatch I noted the absence of Negroes in the streets, which I found surprising when one considers the pervasiveness of slavery in Brazilian homes and industry. Yet, I now recognize that this impression will vary according to the hour of one's observation.

As the masters and their families retreat indoors to escape

the afternoon heat, this leaves the streets inhabited by slaves who have no choice but to continue their work and errands. A traveller strolling through town might conclude that there does not reside a fellow European in the entire land and, ergo, the basis of my declaration above.

At present, a majority of the city's inhabitants own at least one slave, charged with the execution of household duties. The Negroes that avoid these domestic services are sent out into the streets by morning to sell their labour for hire, such profits contributing to the economies of the master's estate. The largest conglomeration gathers around a public fountain known as the *chafariz*, which serves as perhaps the slave's only sphere of social interaction with his own kind, for most pass entire days and much of their lives amongst Europeans.

Considering such invitation into the bosom of even the most notable homes, it should now be clear why our United Kingdom persists in its call to abolish the importation of Negroes to South America, the Caribbean, and other settlements in the New World. If the current level of slaves remains unabated, once European nations may find themselves increasingly mongrelized due to amalgamation. If such a scenario is allowed to occur, this land, so newly independent from Portugal, may become, after Santo Domingo, the hemisphere's second Africanized nation; a state of affairs I doubt will please the shrinking European elite. One wonders at what measures will in future be necessary to separate the races, and at what cost.

The morning after his coronation, Reginaldo sat inside the main living room of the palace shooting the breeze with Marcela and Bebel. Marcela lay across the sofa with her feet upon the arm rest, tiny balls of cotton carefully placed between her toes, as Bebel, seated in a chair beside the sofa, carefully painted her new friend's toe nails.

"They're always asking me about my proposals," Reginaldo remarked out of nowhere.

"Who?"

"The journalists."

"Well, don't tell me you haven't got any bright ideas to improve this city you hate so much," Marcela said.

"I don't hate it."

"Well, you sure do complain a lot," she pointed out.

"What about you?" Reginaldo asked.

"What about me?" Marcela wondered.

"You got any ideas?"

"Ideas?" Marcela echoed with surprise, sitting up. "The King is asking me," she said, dragging the pronoun out for maximum sarcastic effect, "asking me for advice? The Mouth-of-the-South, His Royal High-horse asking a peasant girl like me for her opinion?"

"Sure, a king likes to be amused once in a while. Never heard of a jester?"

"Oh, well Brazil's lucky 'cos we got those two for the price of one this time round..."

"Ok, please!" Bebel cut in, ending the barbs. "Reggie, what kind of changes can a king make?" she asked, bringing the conversation back to its origin.

"Good question, Bebel. King, give this young wench a raise," Marcela said, settling again into her recumbent position on the sofa.

"It is a good question," Reginaldo acknowledged, "since I must admit I don't know the answer."

"Hmmm... let's see," Marcela wondered, staring up at the ceiling. "Who would be able to tell us about the king's powers?"

"How about Mr. Marcos?" Bebel suggested.

"Sir Frets-a-lot? You've seen the way he gets, all nervous and sweaty at the thought of any unwanted media attention," Marcela reminded her. "As soon as we started asking questions, he'd know we were up to something."

"Do you guys know anybody else who works for the government?" Bebel asked them.

"What about that friend of Marcos'?" Reginaldo suggested. "The one who called the other night at the bar."

"Veronica?" Marcela asked. "Right..." she continued, leaning up and resting on her elbows. "Veronica from Brasília!"

"Doesn't she work for the government?"

"I think she works for the courts," Bebel replied.

"The Supreme Court?"

"Yeah, that one."

"You know her?" Marcela asked Bebel.

"More or less. She's called here before, looking for Mr. Marcos."

"Mr. Marcos..." Marcela repeated, chuckling to herself.

"Did she leave a telephone number?" Reginaldo asked, looking to Bebel.

"I think so. Hold on," she said, rising from her seat. "I'll check downstairs."

"PAULO," SENATOR CRUZ said as he walked out into the lobby of his São Paulo office. "Marcos isn't here yet, is he?"

"No, sir. Not yet."

"Be sure to send him to my office as soon as he arrives."

"Yes, sir," the young man nodded.

The Senator started to walk away, but suddenly stopped.

"Paulo," he repeated, turning back around.

"Yes, sir."

"When Marcos gets here, I think it might be best if you didn't mention the work I – we," the Senator corrected himself, "have been doing the last couple of weeks."

"Ok," the young man agreed.

"We have to be careful. Marcos has been away, uninvolved like you've become. He's likely to feel a bit, well, jealous."

"I see."

"Don't worry, when he does return for good we'll fill him in on everything," the Senator smiled.

"Of course," Paulo nodded.

"By the way," the Senator went on, grabbing some mail from the desk and leafing through the envelopes, "Juliana says hello and apologizes for not being able to dine with us last night. To be frank, I suspect she was nursing a hangover. Celebrated too hardily after the end of exams," the Senator explained.

"Poor thing," Paulo sighed.

"Say," the older man continued, putting aside the letters, "maybe next week we could try again. At getting us all together, I mean. How does that sound?"

"That sounds great. Thank you, sir."

"Please, Paulo," the Senator smiled. "You can call me Antonio."

Paulo remained frozen there at his desk as he watched the Senator return to his office, quite stunned at the informality of that last exchange.

"Well, traditionally," Veronica explained, "the power exercised most often by the monarchy was the concession of religious or military titles and other honors."

"Nothing more... substantial?" Marcela asked. "The king can't change anything, make new laws?"

"Well, assuming that the working constitution is that of the former Empire of Brazil, the government, even though a monarchy, is still constitutional and representative."

"And that means...?"

"It means that changes in the law have to be approved by both the Chamber of Deputies and the Senate," Veronica told her.

"Damn. What good's a king, then?"

"To be honest," Veronica confessed, "he's not good for much."

"You're tellin' me," Marcela agreed, looking over at Reginaldo who had parked himself in the chair beside the sofa and was now painting Bebel's toenails.

"From what I've been able to gather from my own research," Veronica continued, "most kings preferred not having too much responsibility for the day-to-day workings of the government. They just reserved the right to interject their opinion whenever they felt strongly about something — the famous moderating power of the monarchy, a version of a republic's checks and balances."

"So, just opinions?" Marcela confirmed.

"Opinions, and those types of concessions I mentioned earlier... cosmetic changes, really."

"Whoa, whoa, whoa... cosmetics?" Marcela interrupted her. "Alright, now we're in my area of expertise. What types of cosmetic changes?" she asked.

"Changes that, theoretically, wouldn't adversely affect the day-to-day administration of the government," Veronica explained. "Like changing the flag or the national colors... even the name of the country I suppose a king could change without Congress' approval."

"Changing the name of the country?" Marcela echoed.

"Sure, I don't see a problem. The constitution doesn't prohibit it."

"Wow, Veronica. Thanks for the civics lesson. This has been... enlightening."

"No problem. If you have any more questions, just call."

"I will," Marcela graciously told her. "Thanks, hon'."

Marcela hung up and looked to Reginaldo and Bebel as she murmured with a conspiratorial air: "I've got an idea."

"Burn down the houses of the rich?!" Senator Cruz interrogated a battered Marcos who drooped like egg yolk in the chair in front of his desk.

"Reggie's got an extremely active imagination," the young man nervously laughed.

"Who?"

"Reggie, I mean, Reginaldo," Marcos clarified.

"Reggie, Regis, Reginaldo... whatever. He needs to shut his mouth and stop spouting nonsense," the Senator warned. "What happened to the speech I prepared?"

"I gave it to him. I asked him to go over it and told him to let me know if he had any questions."

"And?"

"I don't think he even looked at it," Marcos admitted.

"And this didn't give you cause for worry?"

"I just assumed he wasn't particularly interested. I had no idea he was making up his own speech behind my back."

"Things can't go on this way," Senator Cruz decided.

"I know," Marcos nodded.

"That kind of talk scares people."

"I agree," the young man sighed. "Voters will lose faith -"

"I'm not talking about voters," the Senator interrupted, scoffing at Marcos' concern. "I'm talking about investors," he explained. "Do you know how many hours I spent on the phone to business leaders and diplomats after this referendum? How many gringo butts I kissed just so they wouldn't pack up and move to Bolivia? And now, when they were just beginning to grow accustomed to the idea of Brazil as a stable investment, our king decides he's got a few things to get off his chest. Burn down the houses of the rich?! I'm starting to actually miss the radical Left! At least one knew how to argue with them, you knew where they stood."

Marcos remained silent, not knowing how to respond. "I think he's bored," he finally said, offering a cause for Reginaldo's disruptive behavior.

"Bored?" the Senator asked.

"I don't know how it used to be, but these days there's not much for a king to do," Marcos admitted.

"Well, if he's bored let's find something for him to do."

"Good idea, sir. Any suggestions?"

"Let's see," the Senator began to think, pacing back and forth behind his desk. "I could arrange a state dinner or two with officials from the various embassies back in Brasília," he suggested. "Maybe even some heads of state? The Swiss, perhaps? They love that kind of crap," he laughed.

"I don't think you want him eating in front of others, especially heads of state," Marcos warned.

"And especially not fondue," the Senator agreed. "What about that daily routine I sent you?" he asked.

"It was a bit outdated," Marcos told him. "It mentioned physicians and toilettes and stuff."

"Right. Well, from what I've seen so far, this king is a bit awkward. He could surely benefit from some instruction in the delicacies of social interaction. Etiquette, the art of conversation?" the Senator suggested. "Hell, why don't we throw in lessons in piano, French. Latin grammar, even! Whatever it takes to shut him up!"

"Good afternoon to all our listeners out there enjoying a

beautiful day in sunny Rio de Janeiro," the voice breathed, smooth and cheerful through the headphones of a woman riding a crowded city bus, from a loud speaker in a bustling supermarket, and over Jefferson's small AM/FM radio. "Hope you are all outside enjoying this incredible weather."

"We ain't out there enjoying this weather," the supermarket employees complained between themselves, slapping the cash register drawer shut with a flick of the hips and counting out customers' change.

"I have quite a surprise for everyone today," the DJ continued. "We have on the phone Reginaldo Santos, perhaps better known as Reginaldo the First, our new king. Sir, are you there?"

"Still here."

"I have a question for you, Your Highness," she began, "what do you think about this idea of making Rio the country's capital again? Do you agree with the Mayor's proposal?"

"To be honest, I just can't understand this desire to see Rio as the capital. Despite what everyone thinks, I really like this city, and I can't see why anyone would want to spoil it by bringing back the members of Congress. I sleep much better knowing they're way out there in the middle of nowhere, quarantined like members of some leper colony, inmates inside that fully-paved prison we call Brasília. The capital is like our own little Alcatraz for politicians," he concluded.

Inside the offices of the Tele-Journal, Gustavo was seated at the computer, listening to music on the radio, when Flavia burst in and began to search through the stations.

"Hey, hey, hey, what're you doing?" he complained.

"The king is being interviewed on 98 FM."

Flavia quickly found the station and they listened.

"Well, Your Highness -" the DJ was saying.

"Please, call me Reggie," he interrupted her.

"Ok, Reggie. You actually called today to speak about

something in particular, isn't that right?"

"That's right. I called to submit some proposals to the Brazilian people, since so many in the press have been asking me about them lately. And since I don't really like speaking in front of large groups, my... assistant," he decided after a pause, "my assistant Bebel suggested I call the good people at 98 FM."

"Hey Katia, hey Chico!" Bebel shouted into the receiver from over Reginaldo's shoulder.

"Well, without further ado," the DJ said, "I'll give you the floor. Propose away."

"In the last few weeks," Reginaldo began, "my assistants and I have been thinking long and hard about our nation's past, moments in our cultural heritage..."

"Sir, come quick," Paulo cried, poking his head into the Senator's office. "The National Journal is broadcasting a radio interview with the king."

The Senator jumped up and the two ran into another room where the staff had gathered around a television that was broadcasting a radio feed of the 98 FM interview. The echo of Reginaldo's voice filled the room:

"We've discovered, inevitably, certain things, details really," the king was saying, "that we'd like to see changed. And, being king, fortunately I now have the power to make these improvements."

"Jesus Christ!" the Senator cried. "Paulo, I need to speak with Marcos. Has he left already?"

"A couple of minutes ago," Paulo nodded.

"Get him on the mobile, then!" the Senator ordered.

"The first item," Reginaldo continued, "pertains to our country's name, the Federal Republic of Brazil. This surely needs changing since we're no longer a republic, right?"

"Sure, sure," the DJ agreed.

"And I think it's high time we got rid of the reference to Brazil as well. Our country carries the mark of its first export, brazil-wood, a painful scar that reminds us of the raw material foreigners once plucked from our shores."

Back inside the offices of the Tele-Journal, Flavia and Gustavo exchanged an interested glance between themselves, then back towards the radio. The supermarket employees' attention had also drifted from their work and most were now listening more closely. The king continued his discourse:

"At first I thought about replacing Brazil with the name of a person or character from our nation's history, but I soon discovered this would be too difficult. How could I narrow it down from such a wide selection of national heroes: Indians, Jesuit priests, runaway slaves, backwoods pioneers, miners, gauchos, coffee planters, presidents, generals, diplomats, sociologists, businessmen, soccer players ... as you can see, it's almost impossible to choose just one. Besides, the monarchy believes that Brazil shouldn't linger in the past. After all, are we not the country of the future? Well then, let's step boldly into it," Reginaldo decided.

"Have you got him yet?" the Senator yelled across his office to Paulo.

"Not yet, sir!"

"Hurry it up for Christ's sake!"

"I'm trying, sir! There's no answer."

On radio and television stations throughout the country, Reginaldo's monologue continued. Among those still listening was the woman with headphones on the city bus who was steadily being packed in tighter and tighter against the other passengers.

"The politicians in Brasília," she heard the king say, "possessed of such knowledge and forethought, seem to have concluded that the key to a better society lies in the process of privatization, that this will solve all of our problems. So, therefore, in the tradition of brazil-wood, I propose we update our brand name by privatizing it. In other words, put the name up for auction, sell it to the corporate sponsor that's the highest bidder! Thereby replacing the outdated brazil-wood with a newer and more exciting product!" Reginaldo excitedly announced.

The proposal was met with silence inside the studios of 98 FM.

"Wow," the DJ remarked after the pause. "Put up for sale the name of the country?" she confirmed.

"That's correct," Reginaldo told her.

"So, we could end up as the United States of Coca-Cola?" she wondered.

"I prefer *guaraná*, but sure. In theory it could be Coca-Cola. Brazil-wood, Coca-Cola... there's really no difference. Where once they saw riches in our natural resources, companies now see it in our people. But not as a human resource, mind you. In fact, did you know that Brazil doesn't have citizens at all? That's right, it actually has 150 million consumers."

"So, do you think anyone would be interested? Would they pay up for the privilege?"

"Are you kidding? Imagine your product's name on every flag and soccer jersey in the nation! And on every globe as well! Coca-Cola in big bold letters right there above Argentina. You just can't match that level of visibility!"

"And the money from the sale?" the DJ dared to ask.

"We distribute it directly to the fine people of this country," Reginaldo decided there on the spot. "Congress won't even be allowed to sniff at it. Isn't it just the perfect blend of capitalism and communism?"

Even though the proceeds would have meant less than a dollar for every citizen, the supermarket employees began to celebrate the idea of receiving the money, chanting: "Long live the King! Long live the King!"

"Well, Your Majesty," the D.J. continued, "any other proposals?" she cautiously asked.

"Just one more. This one, instead of economic or political, is more spiritual," he explained. "Looking back across our history, it occurred to me that our independence really wasn't ours."

"How do you mean?"

"The famous declaration of independence at the River Ipiranga was given by my great, great, great grandfather Pedro the First. A nice guy, sure, but no Brazilian. He was, of course, Portuguese," he reminded listeners. "So, you might ask yourself: what kind of independence do we have if no Brazilian ever made a similar proclamation?"

"But, surely these days we no longer need to assert our independence from Portugal," the DJ argued.

"Very true. But there are, in our day-to-day lives, much more subtle oppressors. We all experience those moments where we feel less and less in control of our lives."

"Any examples?"

"Oh, from the smallest inconvenience — a vending machine that takes your change and doesn't deliver the goods — to something as complex as this international network of currency traders and speculators that determines the value of our money," Reginaldo offered. "So I suggest that, in these moments of frustration and uncertainty, each and every one should affirm their freedom, both personal and political, with their own declaration: Independence or death!" Reginaldo shouted.

The woman on the bus, hearing these words, was the first to echo his call. "Independence or death!" she shouted, as the others on the bus, hearing this sudden outburst, jumped back with surprise. A gentle smile of relief broke across the woman's face, having thus secured a little more space for her commute.

"Independence or death!" the supermarket workers screamed in unison.

"Independence or death!" a group of surfers on Ipanema Beach shouted between tokes.

"Independence or death!" Jefferson yelled, arms outstretched, clearing traffic near his corner stand.

"Independence or death!" Gustavo shouted at Flavia, grabbing his keys and dancing from the room.

"Independence or death?" the beet-red face of the Senator shouted over the telephone.

"The king does have a quirky sense of -"

"Get back to Rio now!" the Senator ordered, cutting Marcos short. "The thought of him alone out there scares me to death."

"Yes, sir."

"And Marcos," Senator Cruz added.

"Sir?"

"You should know that I consider this his yellow card. One more misstep and our king will receive the red."

"Yes, sir," Marcos mumbled, understanding full well the threat couched in the parlance of Brazil's national pastime.

THE PLAYERS PEERED over the top of their splayed cards, trying to decipher in their opponent's eyes the hand they were up against. The tension was so that the slightest twitch, or undue amount of perspiration upon the brow, was enough to betray.

"I'll see your bet, and raise you ten cents," the king said, tossing several coins into the center of the table.

Hours had passed since Reginaldo's news-breaking interview, and the palace staff had decided to take a well-deserved afternoon break. Across the table from Reginaldo sat Felipe, while a fellow member of his kitchen staff, as well as one of the maids, faced Bebel.

"He's bluffing," she decided.

"Excuse me?" the king challenged her.

"How d'you know?" Felipe asked.

"His hands are far too busy," the maid chimed in. "That's a sure sign."

"Not to mention the beads of sweat running down his temple," the kitchen worker noted.

"It's an especially warm day, that's all," Reginaldo explained, dabbing at his forehead with a handkerchief.

Suddenly, the group heard the sound of the front door, followed by approaching footsteps that echoed down the corridor.

"Marcos?" Reginaldo wondered.

"Back already?"

The kitchen and wait staff threw down their cards and jumped up from the table, quickly scurrying back to their designated work areas.

"Oh well," Reginaldo smiled, shrugging at the dissolution of the game. "I was, in fact, bluffing."

From around the corner, instead of Marcos, a stranger appeared carrying an oddly-shaped briefcase, exaggeratedly flat and rectangular.

"May I help you?" Bebel asked him.

"Yes, I'm looking for the king," the man replied.

"That's me," Reginaldo said, raising a hand. "And it seems someone has driven over your briefcase," he added.

"That's an easel, Your Majesty," the man explained.

"That's an easel mistake to make, Reggie," Bebel joked as the two shared a silly giggle.

"I'm sorry, I'm sorry," Reginaldo apologized to the man. "How may we help you?"

"Sir, my name is Fernando Berrini," he began. "I'm an artist, a painter," he added, lifting the easel. "I've been commissioned to paint your portrait for the National Museum."

"For an exhibit?" Reginaldo wondered.

"For an exhibit, sure," Fernando confirmed. "And for the national archives."

"Your portrait in an exhibit, Reggie? What will you wear?" Bebel worried, looking down at his worn-out cardigan and otherwise unimpressive outfit. "We'll need to go shopping!" she declared with obvious pleasure.

"That won't be necessary. They've provided a wardrobe for Your Majesty," Fernando told them, deflating Bebel's excitement.

"Not bad... not bad at all," Marcela murmured, standing behind Fernando as he worked on the portrait of Reginaldo. "And the painting's also nice," she added, grudgingly taking her eyes from the young man's buttocks and giving the canvas a look as well.

"How much longer?" Reginaldo asked, trying to remain still, and fearing that his crown might come crashing down at any moment. "It's hot under all this stuff," he explained, referring to the velvet robes that draped his entire body.

"Hush!" Marcela ordered. "Stop with your complaining about the heat. This is for the good of the nation," she laughed.

"Just give me a couple of minutes more, Your Majesty, and I'll let you have a break," Fernando assured him.

"Jeez, for the buzzillenth time, Fernando, my name's Reggie."

"Sorry."

"So, Fernando," Marcela said, circling behind him. "You from around here?"

"Nope. From São Paulo," he answered.

"Oh, maybe you know our Marcos?" she wondered.

"It's a pretty big city, so it's probably unlikely."

"Of course, of course," she nodded. "Well, if you need someone to serve as a tour guide -"

"Marcela..." Reginaldo interrupted.

"What, Your Uptightness? The boy's new here in town. You want your ugly mug to be the only thing he sees of Rio?"

"Actually," Fernando interjected, "I've seen all the touristy places in Rio, but I could use a guide to the nightlife around here."

"The nightlife, you say?"

"Oh boy..." Reginaldo sighed.

"That just happens to be my specialty," Marcela explained.

"Really?"

"Uh huh," she confirmed. "A few questions first, though," she told him as she began to pace back and forth behind him.

"Alright," he tentatively agreed.

"First, music: samba, or bossa nova?"

"Samba," he decided.

"Drink: beer, or caipirinha?"

"Caipirinha."

"National hero: Carmen, or Pelé?"

"Carmen," he answered.

"Perfect," Marcela smiled, confident in the accuracy of her gaydar. "Say, by the way, Nando," she said, already assigning him a nickname. "What's this portrait for, anyway?"

"Jesus Christ, Antonio. This king is really a loose cannon," a colleague complained as Senator Cruz poured him a whiskey on the rocks, creating a noticeable dent in the third bottle of Chivas Regal.

"Don't worry, I've found some things to occupy his time for the next few weeks."

"The next few weeks? Can we get the language for the bill hammered out before then?"

"Sure we can," the Senator assured his friend.

"And what about the king?"

"What about him?"

"Can you keep him under control? He seems to have quite a knack for drawing the spotlight."

"We're doing our best. Keeping him out of the spotlight with indoor activities, you might say," the Senator smiled.

"If you say so," his colleague shrugged.

"But look at the bright side," Cruz suggested.

"And what would that be?" the other wondered.

"It keeps the media off our asses," the Senator declared, raising his glass for a toast.

XIX

Clara waited in line for hours before she finally made it inside the palace. Now, at last, she found herself beneath the archway of the large room where the king held the ceremony of the kissing of hands. It was an enormous hall, which one might have thought an abandoned ballroom, if not for the obvious care taken to see that the crimson drapes matched the roses in the carpet and the red velvet of His Majesty's chair. And there he was, seated in the far corner: the king. Not much older than her Jacob, Clara thought to herself. But younger in the face, she decided. From her place in line, Clara could occasionally catch the gist of a fellow subject's petition, but mostly she heard only a submissive whisper, which would soon be met with a rather curt reply from either the king or his aide. Why had she come? she asked herself. Did she really expect her petition to be fully heard and, more unlikely still, granted? She glanced around nervously at the others who waited in line with her. How had she not noticed earlier that she was the only slave who'd come that day to speak with the king? You are a fool, Clara, she told herself, when suddenly a voice summoned her.

"I'm sorry?" she asked in response.

"Next in line," Vieira growled, striking another blow to the poor woman's already thin veneer of courage and self-confidence.

Clara quickly moved forward, dropping to her knees as she kissed the king's outstretched hand.

"What have you to request from His Majesty?" Vieira asked her.

"To request?" Clara stalled, summoning her strength.

"You do have something to say to His Majesty, don't you? Or have you come to merely kiss his hand?" Vieira smirked.

"Let her speak," Pedro said calmly to his aide.

"I am a slave," she began, "I work here in the city, inside the home of my master and mistress."

"I see," the king nodded, still waiting for her request.

"My son, he stays at the house with me. Helps me with things," she explained.

"Your petition!" Vieira demanded, growing impatient.

Pedro held up his arm to silence his aide. "I recognize your station," he told Clara. "You may proceed to the petition."

"Mister Castro, he's my master," she explained. The mention of the name caught Vieira's attention and he wondered if this Mr. Castro and the Assemblyman might be one and the same. "Mister Castro says he knows a man who wants to buy my boy. Someone outside the city," Clara told the king as she began to lightly sob. "There hadn't been one night that I ever passed without my boy," she wept.

"And you don't want your son to leave," Pedro guessed.

"Might I never see him again?" she asked the king, startling him with such a direct question.

"The court recognizes your difficulty," Vieira said to her, "but cannot -"

"Wait," Pedro told him. "We haven't yet heard her petition," he pointed out, looking down at Clara as an invitation for her to continue.

"My petition," she said, wiping away her tears, "is that maybe Your Majesty can make it so Jacob won't have to go away. Make it so that he can stay with me."

"And how would I do that?" Pedro earnestly wondered.

"You're the king," Clara reminded him, confused by his question. "I was thinking you could hand him his freedom."

"Enough!" Vieira yelled down at her. "Come on," he said, grabbing her by the arm. "Off your knees and out of this room."

"Vieira!" the king cried, jumping up from his seat. "Unhand her!" he warned his aide. Both men now stood above Clara, facing each other in silence, as she rested her head upon the floor beneath them, still weeping. The room had gone completely quiet as the attention of each petitioner was quickly focused upon the scene before them. Vieira was fully aware of the spectacle Pedro had created, and grew furious at the impetuous young king.

"Your Majesty," he said between his teeth. "I think we need to talk privately."

After all the slaves that had come and knelt before him, this tiny woman was the first to ask for freedom, and it wasn't even for her own. You're the king, she had said to him, so simply, so directly. Could one man, even while king, contradict an entire system, an entire way of life? But the woman had not asked him to abolish all slavery. She merely requested that her son be set free. Strangely enough, Pedro had never before considered it in his power to grant such freedom. He had always considered slavery something so much larger than himself.

"I think we should grant her petition," Pedro told his aide as they entered the adjoining room.

"I strongly disagree," Vieira countered. "The boy in question is not yours to do with what you will. He has an owner, recognized by law," he pointed out. "Do you wish to undermine the principle of property rights in this country?"

"Come now, Vieira," the boy pleaded with him. "I'm not trying to do anything of the sort. I just feel we shouldn't separate this mother and son."

"If you're truly committed to respecting this owner's rights, as you say you are, what is your solution, then?" he challenged the king.

"Well," Pedro began, stalling to give himself time to think the issue over. "If I understood the woman correctly, her son is being sold to another owner in another part of the country."

"Go on."

"So the current owner is willing to let the boy go," the king pointed out.

"It appears so."

"Therefore it's simply a matter of money, a business transaction."

"Your point?" Vieira asked, hoping the king would hasten to the crux of his argument.

"My point is just that," Pedro told him. "If it's merely a question of money, we'll offer a higher bid and the slave will be released," the king concluded.

"I don't know," the older man said, shaking his head. "Is this going to be the crown's policy?" Vieira asked him. "To buy every young Negro male in the city to do God-knows-what with every time his weeping mother shows up at the Palace door, as we slowly drain the national economy of its most valuable labor resource?"

"That's not my intention," Pedro argued. "I just feel that this particular one should be -"

"Just this particular one, Your Majesty?" the aide interrupted. "What happens when the rest of the empire hears that His Royal Highness is buying the freedom of young, working-age Negroes?"

"The freedom of slaves has always been for sale, if the rightful owner so allows," Pedro reminded his aide.

"To be purchased by private citizens," Vieira pointed out. "Not by their government. And surely not by the king himself. You're letting your emotions get in the way of logic," he warned the king. "The issue is much larger, it goes beyond the fate of this boy -"

"I agree," Pedro interrupted him.

"Then can't you see that it's not simply a matter of purchasing or not purchasing one measly slave?"

"Please don't use such language," the boy frowned.

"This is an extremely complex issue," Vieira again warned the king. "It involves an understanding of certain principles of political economy that, if you'll pardon my candor, I feel you simply do not possess."

"It's just one slave, Vieira," the boy pleaded with him.

"Oh, for heaven's sake," the older man sighed as he bowed his head in frustration. "Your mind's made up, isn't it?" he asked the king.

"It's just one slave," the boy repeated.

XX

Just before noon, Gustavo entered the National Library and approached Milena who was stationed, as usual, behind the

Information Desk.

"Hello Milena," he half-whispered, half-sang to her, leaning across the counter top. "How have you been?"

"I'm fine, Gustavo," she coldly replied, keeping her eyes trained upon the work in front of her. "Have you come to see me, or did you want to check out a book?"

"What's this?" he wondered, looking hurt. "Of course I've come to see you. To take you out to lunch," he explained.

"Yeah?" she asked, eyes squinting with suspicion.

"Yes," Gustavo swore. "So, what do you say?"

"Well, it is almost noon," Milena conceded, glancing down at her watch. "Give me a few seconds, ok?"

"Sure, sure," he agreed.

Turning around with his elbows still resting on the counter, Gustavo surveyed the expansive reading room and its silent clientele. Panning back towards the entrance, he noticed a rather extravagant woman slip into the building, her sunglasses and ornate red hat contrasting sharply with the otherwise dry and studious atmosphere of the library. Insuring with a quick look behind the Information Desk that Milena would not catch him checking out this other woman, Gustavo watched her, or rather the swaying of her hips underneath a tight, matching red dress, as she slowly crossed the main floor.

"She's coming this way," Viana said to himself, glancing up from his book. She's looking right at me, he decided. The Chief of Police racked his brain, trying to remember from just where and how he might know such a woman and why she would be seeking him out in particular. Was she a colleague participating in some on-going undercover prostitution sting operation? Perhaps, but it was difficult to recognize her with the sunglasses.

"Psst," Marcela whispered to Reginaldo. "Hey, Einstein."

"Marcela?" he said, looking up at her.

"The one and only," she confirmed, pulling off her sunglasses.

Relief passed over the Chief as the woman veered right just before reaching him and stopped to speak with someone seated on the other side of the shallow partition that separated the two reading tables. But Viana's curiosity lingered, so he slowly rose from his seat, pretending to take something from his pant pocket as an excuse to peer over the partition. Seeing the person she had come to visit, Viana plopped quickly back down into his chair.

"The king?" he silently mouthed to himself. "What is a woman like that doing visiting the king?"

"I was in the area, so I thought I'd stop by," Marcela explained. "I wanted to see for myself where you spent your days, 'cos I know where you spend your nights," she laughed.

"Speaking of which, are you performing tonight?" Reginaldo asked.

"I go on around nine," she told him. "You'll be there?"

"I'll be there," he smiled back.

Viana sat still for several seconds, speculating as to what could possibly be happening there on the other side of the table. The thought of not being able to observe the pair drove the Chief crazy, so he grabbed the book he was reading and slowly brought it up to his eyes. Then, straightening his back, he lifted himself to where he could just barely see the two lovebirds over the top of both the partition and his book.

"So," Marcela said, looking around the building. "This is where it all happens," she sighed with mock gravity. "The treatise on hot and cold climates, the exposé on Brazilian poverty, the -"

"Hey," Reginaldo interrupted. "Was the snack vendor out front?"

"Ah, so you're really thinking about food the whole time? That explains a lot," she laughed.

"No really," he insisted. "Was Jefferson out there by the front steps?"

"Jefferson? You're on a first-name basis with the snack vendor?"

she smiled.

"Was he out there, or not?" Reginaldo repeated.

"I think so," she shrugged. "Why?"

"Here," Reginaldo said, digging into his pocket and pulling out some bills. "I owe him for a sandwich. Do you mind?" he asked, handing Marcela the money.

"Sure, I'll give it to him. So, we can look forward to seeing you tonight?"

"Just before nine," he confirmed.

"Sounds good, Plato," she winked back. "See you then," she said, standing up to leave.

"See you then," Reginaldo agreed, as Marcela leaned in to plant a kiss on his cheek.

"And don't study too hard," she warned him. "I'm afraid it's going to your head," she smiled, walking away.

Gustavo, eyes wide open in shock, followed Marcela with a fixed gaze as she crossed the lobby and exited the library. What a woman, he thought to himself. They don't make them like that anymore, he was lamenting when Milena sidled up beside him, on the public's side of the Information Desk for a change.

"Ok, I'm ready," she announced.

"Huh?" Gustavo mumbled, his trance still unbroken. "Oh, right," he said, turning to face her. "You know what, Milena, I just realized I forgot to run an errand for the station. Can I take a rain check on that lunch?"

Without waiting for a response, he hustled away towards the exit.

"Son of a..." Milena cursed him under her breath, throwing her purse back across the desk.

Bounding down the library steps, Gustavo hurried across the street towards the nearest phone booth.

"Flavia?" he breathed into the receiver. "It's Gus," he panted. "Come quick! To the library. I'll explain when you get here."

That woman was no undercover informant, Viana decided. She was firmly planted on the opposite side of any possible sting operation; an operation, it suddenly occurred to the Chief, which he may have just been thrown smack dab in the middle of. Apparently Viana's impromptu stakeout had worked, for the couple failed to notice the uniformed policeman sitting so nearby. The king was just far enough away so that Viana was unable to overhear their conversation, but he had kept a policeman's eye on the pair the whole time. He saw the winks, the kiss on the cheek, the money changing hands. The Chief just loved it when a case came together, when all the pieces fit just right. But he would have to be patient; it would be silly to make a move right here inside the library, a well-respected institution of higher learning, after all. No, he would catch the king on the outside, with his hands in the proverbial cookie jar, if you will. And so Viana waited.

Darkness fell and found Flavia and Gustavo also waiting. Parked at a slight distance away along the Avenida Rio Branco, hidden between the spotlight of the streetlamps, they sat in her car just outside the library. Gustavo, seated in the passenger seat, was looking intently through the binoculars, which were trained upon the building's entrance.

"So they kissed?" Flavia asked him, going over the story one more time.

"More or less. She kissed him on the cheek."

"Did she look like a prostitute?"

"More or less," Gustavo answered unenthusiastically.

"Is that all you can say, 'more or less'?"

"Look, I was in a state of shock," he explained. "I can't be expected to notice all these nitty-gritty details."

"But he gave her some money, you saw that, right?" Flavia

pressed him.

"Oh yeah, that I saw."

"Ok, ok, keep looking. Anything?"

"No, nothing."

"What time is it?"

"Almost eight."

"What in the hell can he possibly do there all day?" Flavia wondered.

"Read, sleep?" Gustavo speculated.

"Very weird. And the hooker?"

"A friend of his, right?"

"Sure, Gus, sure. But what kind of friend? From where? Why the hell is the king giving money to a hooker? Is he a client?"

"Actually, Flavia, we don't know for sure that she's a hooker," he reminded her.

"I guess you're right," she conceded. Then, after a pause: "But I'll bet you money she's a hooker."

"Hold on," Gustavo said, looking again through the binoculars. "He's coming out!"

"I see, I see."

"He's coming down the steps," Gustavo began to narrate, "now he's stopping at the corner, no... he's taking something from his pocket. He's got the light, but it doesn't look like he's going to cross the street."

"He's just stopped there?"

"I think he's waiting for the bus," Gustavo concluded, surprised.

"The bus? That's strange. Are you sure?"

"Yep, that's the bus stop alright," he verified.

"What's he doing now, can you see?" Flavia eagerly demanded.

"Well, he's just waiting for the bus," Gustavo shrugged.

"Gimme those," Flavia growled, snatching the binoculars from his hands. "I wanna see for myself the guilty look on his face."

"So...?" Gustavo asked after a pause. "Has he got that guilty look, the big ol' *sem-vergonha*?"

"No," Flavia reluctantly admitted. "Just a blank stare."

"Here comes a bus!" Gustavo shouted.

"It's stopping."

"What's the number?"

"One... seventy-five. It's his, he's getting on."

"The one seventy-five?" Gustavo asked. "What's that... Copacabana?"

"Yep, that's one of its destinations," Flavia responded, handing the binoculars back to Gustavo. "Ok, let's go," she said, as she threw the car into drive and began to follow the bus. As they pulled away from the curb, Viana rushed past them screaming for a taxi.

"Follow that bus," he yelled, flashing his badge to the driver as he jumped into the back seat of the cab.

"You got it," the young man behind the wheel cackled, flooring both the engine and the radio in anticipation of a high-speed chase.

And the taxi driver was not to be disappointed. Since the bus had no scheduled stops until it reached the neighborhood of Leme, a good ten minutes from downtown, it reached speeds of nearly one hundred kilometers per hour as it hugged the curves of the Avenida Infante Dom Henrique, the lights along the beaches of Flamengo and Botafogo all but a blur from the bus' rattling windows. Darting from lane to lane, the taxi struggled to keep up, sending the Police Chief skating helplessly back and forth across a surface of freshly lubed vinyl as he was tossed about in the back seat of the cab.

"Take it easy!" Viana pleaded with the taxi driver. "The key to trailing someone," he explained, "is to remain inconspicuous."

"Sorry chief," the driver apologized, coincidentally using the friendly term that corresponded with Viana's rank.

As the bus finally began to make its stops inside Copacabana, Gustavo struggled to get a glimpse of the passengers as they stepped off.

"What do we got?" Flavia repeated at every stop.

"Old lady with shopping bags. Couple of kids."

"Alright. Keep your eyes peeled. God dammit," she swore as Viana's cab darted in between them and the bus. "Stupid taxis."

"It's cool, it's cool," Gustavo assured her. "With the binoculars, a little distance helps."

All three vehicles inched along in heavy traffic on that now familiar stretch of the Copacabana strip, when the bus made another stop. This time, Reginaldo stepped off.

"That's him! He's getting off," Gustavo announced.

"Yeah, I see. Look for a parking place, will ya? Who knows how long we'll be able to follow him from the car."

The two were able to follow from the car for a while, but soon found a place to park. Just past them, Viana's cab pulled to the curb. The Police Chief stared through the window for a second, making sure that it was, in fact, the king who had stepped off the bus.

"Alright, this is fine," he told the driver, opening the cab door and stepping out. "Uhhh..." Viana stuttered as he rifled through his pockets. "I'm a little low on cash. Call police headquarters," he said, leaning into the car.

"That's fine, boss, but don't -"

"Tell them the Chief of Police owes you," he instructed the driver before slamming the door shut behind him.

"But don't slam the —" the driver said, seconds too late.

Viana stepped up onto the sidewalk, scanning the area around him while keeping an eye trained on Reginaldo. He began to follow the king, yet, being a trained law enforcement professional, he pursued from a safe and inconspicuous distance.

"There's a cop following him," Gustavo said to Flavia, still looking through the binoculars.

"A cop?" she verified. "They must know something," she decided. "And we've stepped right in the middle of their little sting operation. This is gonna be huge," she smiled, imagining the breaking news media coverage she would generate. There was no longer any doubt in Flavia's mind that this story was worthy of interrupting all regularly scheduled programming, even the eight o'clock soap opera!

"He's going into one of the restaurants," Gustavo told her.

"Which one, which one?"

"The king."

"Of course, the king," she scolded him. "Which restaurant?"

"Oh, let's see. Uh... The Pleasure Palace?" he read aloud.

"Holy shit, he's going into The Pleasure Palace?" she asked, surprised.

"Yep, he's in there."

"What about the cop?"

"No, he's still outside."

"The Pleasure Palace," she repeated to herself. "It's not exactly a restaurant."

"Isn't that a gay club?" Gustavo asked, lowering the binoculars and turning to her.

"It's a little bit of everything club," Flavia chuckled. "What's the matter, king? Gone to get your money back from that little hussy?" she laughed.

"So she is a hooker," Gustavo murmured to himself.

"Look, Gus, you go back to the office and grab the camera. I'll stay out here waiting to make sure he doesn't get away."

"Right."

As the two stepped out of the car, Gustavo hurried around to the driver's side and got in.

"This is the best little scandal in a long time," Flavia excitedly proclaimed, leaning in through the car window. "And you and me, Gussy, are gonna break the story. Ok, make it fast!" she said, slapping the roof. "We don't know how long he's gonna stay in there."

"The Pleasure Palace?" Viana wondered aloud. It had to be some sort of joke; the king going into a nightclub called The Pleasure Palace. The Chief speculated for a second if perhaps he weren't being filmed, set up as part of a practical joke. But no one knew about his recent trips to the library, so what he witnessed must be genuine, he argued to himself. He saw the king give that girl the money and Viana was determined to find out why.

"But, The Pleasure Palace," he sighed. How am I going to get in there dressed like this? he wondered, looking down at his police uniform. He couldn't just stand around outside waiting for the king; someone might spot him and advise His Royal Slyness to slip out the back door. Viana would need to gain entrance into the nightclub. It was the only way to untangle this sordid business between the king and the prostitute.

"Evenin' Reggie," Dante called from the bar. "The usual?"

With dance music blaring, Reginaldo gave the bartender a salute as confirmation.

"One lemonade on the rocks, coming up!"

"Have you seen Marcela?" Reginaldo asked, pulling a stool up to the bar.

"Not in the past half hour," Dante told him. "She must be about to go on," he explained, nodding towards the stage.

"Of course," the king agreed, taking a sip of his drink.

"Honey, you can go ahead and put the cuffs on me," the transvestite at the door smiled to Viana as he entered the building. In order to blend into the nightclub environment, the Police Chief had put to use his very best undercover skills, rolling up his already short sleeves in large, thick folds, and unfastening the top four buttons of his shirt to where it burst open, exposing his undershirt and the tuft of chest hair that sprouted from beneath. "Two drink minimum," she winked, handing the Police Chief a ticket that would record his purchases at the bar.

Merely looking around the club made Viana feel dirty, embarrassed to be in the same building as these freakish others. To make matters worse, the place was so packed with dancing, sweat-soaked patrons that he was forced to rub against a good number of them just to make his way across the floor. Suddenly, the Police Chief felt a hand slip ever so gently into his back pocket. He turned around quickly, grabbing hold of the intruder's wrist.

"Easy officer," a second transvestite smiled at him. "It's not your wallet I'm after."

Viana grimaced to let the drag queen know that this particular officer wasn't interested in taking her into custody, and continued on his way. Finally, he spotted the king seated at the bar.

"Probably hitting the booze before he rendezvous with his hussy," Viana decided.

As he turned to head towards the bar, the lights dimmed and the stage curtain was slowly drawn open. The crowd raised its hands in applause, obscuring the Police Chief's view of his target, and prompting him to turn and see for himself what was happening behind him. As an upbeat, Motown-era tune began to play, Viana looked to find Marcela emerging from the darkness of the stage, imitating the arrested gestures of a marionette. Her dress, however, was anything but clumsy. With only a bikini top to cover her upper torso, she wore a tight red mini-skirt with fringe intended to suggest a rag doll's tattered clothes.

"That's her," Viana mumbled beneath his breath, recognizing

in her the woman he had seen back at the library. Then, Marcela began to sing:

Pull the string and I'll wink at you,

I'm your puppet

I'll do funny things if you want me to,

I'm your puppet, she continued, passing her hands across her chest, over her bellybutton and beyond.

I'm yours to have and to hold

Darling, you've got full control of your puppet

Outside the nightclub, a Tele-Journal news van came to a stop along the sidewalk as a man jumped out and began unloading equipment from the back.

"Carlos?" Flavia said with surprise. "How'd you know I was here?"

"Heard a call over the radio from Gus," the young man explained. "I was right around the corner so I decided I'd come over to help you out."

"Holy shit, that's fantastic!" she cried. "Here let me give you a hand."

The two had already started removing the camera, microphone, and other cords and equipment when, out of nowhere, a competing news team pulled up behind them.

"What the...?" Flavia murmured.

Two men, one in casual attire, the other wearing a tie, jumped from the van and began unloading equipment as well.

"What in the hell are you doing?" Flavia yelled as she approached the van.

"Covering a story, same as you," the man with the tie coldly responded.

"What story?"

"I don't know, but a call from the police went out over the squawker, so here we are."

"Jesus Christ!"

Inside, the music continued:

Pull them little strings and I'll kiss your lips,

I'm your puppet

Snap your fingers and I'll turn you some flips,

I'm your puppet

"Can I buy you a nightcap?" a man asked Viana, stepping up behind him.

"No thanks," the Chief told him.

"I said," the man repeated, holding up a one hundred dollar bill between his index and middle fingers, "can I buy you a nightcap?"

"I'm not drinking tonight," Viana brushed him off, turning back towards the stage where Marcela continued her song:

Your every wish is my command

All you got to do is wiggle your little hand

and I'm your puppet, I'm your puppet...

"How about now?" the man said to Viana, his fingers now holding two one hundred dollar bills as he let them glide across the Police Chief's bare chest.

"Are you offering me money to spend a night with you?" Viana asked the stranger, point blank.

"You don't have to stay the whole night if you don't want to. You can slip out after we're done. Out the back," the man added, placing a hand on Viana's left buttock.

"That's it," Viana said, pulling out his handcuffs and slamming them over the man's wrists.

"Whoa, officer," the man laughed, thinking it was a joke. But it was soon clear that Viana was not kidding; the cuffs were not a prelude to further adventures. "Damn, bitch! What in the hell are you doing?" his captive cried.

"It's you that'll soon be someone's bitch," the Chief laughed back. By now the commotion Viana was causing had started to attract the attention of the other clubbers. And when the music finally stopped, every head turned to see what all the yelling was about.

"Help!" the handcuffed man continued to scream.

"Back off," Viana warned people as he dragged his detainee towards the door. Suddenly, three other police officers burst into the club, sending the place into complete panic.

"Police!"

Hurrying off stage, Marcela ran towards the bar.

"Where's Reggie?" she yelled to Dante, seeing the abandoned lemonade on the bar top.

"I don't know," he shrugged. "He bummed a cigarette and walked off."

"A cigarette?" Marcela asked, surprised. Then, a smile broke across her face as she remembered one of the king's stranger habits. "That's perfect," she laughed to herself, as she turned towards the restrooms to keep Reginaldo from coming out while the cops were around. Struggling across the floor against the tide of patrons who were heading for the exits, Marcela caught Viana's eye.

"Chief?" one of the police officers said with surprise, interrupting his visual pursuit. "Chief, is that you?" he laughed, glancing down at Viana's adaptation of his uniform.

"Yes, it's me," the Police Chief grumbled back. "Here, take this tramp into custody," he ordered, pushing the handcuffed man towards his subordinate.

"You got it, Chief," the officer answered back, trying to keep a straight face.

Looking over the crowd, Viana again spotted Marcela and assumed her purposeful march across the floor would lead to something interesting; a misdemeanor, at least.

"I'll cut her off at the pass," he said heroically to himself, hurrying to catch up.

By now the nightclub was half-empty, and a line of reporters had formed along the sidewalk outside to interrogate the frantic patrons as they exited. Among the media, it was confirmed that the king was in fact inside, had attended the club regularly, and had even formed friendships with a number of club patrons. Despite these patrons' denials, rumor quickly spread that the king was involved in some sort of nefarious business, which, according to some press reports, may or may not involve the Swiss.

"Ai!" Marcela screamed with surprise as Viana stepped in front of her.

"Where is he?" the Chief snarled.

"Where is who?" she demurely asked.

"You know very well who," he scolded her. "The king!"

"The king?" she wondered, confused. "You mean that skinny boy with the tiara?"

"No," Viana shot back, becoming impatient. "I mean the fat guy with the cardigan!"

"Oh... that king."

"Tell me the truth and you just might stay out of jail," he told her.

"The truth...?" she confirmed.

"You heard me," he grumbled back.

"The truth is that..." she began, looking over the Chief's head towards the restrooms. "The truth is that the king is happily seated upon the throne," she smiled at Viana.

"Alright, that's it," he cried, approaching to take her into police custody.

"Dante!" she screamed as Viana pulled her arms behind her back.

Inside his tiny stall, Reginaldo had begun to notice the increased activity outside; the music had stopped, the voices seemed louder and more frantic than usual. But when he heard Marcela cry out, he knew for sure that something was awry. He finished his business as fast as he could, threw the cigarette into the toilet, and, despite all the excitement, even remembered to wash his hands.

"Marcela!" he yelled as he burst through the bathroom door. "Marcela!" he called out again, scanning the bar.

"Ah ha!" Viana responded with a smile. "There you are!"

"Run, Reggie, run," she warned him. "Get the hell out of here!"

"What's going on?" he asked, coming towards them, ignoring Marcela's plea.

"Your presence is requested down at City Hall," Viana lied, releasing Marcela's arms and walking towards the king. "Come with me."

"Marcela!" Dante yelled, seeing that she was poised to jump Viana's back, now that she was freed. The interruption kept her out of jail, for when Marcela turned back around to strike again, Viana was already leading Reginaldo towards the door.

"Reggie!" she impotently cried. Turning his head, Reginaldo flashed a look to assure her that everything would be just fine. After all, he had committed no crime.

When Viana led Reginaldo out the front door of the nightclub, Flavia was the first to come rushing up to him.

"Could Your Highness please explain why you are frequenting a gay nightclub?!" she shouted.

"Reporters?" Reginaldo worried to himself, barely registering her question. "Oh no," he moaned. "Marcos is gonna kill me."

Before he could even entertain the thought of explaining this apparent misunderstanding to the media, Reginaldo was ushered into a waiting patrol car and carted off to police headquarters for questioning.

Spurned yet again, Flavia decided that this was the last straw. She would show no more mercy for this crooked king and his over-sexed court. She gave the signal to her colleague Carlos that it was time to hit the airwaves with the story. In a matter of seconds, with the nightclub lit up behind her, Flavia began speaking into the camera as it broadcast live.

"That is correct, Maria," she said, placing a hand over her ear as she communicated with the Tele-Journal studio through an earpiece. "The king entered the establishment approximately twenty minutes ago. Ironically, it is a nightclub called The Pleasure Palace, located on the Copacabana strip in an area known for attracting foreign tourists out looking for exotic sexual adventures while in Rio."

"Flavia, this is Mauricio," the co-anchor cut in, "can you tell us what led you to the club, how you discovered the king was inside?"

"We received an anonymous tip," she explained, "our source saying that they saw the king at a certain location downtown, interacting - exchanging money, in fact - with a woman who appeared, to this source, to be either a prostitute or some sort of exotic dancer. And, following up on this lead, we were led to the nightclub that you see behind me."

SEATED INSIDE *LA Via Vecchia Ristorante* in Brasília's Bonaparte Residence Hotel, Senator Cruz was enjoying dinner with several colleagues, when, in mid-sentence, a waiter approached and discreetly interrupted.

"Senator Cruz," the young man whispered, "I'm sorry to interrupt but you have a telephone call at the bar."

"Very well. Gentlemen," the Senator nodded to the other men, "if you'll excuse me."

Senator Cruz followed the waiter to the bar and picked up the receiver.

"This is Cruz. Hi, Paulo. This is important, I trust. What's that? A television?"

The Senator looked around and noticed a television at the far corner of the bar.

"Yes," he continued, "there's a television here. TV Globo? Hold on. Could you turn to Globo for a second?" he asked the bartender.

"Yes, sir."

The bartender grabbed a remote control and turned the channel. Immediately, the Senator could see news coverage of some event where an unsteady camera revealed a flock of reporters gathered outside a building as police led people away.

"Volume, please," the Senator requested.

The bartender turned up the volume to reveal a different news team reporting the story originally broken by Flavia.

"The nightclub is best known here in Rio for its gender-bending performers and clientele," the reporter was saying. "And, as might be expected, rumors abound of prostitution and even extortion. Among those found inside was Reginaldo Santos, better known to most of our viewers as... well, the king."

Mechanically, without any further word to Paulo, the Senator hung up the phone.

"Is everything alright, Antonio?" a colleague asked, noticing the wan look on the Senator's face as he arrived back at the table.

"Hm?" Cruz asked, distracted. "Ah, yes, everything's fine," he assured them. "Though it looks like we'll have to resort to Plan B," the Senator speculated, taking a long sip from the glass of Chivas Regal in an attempt to calm his nerves.

PART FOUR

XXI

Clara looked up from her work when she heard the carriage come to a stop in front of the Castro home. She idly speculated as to who could be out visiting so early in the morning, when she suddenly remembered her master's mention of a buyer interested in Jacob. Recalling these recent threats of sale sent Clara into a panic that set the poor woman to thinking of a way to hide her boy, anything that might delay the sale until she could devise a more permanent solution. As she stood there weighing her options, Clara could hear two men talking outside the front door and it gave her pause. She drew closer to the house and leaned her ear forward.

"I know that voice," she whispered to herself. "That's the voice of the king!" So the king had come to grant Jacob's freedom, after all? Hurriedly, Clara ran along the length of the house and into the yard to find her boy.

"Come here, son," she called to him, gesticulating wildly. "I want you to get cleaned up, change this shirt," she ordered, pulling on his tattered clothes. "His Majesty is out front."

"His Majesty?" Jacob asked.

"Yes, His Majesty," Clara repeated. "The king! I think he's gonna let you stay," she revealed to her son. "So get cleaned up to where you can thank him proper." Clara looked down at her own clothes and, as if seeing her ragged work dress in a new light, decided she would have to do the same. "Come meet me in the kitchen when you're done, you hear?" she said before heading inside.

The boy agreed with a nod of his head, but didn't turn towards his quarters. Instead, Jacob walked around to the far side of the house so that he could listen in on the meeting taking place inside. By now Vieira and Pedro had been led into the parlor and taken their seats as they waited for the Assemblyman to come downstairs.

"I'd appreciate it if you'd allow me to discuss the offer," the young king whispered to his aide. "At least in general terms," he added. "Later, you two can work out the details."

"Of course, Your Highness," Vieira agreed, but in a tone that failed to hide his contempt for the entire proceeding.

Leaning against the side of the house, Jacob was now close enough to the open windows to hear all that echoed inside the parlor. He listened as Castro entered the room and the three men exchanged their greetings, cordial but rather reserved.

"Assemblyman, I suspect you know why we're here," the king began after the formalities had ended.

"I have some idea," Castro acknowledged.

"The money we... the sum we're willing to offer you," the king stuttered. "We feel it's quite sufficient."

"Far above what the boy would be expected to fetch at market," Vieira couldn't help but add.

"I do hope you'll accept," Pedro admitted.

"With all due respect, Your Majesty," Castro began, "I think it would be foolish to contradict a king's wishes, no matter the price. But Mr. Vieira has mentioned the amount you are willing to pay and, indeed, your offer is more than fair. May I ask," he added, "what you plan on doing with the boy?"

Pedro and Vieira looked awkwardly between themselves, until the king finally spoke: "We haven't quite decided," he admitted. "But we've promised his mother he shan't leave the city."

By now Jacob had stopped listening, but remained there with

his back pressed up against the house, repeating to himself the words that sealed his fate. So he was to be sold, after all. Sure, to a king that might harbor and protect him, but it made Jacob furious that Castro would now profit even more from the transaction. The offer is more than fair, the Assemblyman had smiled, laughing to himself, no doubt, at the fool with the crown that had agreed to pay such an exorbitant amount for a product that cost Castro absolutely nothing. What a good investment the little Negro Jacob had turned out to be.

"Boy, you still not dressed?" Clara scolded him as he came round the side of the house.

"I wanted to hear what -"

"Spying through the windows?" his mother correctly guessed. "Son, I told you to get dressed. Then you can walk into that room like a man – a free man - 'stead of peeping in from outside."

His mother was so happy, even moved to tears. Jacob didn't have the courage to tell her that he wasn't being set free, but instead shuffled from one master to another. And at a price that would leave old Castro even richer than he already was.

"I'm going inside," Clara told her son. "You come on into the parlor when you're dressed."

"Yes ma'am," he mumbled.

"And lift that head up and smile," she said to him, placing her hand under his chin. "This is not a time for moping around."

"I love you, mother," Jacob said, catching Clara by surprise. "I know what you done for me, to get me free and all," he told her.

"Isn't a mother in this world that would of done any diff'rent," she smiled back at her son. "Now, come on. Get going," she said, motioning towards the boy's cabin.

"Yes ma'am."

Clara turned away and stepped into the kitchen, leaving Jacob standing there, motionless, in the yard. His mother's anticipation and misplaced happiness made the boy even more angry for the deception being carried out upon her. God damn the lot of them, he thought to himself. The Assemblyman, the king, and their whole arrangement. Castro's not about to get that money, Jacob shook his head, stubbornly decided. Not if I can help it.

And I can, he wept.

Clara exited her room, pressing the folds in her best dress as she made her way to the swinging door that led into the parlor. Pushing the door slowly open, she heard her name being called.

"Clara!" the Assemblyman shouted. "Oh, there you are," he said as she entered the room.

"Yes, sir?" she politely answered her master, though smiling, instead, at the young king and his assistant.

"Clara, if you would," Castro began, but paused when he noticed that she had changed clothes and was now wearing the one nice dress she owned. "Clara," he continued, "run and fetch Jacob. These gentlemen are here to purchase him."

"To purchase him?" she repeated, turning her eyes to the king, who quickly looked away.

"You heard correctly. To purchase him. Now run along. And remind him to clear the cabin of his belongings," Castro added, dismissing the woman with a wave of his arm.

"But, I thought," Clara murmured, still staring at the king. "I thought His Majesty had come to -"

"It's not your business to speculate on His Royal Highness' affairs," Castro scolded her. "Now run along!"

But Clara just stood there, unable to move. The king had come to the Castro home at her request, but now he wanted to buy her boy, instead of stopping his sale, instead of granting him his freedom?

"Clara!" the Assemblyman shouted, interrupting her questions.

"Ma'am," Pedro cut in, stepping towards the woman who had

now begun to cry. "He'll be taken care of," the king assured her. "He won't be mistreated."

"I told him he was free," she wept. "I can't do it," she told the men, shaking her head. "I hadn't got the strength to tell him I was wrong."

"Clara," her master threatened.

"I can't," she again wept.

"For heaven's sake," Castro grumbled as he pushed Clara aside and headed towards the kitchen. "Jacob!" he shouted.

"Wait!" she cried, heading out after him. With a glance between themselves, Pedro and Vieira decided they had better follow along as well.

"Wait, sir," Clara called out again after Castro. "Let me talk to him first," she begged.

"Jacob!" the Assemblyman yelled, throwing open the back door. "Jacob!" he repeated, ducking under the clotheslines and weaving his way between the trees as he set off towards the boy's living quarters. The others followed close behind.

"Jacob!" Clara wailed. But there was no answer.

"Come now, Assemblyman," Pedro called to Castro. "We're going to scare the boy half to death coming after him like this. Let's turn back inside and we'll finish this later," the king pleaded. But the slave's owner kept on walking, batting away the hanging linens and other laundry that obstructed his march.

"Jacob," Castro said again in a quieter, almost reassuring tone of voice, as he came to a stop just outside the cabin door. "Jacob, could you come out here please?" Hearing no response, the others looked nervously between themselves. "Jacob, damn it!" the Assemblyman yelled, losing his patience. "Come out here, now!"

"Come, Mr. Castro," the king again pleaded with him. "We can do this another time."

Ignoring the king's entreaties, Castro stepped back and raised his foot as he prepared to force his way inside. Such measures were unnecessary, for, upon impact, the door swung violently open, as if it had not been fully closed, as if inviting someone to enter. The others gasped in horror as they saw Jacob there inside, hanging by his neck from one of the three wooden girders.

"Jacob!" Clara cried as her body began to convulse uncontrollably. "My boy, my beautiful boy!" she screamed as she looked up at the child's body that still swayed slowly from left to right, as if having fallen just seconds ago. Initially, Pedro hid his face, but now the king looked up at the figure hanging there before him. Perhaps he expected to find an accusatory stare from his childhood acquaintance, but the boy had donned an old carnival mask, possibly to shield his mother's eyes from the grotesque image of a hanged man's bloated face. Surely he wouldn't want her to remember him this way, but would prefer that she instead guard in her memory the features of a smiling, innocent child.

"Jesus Christ!" Castro cursed. "All right, everyone out," he ordered, forgetting in his moment of anger that he was speaking to a king. "Out!" he waved his arms, pushing Clara away from the cabin. The force of the blow caused her to stumble backwards and Clara continued to recoil from the scene until she found herself caught up in the hanging linens, which she pulled violently as she writhed in grief and anger, wrapping herself completely in their folds.

As Castro prepared to close the cabin door, Pedro noticed him inspecting a tiny satchel that was tied around the boy's wrist. As Castro pulled the string, the package fell to the floor, spilling several coins all around. The master ignored the petty amount of change, looking up at the boy's body one last time before he pulled the door shut behind him.

Pedro ran to comfort the grieving mother, peeling away the layers of her linen cocoon and embracing Clara's body as she trembled and sobbed violently into his chest. With her head there beneath his chin, he could detect something akin to perfume; a scent she must have put on to honor his visit. How often had she worn the fragrance in the past? Pedro found himself wondering. Once a week? On Sundays, perhaps? No, not even for worship would she allow herself such extravagance. This was to be the most beautiful day of her life. And I have destroyed it, the king told himself.

Pedro led the woman back into the house and sat beside her in the kitchen, clutching her hand as she wept.

"I'm sorry," she apologized after a few minutes of silence. "I won't keep you," she told him, patting the hand that was holding hers as if to grant the king his leave.

"I'd like to stay if you'll let me," he told her.

"Alright then," Clara agreed.

"What is your name?" Pedro asked after a pause.

"Well, I hadn't got a family name," she explained to the king. "Folks just call me Clara."

"Right, Clara," he remembered. "Clara, I'm Pedro," he introduced himself.

"Yes, I know," she nodded between sobs.

"Clara," he whispered to her. "Would you like to leave here?"

She looked up at Pedro, confused by his question. "How do you mean?" she asked him, wiping away more tears.

"I've set the money aside," he explained. "I'm sure the Assemblyman would -"

"Good Lord!" she cried, knocking her chair to the floor as she recoiled from the king. "Hadn't you learned nothing from my boy's killing hisself?" she demanded through her tears.

"I thought you would...," he stuttered. "I was only trying to help."

"Trying to help?" she said. "Ask yourself if it's right for a king to go running from door to door, offering money for slaves like some kinda Negro trader?" Clara challenged him.

"But ..." Pedro again stumbled through his argument. "Wouldn't you like to be relieved of your duties here?"

"I swear to the Lord yes, but ..."

"But?"

"But this is the only home I got! Where does Your Highness think I got to go if I leave this here house? Am I any freer out there in the street, like slavery somehow disappear when I walk out through that door? Like folks'll just welcome me in when I hadn't got a place to stay?"

"You can come live on the palace grounds, with no obligation to work," Pedro suggested to her.

"And how're the other slaves gonna take that, having a free Negro laying round why they's all working? Sorry," she shook her head, "but you telling me I can go free is just the beginning of my troubles, not the end."

The king could only sit there dumb, not knowing how to respond to the woman's reasoning.

"I know I am not showing the proper respect," Clara admitted, "denying a king's request. Maybe even crazy, too, when it's freedom he's come offering. Oh heavens," she sighed, "I used to say 'give me liberty, or give me death,' but I just can't think straight right now -"

"What was that?" Pedro interrupted her.

"I... I just can't seem to think -"

"No, I'm sorry. Before that. What did you used to tell yourself?"

"I told myself what every slave learns to tell hisself," she told the king. "Give me liberty or give me death."

Give me liberty or give me death, Pedro repeated to himself, mouthing nearly the exact words his father had uttered when he called for the nation's independence. And this woman was to tell him what he should have realized long ago: that the call was, of course, still ringing unfulfilled in the throat and heart of every slave in Brazil. What had the declaration meant so many years ago, if nearly half the nation still felt the need to repeat it? Who was it meant for? Pedro asked himself, but he knew the answer immediately. And with the response echoing in his head, he suddenly sensed his entire kingdom shrivel up before him to the point where it was no bigger than an island, a tiny strip of sand that rose up as a mountain to finally become a throne. And from that abandoned and irrelevant post the king could see, as he looked down, the tide that now separated him from his subjects.

"If you'll pardon me, Your Highness," Clara quietly said, dispelling the image and bringing Pedro back to their conversation. As she rose from her chair, the king took her hand and stopped her.

"I appreciate your talking with me," he said, leaving his chair and coming to rest on one knee. "Please accept my sympathies," Pedro begged her, leaning forward to kiss her hand. Clara looked down into the king's eyes and smiled.

"Well, if you'll pardon me," she repeated. "I got a child to bury."

"JESUS CHRIST, VIEIRA," the king said to his aide as they entered the older man's office back at the palace. "Don't pretend there's not blood on all of our hands from this boy's death."

"How so?" he wondered.

"The mask, the sack of coins tied around his wrist," Pedro recalled. "He was mimicking the lynching of Judas on Hallelujah Saturday. He knew why we were there."

"So why hang himself? We were there to set him free," Vieira argued.

"The boy didn't know that. If he knew anything he knew that two white men had come to purchase him. How would he know what our intentions were?"

"But hang himself? Why?"

"To prevent the Assemblyman from receiving our payment," the king had finally come to realize. "To liquidate the investment, as you might put it," he told his aide.

"Your Majesty, this was your idea, not mine," Vieira reminded him.

"You're right," Pedro agreed. "His message was meant for me. I'm the Judas, I'm the traitor," he sighed, falling back onto the sofa. "Clara is also correct," the king murmured to himself. "Is it right for a king to go from door to door offering money for slaves like just another of so many Negro traders?"

"Oh, for heaven's sake, Pedro," Vieira laughed, shaking his head at the young man's melodramatic tone. "You're letting your imagination -"

"Why did I believe that by imitating the system I might resolve its injustices?" Pedro interrogated himself. "A more permanent solution must be found."

"You're taking this far too personally. Who knows what the boy meant by killing himself?"

"I'm going to endorse Abolition," the king suddenly announced, ignoring his aide's comments.

"I'm sorry?"

"I said I'm going to endorse Abolition," Pedro repeated.

"You know how I feel, Your Majesty."

"I do."

"I can't stop you," Vieira admitted. "I only ask that you think carefully before making such a decision. Put some distance between this incident and yourself," he counseled the boy. "Let your emotions settle. Afterwards, you'll be able to reason more clearly."

"My thoughts have never been clearer," Pedro assured him.

"So you're prepared to leave behind a nation in ruin?" Vieira asked him, betraying his anger.

"Ruin?"

"Yes, ruin, Your Majesty. Could you live with yourself knowing that you'd crippled the nation's economy? For this is exactly what will happen if you agree to Abolition."

"Please, Vieira, you exaggerate —"

"Haven't you considered the fate of farmers and their plantations when you emancipate the slaves?"

"The workers can stay on and earn a just wage for their labors."

"A just wage? Do you realize how much capital is already invested in each worker?" Vieira berated him.

"I can't help that."

"And when the slaves walk away, that investment will turn to smoke," he concluded, shaking his head.

"I'm sorry," the king apologized.

"Look," Vieira said, changing his tactic. "Think about your own future, Pedro. What's going to happen to you?"

"What do you mean?" the boy asked.

"Think about it," the king's aide warned him. "The deputies who maintain the monarchy's tenuous hold on power are the same ones who oppose Abolition. You know that."

"I do," Pedro acknowledged.

"If you contradict your supporters, they will abandon you. That's certain. Quite frankly," Vieira added, "if slavery goes, so do you. Please, Pedro, think hard about what you're doing. It's either you or them," he concluded.

"Without them, Vieira," the king sighed, "there is no empire, no emperor. Not one that matters, anyway. As long as slavery persists among my subjects, it will be like reigning over a deserted island."

"Deserted island?" Vieira scoffed, finding the king's words almost humorous. "A country nearly the size of an entire continent, overflowing with natural abundance, and a coastline that is the envy of all sea-faring nations? Imagine what the future holds for Brazil?" he challenged the king.

"The same thing it offers today," Pedro suggested. "An earthly paradise inhabited by an enslaved people. Unless something changes," he told his aide. "And right now that change is Abolition. Even if it means the establishment of a Republic."

"So, this is it?" Vieira sighed, tired of arguing with the boy. "It's all over?"

"It's not over," Pedro countered. "There may not be a king, but I'd like to believe there's still a me."

"They won't let you stay," Vieira warned him. "They'll insist upon your return to Portugal."

"Portugal? But I'm -"

"No matter how Brazilian you may feel."

XXII

Reginaldo sat there, silent, in the tiny leather chair closest to the wall, to the left of the Mayor's desk as one entered the room. The other chair remained empty, for Police Chief Viana preferred to stand near the door, keeping an eye on the king's every move. It was a needless surveillance, for Reginaldo had barely stirred a limb the entire time they had been waiting for the Mayor to arrive. Occasionally, Reginaldo would look back over his shoulder at the Police Chief, as if inviting him to give his legs a rest and take the seat next to him, but Viana's straightforward stare was enough to let the king know that the head of law enforcement was not in the least bit interested in cozying up to a criminal.

"Am I going to be charged with anything?" Reginaldo finally asked him.

"That's for the Mayor to decide," Viana coldly responded.

"Is he coming soon?"

"He'll get here when he gets here," the Chief enigmatically answered.

Finally, footsteps were heard in the hall as Viana stepped back from the doorway to clear the Mayor's path to his desk.

"Mayor," he nodded with respect as his boss entered the room.

"Chief Viana," the Mayor nodded in return. "And the king..." he sighed, walking behind his desk and coming to a stop in front of Reginaldo. "So nice to see you again," he said with more than just a bit of sarcasm before taking a seat. "What's it been? A couple of weeks since the coronation?"

"Something like that," Reginaldo mumbled back.

"Well, no matter how long it's been," the Mayor smiled, "I think we can safely say that each meeting has certainly been – how should I put it? Interesting, perhaps?"

"I'd like to know why I'm being held here," Reginaldo demanded.

"You're being held here because you were picked up at a nightclub that is well-known as a meeting place for prostitutes and their johns," the Mayor explained, opening a manila folder full of reports that had been left for him on his desk. "And to make matters worse," he continued, looking down at the papers, "you were seen earlier in the day handing money over to one of these afore-mentioned ladies of the night."

"But I didn't ... Marcela's not a -"

"Save your breath, king," the Mayor stopped him in mid-explanation, closing the folder and looking up. "I don't really care what you did or didn't do. Just see to it that you stay out of the police's hair, out of the media's spotlight, and out of that chair. Because, when you fail to stay out of these things, it makes my city look bad and makes me look like a fool. Got it?" he asked.

Reginaldo simmered in his chair, unsure of how to respond.

"You can go now, king," the Mayor concluded after a pause.

"I don't seem to be receiving the treatment I feel a king deserves," Reginaldo finally blurted out, ignoring the Mayor's invitation to leave and remaining in his seat. "Dom João was carried in a sedan through the streets, but you think it's ok to let me ride in the back of a patrol car and stay locked up for hours. Pedro the First declared independence against his own homeland, but I can't even criticize our government? Pedro the Second regularly attended the theater and was glad to be seen among his subjects, but I am arrested when I merely visit a friend who just happens to work at a nightclub! I ask you, Mayor, does this seem fair?"

"You're right," the Mayor nodded. "You're not receiving the so-called royal treatment. But do you honestly believe you deserve it?" he asked. "Dom João turned this colony into an empire, Pedro the First won our independence from Portugal, and Pedro the Second freed the slaves. What did you ever do? Visit a nightclub or two? Prank call a radio station? Break bread with a bunch of hookers?"

"They're not prostitutes!" Reginaldo again corrected him.

"If you say so," the Mayor shrugged.

"I think I'll go now," Reginaldo decided, jumping to his feet and heading towards the door.

"Mayor?" Viana asked, stepping out to block the king's path.

"It's alright, Viana. Let him go," he told the Chief, dismissing Reginaldo with a wave of his hand.

After Reginaldo had stormed out of the room, Viana looked back at the Mayor, surprised that his boss had not questioned him more, shocked that no penalty was handed down to the errant king.

"You want me to trail him?" Viana asked.

"Nah," the Mayor shrugged. "Don't worry about him."

"No?"

"No, Viana. Let it go," he repeated, but noticed that Viana was still waiting, as if expecting an order. "Is there something else?"

"Kind of," Viana nodded. "You see, I've still got a few men at that nightclub, and I was considering widening our dragnet – no pun intended, sir. You know," he explained, "maybe closing down several of the other strip clubs along the Avenida."

"Say what?" the Mayor asked, looking up from his work.

"You know," the Chief repeated. "Clean up the area along Copacabana Beach. Like you said, it's full of these women that -"

"Look, Viana, you pull your men out of that nightclub and tell them to leave well enough alone," the Mayor warned him.

"But I thought..." Viana stuttered. "What about what you said to the king, about the prostitutes and all?"

"I just don't want the king down there, that's all," the Mayor clarified. "But I'm not trying to close them down. Are you crazy?" he laughed. "Do you know how much revenue from tourists the city pulls in from down there?"

"I guess I never -"

"A hell of a lot," the Mayor informed him. "Stay out of those boys' way," he again warned. "What they do behind closed doors is their own business, as long as they keep spending their dollars and deutschemarks right here in Rio. Do you know how much money we've been losing in the past few years to places like Cancun and Bangkok?"

"I hadn't really -"

"Too damn much! So stay down there if you want. But no arrests, you hear me?"

"Yes, sir," Viana nodded.

"Alright, well, I've got to get back to work," the Mayor growled, abruptly dismissing the Chief.

Viana left the Mayor's office both angry and confused. How could his boss ignore such a blatant public menace as the Copacabana strip? The increased traffic, the heightened consumption of alcohol, those thumping bass beats that shook the entire neighborhood. And these were just a few of the more blatant public disturbances, which left unmentioned such unmentionables as the house of mirrors-like sexual play that went on inside that enchanted palace, where one wasn't sure if their hand was brushing up against a male or female buttocks, and if the hand on one's own rear-end was attached to either man or woman. And the Mayor wanted to preserve this Carnival atmosphere for the sake of foreigners? Just as he had done at the king's coronation, the Mayor was once again displaying a reckless disregard for public safety and all that it stood for.

The mistake, Viana decided, was tactical in nature, for the Mayor was constantly erring in his placement of troops, or officers, we should say. Again, the coronation was the perfect example. Why bother securing downtown when the real action was at the beaches? Sure, there could have been some disturbance from people coming down the hillside to see what all the fuss was about, but did such a scenario really require the number of officers the Mayor had demanded? What, besides a few hecklers, had the Mayor feared?

As he stepped out of City Hall, the sight of Reginaldo, seated alone on a bench, interrupted the Police Chief's questions.

"I believe I owe you an apology," Reginaldo heard Viana say, as the Chief approached him from behind.

"An apology?" Reginaldo wondered, turning around.

"Yes, an apology," Viana confirmed, taking a seat beside the king.

"For the arrest?"

"Well, yes. First of all, for the arrest," the Chief agreed, "and then, more generally, for my behavior since you arrived," he added.

"The G-string incident?" Reginaldo guessed.

"I was thinking about other things," Viana confessed. "Like rounding up pedestrians during your coronation, threatening the hillside residents so they wouldn't make a scene on TV, that kind of thing," he explained.

"I see," Reginaldo nodded. "We all make mistakes," he comforted the Police Chief. "But why apologize to me for what you did to others?"

"I don't know," Viana admitted, shaking his head. "I guess it's because, well... because you're the king," he shrugged.

"Well, either way, apology accepted."

Slowly, Viana began to take in his surroundings and realized that he and the king were seated at a bus stop.

"Are you waiting for the bus?" he asked the king, surprised.

"Uh huh," Reginaldo confirmed.

"And you were on a bus last night, too," Viana recalled. "Do you always take the bus?"

"Yep," the king nodded. "I don't own a car," he explained.

Viana looked around at the others who were also waiting there; men and women on their way to work, mostly, already wearing a look of total exhaustion, even before the day had begun in earnest.

"You know," the Police Chief said after a pause, "it's amazing the things I've learned since abandoning my patrol car. You must have experienced the same thing by taking the bus," he guessed.

"You think? What kinds of things?" Reginaldo wondered.

"Well, personally," Viana began, "by walking the streets I've come face to face with all kinds of people that I wouldn't ordinarily deal with, except in a law enforcement situation. You know, some sort of confrontation," he explained.

"I see," the king nodded.

"Our society has so many inventions to insulate us from the world outside."

"Right," Reginaldo agreed.

"It's our own fault, really," Viana admitted. "Just like you said in your speech, you know, at the coronation."

"Mm Hmm."

"We choose to go blind because we're afraid of what we might see."

"Then show them," Reginaldo suggested.

"Show who?"

"The insulated."

"The insulated?" the Chief asked.

"Sure, show them that which they'd rather avoid."

"How?" Viana wondered. "Won't people just look away?"

"Make it so they can't. This car idea, for example."

"Car idea?"

"You said you were insulated inside yours, correct?"

"Yes."

"Well then," Reginaldo said, as he slowly began to lose himself in thought. "As it stands today, the down and out choose to steal the cars they cannot own. It's the have-nots taking from the haves, which must seem to them like the quickest way to even things out. But what if, instead, they jumped into the cars and just sat there, obliging the driver to take a few minutes out of his or her day for a chat? The car guarantees a captive audience," he pointed out. "That would be one way of showing them what they'd rather avoid."

"Encourage car-jackings? Hmmm, I don't know..." Viana worried.

"Yes," Reginaldo sighed in a moment of self-appreciation. "It would be an updated version of the Reverend Martin Luther King's sit-ins. Only this time people can't just get up and leave the diner."

"Well, I'll keep your suggestion in mind, but -"

"Say, Mr...," Reginaldo interrupted.

"Call me Viana."

"Viana, instead of them coming to us, why don't we go to them?"

"What do you mean?"

"You know," Reginaldo explained, "why don't you and I go see this other side of Rio?" he suggested. "I assume a favela would be the place to start."

"Oh, I don't know, Your Highness -"

"Please, you can call me Reggie."

"I don't know, Reggie," Viana continued. "The favelas aren't exactly a tourist attraction. They're very dangerous," the Police Chief warned.

"Ma'am," Reginaldo called out to a fellow commuter. "Ma'am, do you know how to get to the nearest hillside slum?" he asked her, ignoring the Chief's warning.

"Slum?" she verified. "You're trying to get to a slum?"

"Yes, you see I'm new in town, and I just thought... well, it's a long story," he told her. "Anyway, do you know if there's one around here?"

"How about that one?" she said, pointing to a nearby hill.

"Perfect!" Reginaldo exclaimed. "We can walk there!"

"Reggie, I still don't think this is a good idea. Folks in the favela don't exactly welcome cops with open arms," Viana pointed out.

"And whose fault is that?" the king pressed him.

"Well, now that's... it's complicated," the Chief stumbled.

Then, glancing down at the navy blue outfit the Chief was wearing, Reginaldo asked: "Do you have a change of clothes, you know, something besides the uniform?"

"No."

"Nothing?"

"I usually wear the same thing all day," the Chief told him, somewhat impatiently.

"Don't worry," Reginaldo assured him. "I have an idea. We'll buy you a shirt from a street vendor on the way there," he said as they prepared to walk away. "Oh," he stopped. "You should probably leave your gun behind as well."

"No Your Hi- No, Reggie. Without a gun we're helpless," the Chief argued.

"Viana, if we show up armed to the teeth they'll think we want trouble. Our mission must be in peace," Reginaldo countered.

"Fine," Viana said, shaking his head as he removed his belt. "But you can't blame me if, God forbid, something were to – "

"We'll be fine," Reginaldo scoffed, dismissing the Chief's concerns.

"Here we are," Reginaldo said, as he stared at the seemingly endless trail of steps that led up into the favela *Morro do Pinto*. The walk had proved longer that our duo initially predicted, the problem being that immediate access to the hillside was cut off by a commuter railway line that ran along the mammoth Avenida Presidente Vargas. Rightly or not, Viana cursed the pretentious boulevard.

"Yep, here we are," the Chief finally echoed.

"By the way, the shirt looks nice," Reginaldo told him, glancing down at Viana's brand new, paper-thin, sleeve-less red T-shirt with the image of Ché Guevara emblazoned upon the chest. "You see," he smiled, "I told you we'd find something."

"Thanks," the Chief smirked. "You sure you want to go up?" he asked the king, raising his head as he tried to see where the steps might end.

"We've made it this far," Reginaldo sighed. "We might as well go on."

"I guess I'll go first," Viana said, "in case there's trouble."

"Good idea."

At that early morning hour, all was quiet inside the favela. Reginaldo thought the place completely deserted until he finally caught sight of a pair of eyes that followed him and the Chief through the narrow trails that wove in and out between the tightly-packed houses. Despite the lack of sophistication in the methods used for their construction, these man-made shelters were true marvels of what was possible when one had only recycled materials to work from – an elaborate patchwork of metal and brick that clung to the hillside by miracle alone. Again, Reginaldo noticed the pair of eyes peering from a void between the slabs.

"I think we're being watched," he whispered to Viana.

"Of course we're being watched," the Chief responded. "We must look extremely out of place."

"Look at these homes, Viana. How do they keep from washing away every time it rains?" Reginaldo wondered.

"Actually," the Chief told him, "they're very well-constructed. They can withstand quite a lot. You see -"

Suddenly, the pair of eyes in the window came to life as a young boy stepped out of a doorway wielding an over-sized pistol that his tiny hands could hardly keep raised. He was shirtless; a pair of Ocean Pacific shorts and tattered flip-flops were his only clothing. It was a youth nearly identical to the hundreds Reginaldo had seen roaming the city.

"Please, don't shoot," Reginaldo begged him. "We'd be more than happy to purchase some candy if you'll just put down the gun."

"I don't think this kid's too concerned with candy," the Chief mumbled from the side of his mouth.

"What do you want?" the boy asked the two men.

"We mean no harm!" Reginaldo cried.

"Listen, son," Viana said to the boy. "Why don't you put the gun away and we'll forget all about this little misunderstanding."

"How old are you?" Reginaldo asked him.

"You grow up fast around here," a voice announced from a nearby window. This time the person holding a gun was a bit older, although this did little to calm the two visitors.

"What in the hell do you want?" a second man asked, emerging from one of the homes. Now there were three pistols pointed at Reginaldo and Police Chief Viana. More than plenty.

"Look, gentlemen," the king pleaded with them. "I can explain."

"You cops?" one of the men asked.

"Cops?!" the two laughed as they nervously looked at one another. "No, we're not cops!"

"Those pants you've got on," the oldest one said, pointing to Viana. "They look like the kind of pants cops use."

"These?" Viana asked, looking down at his clothing and cursing himself for ever having agreed to the king's idea of visiting a favela unarmed. "I borrowed these from a friend," he explained.

"I hate friends of cops almost as much as I hate cops," the gunman laughed to the other. "How about you?"

"Uh huh," the other agreed with a chuckle. "And, you know, if we took you two out, right here and now, no one would ever know."

"Why not?" Reginaldo wondered.

"Reggie..." Viana mumbled, finding it unwise to press the gunmen for explanations.

"Why not, what?"

"I'm curious to know why no one would know."

"Because no one would bother coming up here to look for you," one of the gunmen explained.

"Cops don't care what happens up here, as long as it stays up here," the other man added. "And when they do come round, it's to bust some drug dealer 'cos he's probably cutting in on some of their business," he laughed.

"Look, maybe we can —"

"I'm tired of talking," the gunman interrupted the king, slowly raising his pistol into line with his one open eye.

"Please!" Viana called out. "Let him go and take me as a hostage."

"Hostage?" one of the gunmen laughed. "What the hell I want with a hostage?"

Viana was prepared to reveal his identity, to let these thugs know they had captured the Chief of Police, unarmed, in their own backyard. As a hostage Viana would be worth his weight in gold. As the Chief began to speak, the sound of rickety wheels scraping along the stone path made him stop. Someone was coming and the others heard it as well. But Viana was wise enough to know that an intruder wouldn't mean salvation. At best, just a momentary interruption of the inevitable. At worst, another innocent victim. Slowly, the wheels rolled closer.

"Look," Viana began, "I think you should know that -"

"Reggie?" a voice suddenly called out. "Reggie, is that you?"

"Jefferson!" the king shouted.

Pulling his cart behind him, the snack vendor was shocked to find Reginaldo standing in the middle of the path, his hands raised. He had yet to notice the men that held his friend there.

"What are you doing here?" the king asked, surprised.

"I live here," the other explained. "Question is, what are you doing here? And why are you boys -"

"You know these guys?" one of the gunmen asked the snack

vendor.

"I know that one," Jefferson said, pointing to Reginaldo. "He's a friend of mine. From the library," he explained.

"Jefferson," Reginaldo begged him. "Tell them we're not cops."

"Cops?" he laughed. "Boys, put your guns away, these ain't cops."

Satisfied with Jefferson's testimony, the two young men and the boy lowered their guns and disappeared into their respective homes without uttering a single word.

"You two headed down the hill?" Jefferson asked them. "If so, we can walk together."

"That would be great!" the other two agreed in unison.

XXIII

Excerpt from Gregory Neeld, *Diary of the Revolution at Rio de Janeiro, Brazil, Kept by Commander Neeld, H.M.S. 'Beagle,' Septembre 1887 to March 1890.*

... and of late there have been rumors of military unrest and much public pressure besides placed upon His Royal Majesty to, once and for all, abolish the institution of African slavery practised here in Brazil for the almost four hundred years of its existence. It remains foreign to my purpose to here suggest that these poor souls will have been more secure in chains, but one cannot but dread the fate that awaits when the citizens of this nation, who so despise these servants, are no longer obliged to house, cloth, and feed them. With humility, I can only assume my worries are the folly of one who has never felt the tug of the shackle cuff at his ankle, or wrist. And so, for today, this hand rests.

The three men walked side by side through the city streets, the snack vendor and the Chief of Police on either side of the king. Despite their proximity and their common destination, none said a word. One would guess that, taking into account the ordeal Reginaldo and Viana had just been through, neither man was feeling particularly chatty. Yet, there was another, less defined, motive for their silence.

"This here's my stop," Jefferson said, as he began to set up his things at the corner of the Avenida Rio Branco and the Rua Pedro Lessa.

"You know," Viana said, also stopping, and glancing up at the National Library, "I think I might go inside here for a little while before heading back to the station."

"Really?" Reginaldo reacted with surprise. "I hadn't pegged you as a, well...," he hesitated, not wanting to offend his new friend.

"Go ahead, say it. A thinking man?"

"I wouldn't go that far, Viana. I just envisioned you as more of a ... man of action, let's say."

"Well, it's your fault, really. Ever since you arrived the Mayor's been asking the impossible of me, and so I ended up here, looking in vain for ideas on how to turn this place into an empire."

"Any luck?" Reginaldo wondered.

"None at all. But, to be honest Your Highness – sorry, Reggie – after today's little adventure I think I've lost my appetite for the Mayor's vision of the city."

"Hmm. Really..."

"How can he think he has the right to preserve the streets for only those he sees as fit?" the Chief of Police continued. "Does any one man own a street corner? A plot of land? The right to walk the beaches?" Viana demanded, growing quite vehement. "Oh dear," he sighed, shocked by his own words. Glancing down at the image of Ché Guevara on his T-shirt, he wondered if the old revolutionary weren't somehow influencing his thoughts.

"What we saw today, Reggie... this city... those people... how did things get to this point?" the Chief despaired.

"Well, we might find some answers inside," Reginaldo predicted, motioning towards the library.

"I've tried, but the history books just leave me with even more questions."

"I know what you mean, my friend. This is serious and we need help. Ok, come with me!"

"What about your sandwiches?" Jefferson called out after them.

"They'll have to wait," Reginaldo decided.

"Wow, this is serious," the vendor noted with surprise.

"We're fed up."

"Fed up?" Milena asked.

"With History, we mean," Reginaldo explained.

"You two still looking at the monarchy and what-not?"

"Uh huh."

"And the titles under History ... ?"

"They're not really discussing the things we're interested in," Reginaldo explained.

"I think travel narratives are what you want," she decided.

"Travel narratives?" the two men questioned in unison.

"They're an ideal resource for those details of daily life that most History books overlook," Milena explained. "I'm guessing this is your complaint?"

"I think that's about it," the two men decided.

"Ok, follow me. But we'll have to go down into the Archives. No more comfortable reading tables and soft lighting."

"I think we're willing to make a few sacrifices in order to get to the truth. Right, Viana?"

"Please lead the way, miss," the Police Chief said with more conviction than he'd felt in years.

"AND ONE MORE thing," Milena warned once the three were among the archives. "Most of these were written by foreigners, Englishmen mostly," she explained as she ran her finger along the spines of the old volumes.

"Foreigners, eh?" Viana hesitated, looking towards Reginaldo.

"Is that a problem?"

"What about Brazilians? Didn't any of us write this stuff down?"

"Some did, sure, but the Europeans tended to write about the more mundane culture and surroundings, which stood out to them as foreigners," Milena explained.

"I haven't had much luck with foreigners lately," the Chief whispered, leaning in towards the king. "Mostly at that club of yours. How do we know we can trust them?"

"We don't. But we've got no choice."

And so Milena began dusting off volume after volume of the leather-bound journals the various Europeans had published of their travels to the tropics. She was right: it took a foreign eye to record the banalities of daily life that a permanent resident would involuntarily ignore. And the banalities were many: the food, the dress, the height of a verandah, or the shape of a front door, men who spat, and women who spat even farther. They were the candid impressions of this city's earliest tourists, the few who saw Rio before there existed a single tourism board to shuffle them safely from one spot to another in air-conditioned minivans.

Amid such details a biography of Rio de Janeiro began to emerge, and Viana found himself a reluctant protagonist in this story, for the tale of the city was also that of the Police. And so, between these yellowed pages, Viana began to uncover his own roots. Most troubling was the realization that the policeman's career began where slavery had ended, as the aloof Royal Guard was transformed into a meddling City Patrol in the years after Abolition, when control moved from the private to the public sphere. Under slavery, the master had controlled every aspect of his slave's existence, a vigilance that extended even beyond the boundaries of his estate. But when slaves were declared to be no longer the property of such families, the streets were inundated as servants were expelled from the elite's homes. Thus, the modern-day police force was born, as it harassed and corralled the newly displaced.

One hundred years later, little had changed, Viana decided. He was being paid to do exactly that which had been done by his ilk a century ago: to keep well hidden and contained the true nature of Rio de Janeiro. Perhaps it was overly cynical to characterize these poorer districts of Rio as the true nature of the city, but it was certainly a reality just as authentic as that of sea, sand, and sun. And just as the City Patrol and the Royal Guard had done after the first king's arrival, Viana was also trying to transform a Brazilian city into an idealized metropolis by sweeping its unpleasantness under the rug. Today he saw just where such unpleasantness was being swept. The extra guards around the favelas were always "extra" guards, for - if not a coronation - there was always another rationale in waiting as an excuse to maintain the heightened level of security. Ashamed, Viana gently closed the volume of memoirs.

"What sad ol' bug bit you two?" Jefferson asked the two forlorn faces that stared blankly back at him.

"Hmm?" the men mumbled back.

"Looks like you two just seen a ghost."

"I'll take a hot dog," the Chief said absent-mindedly, digging some bills from his pocket.

"No hot dogs," Reginaldo told him. "Just sandwiches."

"Just sandwiches?"

"Just sandwiches," Jefferson confirmed.

"Fine."

"Make it two," Reginaldo chimed in.

"Ham alright?"

"Ham is perfect," the king smiled, handing the Chief his lunch. "Thank you, Jefferson. You know, Viana," Reginaldo said as the two men turned to walk away, "you and I have another enemy in common. That is, besides the automobile."

"We do? What's that?"

"The heat," Reginaldo declared.

"The heat?"

"Sure, you don't think the heat is behind your G-string problem, if you'll pardon the pun."

"I guess I see your point, but what can one do about the heat?"

"Nothing, so we must learn to work with it instead of against it," Reginaldo explained.

"Right," Viana agreed, "so how do I work with the heat to prevent the use of the G-string?"

"That's where our problems differ, my friend, for mine has a solution. Yours, no. I think the G-string is here to stay. But I could use your help with solving my problem."

"My help?" Viana worried.

Later that afternoon, Marcos burst into the palace, running through the corridors as he frantically searched for the king.

"Bebel, where's Reggie?" he asked, stopping in front of her desk.

"He went out. Say, how was your trip?" she asked him.

"Where, Bebel, where?" he pleaded with her.

"You went to São Paulo, right?"

"Focus, Bebel," Marcos said condescendingly. "Where did Reggie go?" he repeated, dragging out the syllables.

"I don't know Mr. Marcos, he didn't say."

"God dammit. Ask him," he scolded her. "Ask him where the hell he's going!"

Marcos stormed away from Bebel's desk, whispering to himself as he tried to work out where Reginaldo might be. Suddenly, he raised his head and snapped his fingers as if remembering something.

"My notepad," he mumbled. "Where's my notepad? Bebel?" he asked.

"Yes?" she timidly responded, wary of another outburst of anger.

"Have you seen my little notepad?"

"I saw it upstairs by the couch," she told him.

"Oh, thank God," he sighed with relief, heading towards the stairs.

"So I put it back on your desk," Bebel added. "I thought you'd be more likely to find it there," she explained.

"On my desk?" Marcos confirmed.

"Yes, sir," she nodded.

"Thanks, Bebel," he said to her. "That was... that was real smart," he conceded.

Marcos ran into his office and grabbed the notepad from his desk. Leafing through its pages, he finally found the one he was looking for, which read:

MONARCHY ?!?

NOT TEIXEIRA

THEN WHO?

REGINALDO SANTOS

CONJUNTO BELA VISTA, 147

CRUZILIA (MG)

(LOTS OF...)PORK RIBS & "WHIPPED" POTATOES

ISABEL (34) 256-1808

LIBRARY ???

"Bebel?" he called out to her, exiting his office.

"Yes, sir?"

"You're probably not," he began, but suddenly stopped. "You really wouldn't...," he again stuttered.

"What?" she asked.

Finally, not wanting to offend her, he asked the question: "Are you familiar with any libraries here in Rio?"

"Sure, there's one at school, you know, at PUC," she explained.

"Uh huh, ok, PUC," Marcos nodded.

"But then there's also one at the federal university, and at state, I guess," she continued.

"Christ, that's three already," Marcos sighed, fearing it may take hours to locate Reginaldo.

"Reggie prefers the National Library, but I think it's a bit too —"

"What was that?" Marcos interrupted her.

"The National Library, downtown," Bebel repeated.

"Reggie likes that library?" he confirmed.

"He's like always there," she laughed. "Hey, you know, come to think of it that's probably where he —"

But before Bebel could finish the thought, Marcos had turned on his heels and was already racing back down the corridor towards the door.

It had been a busy morning and, quite frankly, Reginaldo was tired of leafing through so many delicate historical documents. In fact, he was starting to show signs of fatigue in relation to History in general. Sure, this morning's exercise had yielded many answers as to the lamentable fate of slaves after Abolition, but not knowing what had happened to a few certain individuals kept nagging at the king. The realization was sinking in that he might never know.

Perhaps such frustration explains the decision to abandon his habitual drawer of the card catalog and instead peruse a collection of disciplines that, unlike History, never promised any answers in the first place. So, like a jilted lover, Reginaldo moved on.

Wasn't there a reputed consolation to be found in philosophy? Reginaldo thought he remembered.

"Philosophy?" Milena confirmed. "Right, no more History," she remembered. "Anything in particular?"

"Not really," he shrugged.

"Ok, I'll just grab a handful at random," she decided.

His arms again filled with Milena's choices, the king walked upstairs, headed towards his left, and waded deep into an unexplored section of the library. Settling into a private desk, he once again scanned the titles for a phrase, or even a unique binding, that might call out to him. Strangely enough, the title that caught his eye was really quite mundane, although Reginaldo found its simplicity rather enigmatic.

"Essays," he read aloud. "Hm. Essays on what?" he wondered.

Opening the book, Reginaldo was surprised to find that one of this Frenchman's essays was on Brazil. It seemed that, no matter how hard he tried, he couldn't get away from the nation – his nation, he remembered, for he is, after all, its king – and its history.

"Have you seen a big guy, blondish hair?" Marcos panted as he reached the Information Desk.

"You mean Reggie?" Milena asked him.

"Yeah, that's the one," Marcos acknowledged.

"He was downstairs, but he's gone up to the second floor now," she said, pointing towards the stairs.

"Thanks."

Topping the stairs, Marcos moved hurriedly in search of Reginaldo, darting between shelves, and weaving in and out between rows. Meanwhile, the king found the essay on the philosopher's travels in Brazil and began to read when the following words suddenly caught his attention: *This man who stayed with me was a plain, simple fellow, and men of this sort are likely to give true testimony. Men of intelligence notice more things and view them more carefully, but they comment on them; and to establish and substantiate their interpretation, they cannot refrain from altering the facts a little.*

Frustrated by the library's enormity, Marcos felt he was traveling in circles and worried he might never find his friend. Nearby, Reginaldo continued to read: *We need either a very truthful man, or one so ignorant that he has no material with which to construct false theories and make them credible... a man wedded to no idea.*

Then, Reginaldo thought back to the night before and the song Marcela had opened with. There was a reason, he now realized, it had stuck in his head.

Your every wish is my command

All you got to do is wiggle your little hand

and I'm your puppet, I'm your puppet...

"Reggie?" Marcos said, happening upon a row of reading desks, where at last he found Reginaldo.

"Marcos? What a surprise, what are you doing here?" the king asked him.

"I need to talk to you," the young man said in a rather serious tone of voice.

"Look, Marcos," Reginaldo began, pulling out a chair for him. "I apologize about the confusion at the club. I explained everything to the authorities and -"

"It's not that, Reggie."

"No? Then what is it? What's wrong?"

"Reggie..."

"Yes...?"

"The Senate, Reggie. They've voted to dissolve the monarchy."

"Dissolve... what do you mean?"

"Dissolve, abolish, cancel... whatever. They passed an amendment this morning to annul the referendum. I just got word from the Senator. He's dissolved my position as well."

"Oh, Marcos. I'm so sorry," Reginaldo comforted him.

"Sorry for me, what about you?" Marcos angrily asked, leaving his chair. "You're the king for Christ's sake! They can't just vote you out."

"Shhhh," Reginaldo tried to calm him, motioning for him to sit back down. "Well," he laughed after a pause, "I had a feeling they might do this."

"What do you mean you had a feeling?" Marcos wondered, looking up at him.

"I just figured they would do it sooner or later."

"I don't understand."

"Here, read this," Reginaldo said, sliding the book over to his friend.

"Montaigne?" Marcos asked, turning it over and reading the name along the spine. "Who the hell's Montaigne?"

"A French philosopher who apparently spent some time in Brazil, but that's not important. It's what he has to say that's enlightening."

"This is not about naked women again, is it?"

"No, now go on," the king urged his friend.

Reluctantly, Marcos read the indicated paragraph.

"Reggie, that's great but what the hell does this have to do with - "

"They wanted an idiot," Reginaldo told him. "A puppet. Someone without opinions."

"Who? The French?"

"No. Our government, Senator Cruz. Maybe others as well," he speculated.

"What?!" the young man scoffed in disbelief. "I can assure you that Senator Cruz hasn't been reading any French philosophers," he laughed.

"The facts were there in front of me the whole time," Reginaldo reflected, ignoring Marcos' comment. "But I was blind," he concluded. "Oh jeez, how could I have not seen it?" he scolded himself. "They did the same thing to Pedro the Second," he explained to Marcos. "His father had abdicated the throne, but the people still wanted a king. The Congress was all too happy to agree, for they saw in the young king an innocent and naïve young man whom they could smother with ceremony and useless training, making him irrelevant. 'A man wedded to no idea,'" he concluded, quoting the philosopher once again. "Remind you of anyone?"

"But you're full of all kinds of... interesting ideas," Marcos noted, choosing his words carefully.

"Ah, but that's the beauty of the story," Reginaldo sighed with visible delight. "Pedro, too, was wedded to his own ideas. And like him, the very ones that set me up have come to knock me down."

"But, what does it matter what somebody wants?" Marcos asked, becoming frustrated with this overly complicated explanation of events. "You're the heir and that's that. Use that power to stop them," he suggested.

"Marcos," Reginaldo laughed. "Do you really believe that I am the heir of the royal family?"

"I already told you, Reggie, it's probably from an illegitimate line."

"So then it's more improbable still. Who's going to be able to trace the genealogy of a bastard child back one hundred and fifty years to the Portuguese royal family? Who can and who would?"

"The government, Reggie. They collect this type of data."

"The government, Marcos, can't even collect our garbage."

"Fine, you're not the king," Marcos conceded. "The Senator lied, it's all been a hoax. So what the hell are we going to do now? Just let them claim victory over us? You know he'll probably run for President."

"Fine, let him," Reginaldo shrugged. "We can't fight him for the rest of our lives."

"It wouldn't be for the rest of - "

"Look, Marcos," Reginaldo interrupted him. "This has been fun, but I'm tired. I miss my friends back home, my house, karaoke at the Apolo... the pork ribs. You remember those ribs, don't you?" he asked, nudging his friend's elbow. "Weren't they some good ribs?"

"Sure, they were good ribs, but..."

Marcos lost his enthusiasm before he could finish the thought.

"Come on," Reginaldo whispered. "Let's head back to the palace, have a nice last supper prepared by Felipe, and pack up our things. What do you say?"

"Fine," Marcos acquiesced.

Thus resolved, Reginaldo gathered his books, threw an arm around the young man's shoulders and the two walked towards the stairs, Marcos with his head still lowered in defeat.

XXIV

Outside the palace, the rain was falling hard as Flavia sat alone in her car. She had left the engine running, the whisper of the radio and the hum of the windshield wipers her only distraction as she waited along the opposite side of the street. Her eyes darting between the building's various exits, she took a cigarette from the pack lying on the dashboard and lit it, releasing the smoke through a tiny space she created when lowering the window. Between the back and forth of the windshield wipers, she finally saw a red sports car drive across an area usually reserved for pedestrian traffic.

That's gotta be them, she said to herself when she saw someone throw a suitcase into the trunk. She put the car into drive.

Flavia hadn't once taken her eyes from the red sports car when it finally pulled over at the corner of the Rua Barata Ribeiro and Republica do Peru, a busy, yet residential, area inside the Copacabana neighborhood. After the car parked, she saw a young man get out and open a single umbrella for both himself and the other occupant, as they began to remove their luggage from the trunk. When they started walking down the sidewalk, Flavia got out of her car as well and followed on foot from the opposite side of the street. All three walked along for a while before the two men entered an apartment building. Flavia stood there for a moment beneath a tree, just watching. Then, after waiting for some cars to pass, she crossed the street and entered the building.

Inside, a doorman seated behind a table in the lobby fought off sleep.

"Excuse me, sir," she said, jarring him to attention. "You wouldn't be able to tell me which apartment those two men just went to, would you?" she asked, flashing an ID card. "I'm from the Tele-Journal, channel 4," she explained.

"They asked for Miss Seville," the doorman answered. "Number 510."

"Thank you," Flavia said, handing him a few crumpled bills for his trouble.

Upstairs, Marcela opened her front door to find two pitiful figures dripping water there in the hallway.

"Oh, you poor things," she gasped. "Soaked to the bone. Hurry, come in."

"Thanks, Marcela," Marcos said while Reginaldo remained glum.

"Of course, of course. Here, take off these jackets, give me your bags," she said, taking their clothes and suitcases into her bedroom. It was a modest apartment; from the entrance one could see the entire place – a kitchenette, another area made into a living room by the opposing placement of a couch and television, a bathroom off to the right, and the bedroom to the left of the front door. Marcela's fellow dancers, Luzia and Claudia, were at the apartment as well — Luzia preparing some food in the kitchen, Claudia on the couch watching television. Exiting the bedroom, Marcela nearly bumped into Reginaldo.

"Oh. Sorry, honey. Whatcha need?" she asked him.

"I'm not feeling too well, mind if I lay down for a while?"

"Sure, of course. Can I get you anything? Water, juice?"

"No, I'm fine," he told her. "I'd just like to rest a bit."

Reginaldo slinked into the bedroom as Marcela closed the door behind him.

"I'm worried," she whispered to Marcos. "He doesn't seem

well."

"It's strange, he was fine earlier. When I told him the news he took it so well, said that he even expected it."

"Expected it?"

"Yeah, he claims he's not the heir," Marcos explained. "Then he insisted on showing me a book by Rousseau, no, Montaigne, somebody... Anyway, he thinks he was picked — "

A sudden knock on the door interrupted Marcos' explanation.

"Hmm, who could that be?" Marcela thought aloud. As she walked over to answer the door, the others looked on, curious. As the door swung open, there stood Flavia, arm still raised, poised to knock again.

"Yes?" Marcela asked.

"Uh... Miss Seville?" Flavia stammered.

"Yes?"

"You don't know me," Flavia began, "but I've come to apologize for-"

"Hey!" Claudia shouted from the couch. "It's the reporter bitch from the other night!"

"What!? What the hell—" Marcela cried out, preparing to slam the door in Flavia's face.

"Please, Miss Seville," the journalist begged, her arm outstretched to block the door. "Give me a chance to explain."

THE NOISE OF a slamming door was instead replaced by that of a falling gavel. On the floor of the Senate chamber, Senator Cruz approached the standing microphone to announce the introduction of a bill he was sponsoring: the 1993 Banking and Securities Reform Act.

"You thought Reggie was in business with Senator Cruz?" Marcos laughed.

"Nothing else made sense," Flavia tried to explain. "How else could I account for his not knowing about the clause in the constitution? I smelled scandal and I really wanted to pin it on that bastard," she confessed. "But when the Senate abolished the monarchy, well," she shrugged. "Then it was pretty obvious that they weren't in cahoots."

"I can't believe this," Marcos sighed.

"Look, I wanna make it up to you, and to the king."

"He's not the king anymore, remember?" Marcos reminded her.

"I should go," Flavia mumbled, lowering her head and walking towards the door.

"Wait," Marcela stopped her. "How would you make it up to us?"

"Investigate the Senator, I guess," she shrugged. "Find out the truth behind this whole scam."

Marcela looked to Marcos. "We don't really have a whole lot of options here, hon'. So he's not in cahoots with Reggie... but we could catch him in some other kind of scandal," she suggested, turning back to Flavia.

"Like what?"

"How about: 'Distinguished Senator caught with exotic nightclub singer'?" she excitedly announced, extending her arms as if flashing each word of the possible newspaper headline.

"Sex scandal?" Flavia asked. "It doesn't play here like it does North of the Equator."

"You tried it with Reggie," Marcela reminded her.

"I was desperate."

"Aren't we?"

"No, there's gotta be something better," Flavia sighed. "We Brazilians aren't so hung up on sex like the Americans."

They paused to think.

"Wait a second," Marcela said, breaking the silence. "Let's back up. Marcos says Reggie claims he's not the heir. So why did they pick him?"

"He believes they needed a puppet."

"A puppet?" Flavia wondered.

"Yeah, someone too simple to get in the way or cause problems," Marcos explained. "So he did just the opposite."

"I'll say."

"But, get in the way of what?" Flavia asked. "What would he have gotten in the way of?"

Back on the Senate floor, a motion to dispense with the reading of the bill was agreed to and Senator Cruz was now calling for a full vote on the measure.

"So," Marcela began as she played the scenario out in her head once again. "The Senate chooses Reggie 'cause they think he won't get in the way. Who was in the way before?"

"Well, the king replaced the President so it must have been him," Marcos concluded.

"The President was in the way? Great, he probably had his hands in all kinds of stuff. That doesn't really narrow it down too much."

"Sure it does," he assured them.

"Please, enlighten us," Marcela sarcastically requested.

"I've always argued that the President doesn't really have that much power. More like a show thing."

"A show thing?" Marcela confirmed. "Honey, you've been hanging around me too long," she warned Marcos.

"Yeah, the President is the leader of the nation. He's got all kinds of power," Flavia countered.

"Sure, I agree," Marcos nodded. "But what I'm saying is that he doesn't have much direct power. He's got that with Executive Decrees and what-not, but his real power is indirect, in his ability to veto legislation that comes from the Congress. He's the final 'say so' that can make or break a proposal."

"So they get rid of the President," Flavia said, "and they can pass whatever they want..."

"No veto so what's to stop them, since they predicted Reggie wouldn't get in their way." Marcos concluded.

"Oh my god," Marcela sighed, "somewhere out there Sherlock Holmes is just turning over in his fictional grave with the lameness of this plot. Is politics always this boring?"

Flavia and Marcos shrugged their shoulders as if to confirm her suspicion.

"So," Marcela said, turning to Flavia, "have they been taking advantage of our little puppet? Have they passed any laws lately?"

"I guess they're always passing laws. I haven't been keeping up," she confessed. "I've been following the king for the last month."

"Wait, wait, wait," Marcos interrupted. "Flavia said earlier that we Brazilians aren't concerned about sex scandals."

"Yeah?"

"So, what's so serious that the Senator would have to go to such lengths to hide? If not sex, what do we worry about?"

As they were pondering this question, Claudia exited the bathroom, smartly dressed for the evening ahead.

"Look at this!" she said, digging up a few crumpled bills from the bottom of her purse. "Customers sure don't tip like they used to."

The others looked to one another excitedly. "Money!" they cried out in unison.

The gavel fell again as the Senate President pro tempore announced passage of the financial reform bill.

"So, what do we do now?" Marcela asked the others.

"I've got some contacts in the capital," Flavia said, moving towards the door. "I'll get in touch with them and see what's going on, see if they've introduced any budget requests, projects for funding, anything like that."

"I've got some research to do as well," Marcos sighed. "Here's my mobile number," he said to Flavia, handing her a business card. "Please call me as soon as you find something and I'll do the same."

"Sure thing," she agreed. Then, turning to Marcela: "Bye for now, Miss Seville. I will make this up to you," Flavia assured her.

Marcela nodded as Flavia took her leave.

"What about Reggie?" Marcela said to Marcos, glancing towards the bedroom.

"Can he stay here with you for a few days?"

"Of course."

"Great. I'd better get going then as well, but I'll be back in a few days. You've got my number?"

"Sure do."

Marcela extended her arm for a handshake, but instead Marcos took her hand and kissed it.

"Thanks, Marcela," he smiled.

"Hello?"

"Veronica?"

"Yes?"

"It's Flavia Mores again," the journalist announced loudly into the receiver, talking above the sound of rain as she stood at a pay phone outside Marcela's apartment. "From the Tele-Journal in Rio," she added.

"Yes, I remember you. How's it going?"

"Things could be better," she admitted. "Look, I need to ask you a question."

"Alright."

"How illegal is it to lie about the true identity of the heir?" Flavia asked.

"The heir?" Veronica wondered, confused.

"The heir to the throne. The king," she explained.

"He wasn't the heir?"

"That's what we're trying to sort out."

"Well, I can't give you an exact legal penalty at the moment, but I imagine the offense would prove very serious."

"That's what I'm hoping," Flavia confessed.

"But, just like in all cases," Veronica reminded her, "you'll need some fairly convincing proof."

"Right," Flavia sighed, already somewhat disappointed. "Proof."

CLOSING THE DOOR behind Marcos, Marcela moved towards the bedroom to check on Reginaldo. Slowly opening the door, she peaked her head in.

"Reggie?" she whispered.

"Yes?" a timid voice responded. The dismantled king was lying on the bed with his back facing the door.

"You asleep?"

"No."

"Wanna talk?"

"Sure," he agreed.

Marcela gently closed the door behind her, and took a seat on the bed across from Reginaldo. Feeling her weight upon the mattress, he turned over, rose a bit, and rested his head against a pillow that he'd propped up against the headboard.

"You know," she began, "it's alright to be upset about the whole monarchy thing."

"It's not that, not really," he admitted.

"No?"

"It's related to that, but it's something different."

"Well... wanna tell me about it?"

"It's just that, when I found out I was the heir, I had my entire history handed to me, most of it anyway," he told her. "I may not have known about my grandparents and their parents, but I did know something about the generations before them."

"Right," Marcela sighed.

"For so long it had been just mother and me, even after she died. Then, all of a sudden, I was reading about Dom João's voyage to Brazil, Pedro the First's illicit encounters with burlesque actresses, the coronation of Pedro the Second at age fifteen, and I felt like an intimate part of it all. I guess I always knew the adventure was too good to be true. This whole time I've been doing nothing more than playing dress-up, just another Carnival king."

"Oh, Reggie," she said, running her hands through his thinning hair in an effort to console him.

"Turns out that the only thing Pedro the Second and I really share is a similar fate, both of us duped and manipulated until the truly powerful find a way to toss us out into the street," he explained.

"Don't feel too bad, hon'. Politics is a business that rewards cunning and deceit. I'd be worried if you were actually good at it."

"The Mayor's right," Reginaldo conceded. "Pedro freed the slaves. What did I ever do?"

"You didn't have time," Marcela argued. "Who knows what you could have done with a few more months as king? Oh dear," she laughed, "I just got chills thinking about that."

Reginaldo smiled, appreciating her mildly serious joke.

"Have you ever noticed, Marcela," he asked, looking up at her, "how everything exciting happened in the past and there's nothing more to be done? Not nothing, really," he corrected himself, "but nothing very big."

"You trying to say there're no more battles to be fought in this world? That we don't have anything to fix, that Brazil's a country without problems?"

"Certainly not, Marcela. But the country's won its independence, slavery's been abolished..."

"So what about that whole 'independence or death' speech?" she wondered.

"On the radio?"

"That's the one."

"I don't want to say that I was kidding, but I was having some fun with the whole thing," Reginaldo admitted.

"People took it seriously," she told him. "I think you struck a chord."

"Really?"

"I know it's hard to imagine, and I can't believe I'm actually admitting as much, but sometimes your silly little speeches do make sense. Sometimes," Marcela added with a wink.

"Now that you mention it, I was serious about the whole brazil-wood thing. Before becoming king I had never really thought about it, but doesn't it seem a little insulting to be named after a raw material?"

"Just like Argentina for its silver?"

"And the Gold Coast, the Ivory Coast," Reginaldo noted.

"Why do you think the first thing most countries do after independence is change their name? There's a lot of power in a name," Marcela concluded. "But, I don't know..." she sighed after a pause.

"Don't know what?"

"Maybe I'm a cynic," she shrugged, "but sometimes I wonder if changing those names really changed anything else?"

"Psychologically, perhaps?" Reginaldo suggested.

"I guess you're right," Marcela conceded. "But I'd like to believe that people are strong enough to be themselves no matter how others define them."

"Like being told you're a king, for example."

"Or a queen," Marcela winked. "Oh jeez...," she sighed.

"What?"

"I'm not a cynic."

"No?"

"Worse," she concluded. "I'm an idealist."

Reginaldo smiled, nodding his head.

"Marcela?" he asked after a pause.

"Yes?"

"Mind if I use your phone?"

"Of course not, hon'. Know where it is, in the TV room?"

"I'll find it," he assured her, lifting himself up from the bed.

Leaving the bedroom, Reginaldo stepped quickly across the apartment towards the telephone, finally regaining his usual animation. Reaching into his back pocket, he pulled out a business card and dialed the number that was scribbled on the back.

"Fernando? Hi, it's Reggie. Yes, well, the former king anyway," he laughed. "Look," he said, becoming more serious. "I need a favor," he explained, staring across the room towards a photograph of Marcela.

"A favor?" Rafael repeated. "When did I do you this favor?" he asked the king.

"Years ago," Pedro told the old man. "I must have been no older than eight or nine."

"I must admit," Rafael laughed, "I'm curious to find out what kind of favor a poor old man like me did for a king."

"You laughed at me," the young man said.

"I laughed at you? You sure?"

"Positive."

"Doesn't seem very respec'ful on my part," Rafael admitted, somewhat embarrassed.

"It was just what I needed," the king acknowledged.

"Well, if you say so," Rafael shrugged. "Why'd I laugh at you, anyways?"

"I told you that I wanted to live on a deserted island, and you asked me what kind of king I would be with no one to rule over. Do you remember?" Pedro asked him.

"I think so," the old man guessed, searching his memory.

"Well, today I was shown the answer."

"Oh yeah, how's that?" Rafael asked.

"I couldn't have been a king on that island because a king's power doesn't come from within himself," Pedro said. "It's a gift granted to me by my subjects. But what happens when those subjects aren't even free to exercise their own will?" he rhetorically asked. "How could they ever grant me the right to act on their behalf when they themselves are not free to act? So they're not citizens at all, really. And, well, the monarchy's as hollow as if I, or any king, ruled over a deserted island," Pedro concluded. "Now I know that's why you laughed at me that day. You realized it long before I did. I only wish I could have figured it out sooner," he confessed. "Maybe, then, a life could have been saved today."

PERHAPS HIS LIFE could have been saved, if only she'd waited to tell Jacob about the king's visit, Clara accused herself. He would have never run around the house and overheard their conversation. He would have been resting peacefully in his cabin when Castro called for him, instead of swinging from its – No, she wouldn't allow herself to visit the scene again. There was no use playing it over and over and over again in her mind. She had work to do. Clara must bury her child and move on for, in this life, a slave wasn't afforded the luxury of mourning.

Clara wrapped the boy tightly in the linens he had always slept in, and placed his body down upon the hammock that would be used to carry him off to the Santa Casa da Misericórdia. When the two men from the cemetery arrived, they tied each end of the hammock to a pole, which they then placed over their right shoulder, carrying the boy away with the diligence one would display with any other cargo. There was no master of ceremonies to accompany her to the cemetery, no priest to console her, nor to lift the boy's soul unto heaven. In this procession of one, there was no carriage in which Clara might hide her grief from onlookers, no sentry to escort her through the streets and to the gates of Misericórdia. Reaching the graveyard, the two makeshift pallbearers placed the body along the outside wall, and left to make other rounds as Clara waited for an attendant to arrive. She was not alone, for an old black man was also there, a candle lit to mourn the loss of a woman that must have surely been his wife. Passers-by would occasionally toss a coin into his upturned hat; alms to cover the cost of burial. Before leaving the house, Castro had given Clara a few coins to pay for her expenses at the cemetery, the same coins that had fallen from the sack bound to Jacob's lifeless wrist. Fortunately, Clara was not aware that her boy was paying for his own burial with the money he had, over the years, managed to save.

Look at him, she thought to herself, as she gazed down at the boy's face that was framed by the burial garments. He lay there so peaceful, swaddled in blankets just as on the night he was born, Clara recalled. His face, already so light-skinned in life, was now even more pale in death. What if I had refused when they placed him into my arms that night? Clara asked herself. It was selfish of me to tie this child to a slave woman's fate. He would have been better off as an orphan, she argued, maybe even picked up and adopted by a rural white family that wouldn't mind the additional mouth to feed, knowing it would soon provide an extra helping hand in the fields. With that light complexion, he could of perhaps even passed as white and his life would have been that much easier. Could of walked out into this world as a man and never known hate, or ridicule; no one to discover the truth of what was within. I could live with that, Marcela thought to herself. I, too, could have passed, she decided, as she let the straps of her brassiere fall across her shoulders. She stared into the mirror at the other that perhaps she was, or perhaps could have been. Could she really choose, just like that?

Suddenly, Reginaldo opened the bedroom door.

"Thanks, Marcela," he said, closing the door behind him before looking her way. Quickly, Marcela grabbed the brassiere that was lying on the dresser and covered her bare chest. "I just had to —" he continued, stopping short when he saw her there at the mirror. Their eyes met, each one waiting for the other to speak first. It was Reginaldo who broke the silence: "I'm sorry, I can come back —"

"It's alright," she told him, lowering the bra. "You're not so naïve as to not already know the truth."

For the first time, Reginaldo looked upon her naked chest, which was as concave and flat as any other man's.

"Marcela?" he asked after a pause. "Have you been crying?"

"No, I haven't been crying," she lied. "This is just me without the make-up. Horrible isn't it?"

"I don't think so," he told her.

"Well, you've always been too nice," she laughed.

Reginaldo remained standing before her, as if waiting for the truth.

"Fuck it," she sniffed. "You're right, I have been crying," she finally admitted to him.

"Why?" he asked her, coming closer.

"I don't know," Marcela shrugged. "It's just something I do from time to time."

"I see."

"I know it must seem like all fun and games," she said to him, "but it's not always so easy being me."

"I understand," Rafael nodded.

"And, now, who knows maybe tomorrow, next week... that me will be gone," Pedro said. "I told Vieira that there would still be a me even when there's no king, but now I'm not so sure," he confessed. "Who would I have been on that deserted island, with no title, no crown?"

"Didn't you jus' tell me that you were already on that deserted island?" Rafael pointed out. Pedro nodded his head in agreement. "Well, then, I think you got your answer," he told the boy. "A true king or not, sounds like what you did today took real courage. And that's what makes you a great man, Pedrinho. I wouldn't think that would change - with, or without, a crown."

"For example, am I any different today?" Reginaldo asked Marcela.

"How do you mean?"

"You know, any more or less regal?" he clarified.

"Regal?" Marcela laughed. "Oh, I'm sorry honey. I don't mean to —"

"No, it's perfect," he assured her. "You're right. I was no more regal yesterday than I am today, only difference is that yesterday they said I was king and today they took it back."

"This is probably going somewhere, right?"

"Marcela," he said to her. "Put your clothes back on, do your make-up. Just because I've seen you without them doesn't mean I've seen the real you. Quite the opposite," Reginaldo concluded.

"Let me guess," she said. "We have to have the courage to be ourselves no matter how others define us."

"I think so," he nodded.

"I knew that comment would come back to haunt me," Marcela sighed.

"Independence or death, Marcela. It's the only way."

"That one, too," she laughed, dropping her blouse back over her head. "Right... independence or death," she chuckled, reaching out to Reginaldo for a hug. "Oh, Reggie," Marcela sighed, "I guess you and I have more in common than we thought."

"Yes, I guess so," he agreed. "Well, except that I still don't like the heat," Reginaldo pointed out, his voice slightly muffled by Marcela's blouse.

"Please, king, just shut up and hug me."

XXV

Excerpt from Hermann Mansfeldt, *Meine Reise nach Brasilien im Jahre 1887*.

This day I observed a spectacle unlike any other I have seen. As if lost in a collective dream, a state that temporarily ignored the reality of their surroundings, a race of servants and otherwise oppressed beings elevated themselves to royalty. The ceremony here is known as the crowning of the Congolese king, and residents tell me it occurs once a year. To the European observer, such as myself, it will remind one of our fava bean king celebration at Lent, where the celebrant who is fortunate to find the bean in his slice of cake shall reign as king for a day, dressed in the robes and adornments that seek to mimic those of His Majesty, often accompanied by an equally ornate gathering of imaginary courtesans. Yet, it is here where the similarities end.

These crowds invade the streets, their rejoicing supported by a native music they beat out of instruments that presumably derive from their distant lands. Above their heads, they wave banners that celebrate nations and peoples that few here can recognize. Similarly, in a cacophony of foreign tongues, the celebrants chant a refrain that must be an integral part of this tradition, for the participants know every word and actively sing in unison. Those not carrying standards instead dance about with colorful umbrellas, perhaps celebrating their temporary sanctuary from the sun and its heat. These dances, too, must have their origin in far-away lands, for they in no way resemble our more elegant movements. These, by contrast, seem quite erratic and disharmonious, a shaking without symmetry, where the lower and upper halves of the body seem unable to communicate between themselves, each carrying out its own wishes.

Strangely enough, and unlike other spontaneous gatherings of Negroes, the Crown does not oppose this celebration. Perhaps they judge it to be an acceptable release of erstwhile energies, an act smothered in ceremony that holds no true political or rebellious significance. It is also possible that the Crown sees the parade as an imitation of its own ceremonies, and is far too flattered to bring it to an end.

Yet, while observing this procession I wondered if these temporary monarchs, these Carnival kings, do not carry a meaning and significance that is beyond our comprehension. For are they not made more powerful by the fact that they are willingly obeyed and have no need to resort to coercion? The same cannot be said of the Monarchy.

On this, his second trip to Cruzília, Marcos knew better than to bring his mobile phone out into the countryside. He found, not surprisingly, that when he wasn't busy fidgeting with its buttons or waving his arm about for maximum reception he had much more time to appreciate the drive through the mountains. He considered stopping at the Big Pig Café for another plate of pork ribs, whipped potatoes, and a large side of conversation, but thought it best to locate Isabel as quickly as possible. After all, he didn't even know where she lived. His instincts didn't fail him, however, for when he pulled up outside of Reginaldo's tiny house, there she was, once again, in the garden tending to the plants. Hearing the car behind her, she turned her head but the sight of Marcos' red convertible wasn't enough for her to abandon her work. He got out of the car and stood just outside the gate, waiting for her to acknowledge his arrival.

"I need your help, Isabel," he finally spoke.

"I'm doing fine, thanks. And you?" she sarcastically responded.

"Isabel, please," he begged her. "They've dissolved the monarchy and kicked Reggie out of the palace," he explained.

"What?" she said, finally turning to face him.

"The Senate voted yesterday," he said. "I take it you haven't heard."

"I haven't really been following the news," she murmured, turning back to her work.

"I'd like for you to come with me to Leopoldina, to find Reggie's family."

"Find his family?" she wondered. "How?"

"We know their last name and a little bit about them. We'll start from there," he suggested.

"I know you think every town out here has about fifteen people in it, but do you realize how many families named Santos there are, even in Leopoldina?" she asked, turning to Marcos.

"I think I know how we might be able to narrow it down," he told her. "Look, if you won't do it for me, do it for Reggie."

"Oh jeez."

Marcos responded with his best pitiful smile.

"Hold on," Isabel sighed, "let me wash up."

Nearly an hour later, Marcos and Isabel pulled up outside a tiny country café.

"The Divine Swine," Isabel read. "Please tell me what we're doing here?"

"Think of it as a welcome center," Marcos suggested.

"Hi there," a woman greeted them from behind the counter as they stepped inside the restaurant. "What can I get for you all today?"

"I bet you make a mean pork rib plate," Marcos guessed, "maybe with some whipped potatoes on the side?"

"Well, I'll be," the woman chuckled. "Word must of got out. Will that be one rib plate, or two?"

Marcos looked to Isabel who merely shrugged in response.

"Make it two," he announced.

The woman yelled the order to a cook somewhere in back as Marcos and Isabel took a seat at the counter.

"Mind if I watch some TV?" the woman asked, turning back to them.

"No, go right ahead."

In a corner behind the counter she turned on a tiny television, then arranged the antenna, but to little avail. The picture remained fuzzy.

"Can I ask you a question?" Marcos said to the woman.

"Sure," she agreed without turning her head, still fidgeting with the antenna.

"Have you lived for a while here in Leopoldina?"

"Since I was born," she told him.

"Ever know a family by the name of Santos?"

"Oooh, lots," she nodded, returning to the counter.

"Told you," Isabel said.

"This was an older couple," Marcos clarified. "Had just one daughter, no other kids. The daughter moved away maybe... what?" he asked, turning to Isabel. "Maybe thirty-five years ago?"

"Let's see," she sighed. "Reggie's thirty-five, so maybe thirty-six years ago," Isabel decided.

"Thirty-six years ago?" the woman repeated. "I would of been just about twenty then."

"About the same age as this daughter," Marcos noted with increasing hope.

"No," Isabel corrected him. "I think Reggie's mom was nearly thirty when she had him."

"Why'd the girl leave?" the woman wondered.

"Uh..." Marcos began, hesitant.

"She got pregnant," Isabel told her.

"So," the woman recapped, "we got a daughter almost thirty years old that gets pregnant and has to leave?"

"Well, she didn't have to leave," Marcos corrected her. "She... well, never mind."

"I'm gonna guess you mean Zé and Maria Santos."

"José and Maria?" Marcos verified, scribbling in his notebook.

"Uh huh. Yeah, that sounds right. Older girl got knocked -, I mean, got pregnant," the woman corrected herself.

"Do you know if this Mr. and Mrs. Santos are still —"

"Oh, honey, I'm sorry," she said, shaking her head. "They both passed some time ago. Been three or four years now."

"And no other family named Santos that meets the description?" the young man asked, grasping at straws.

"No," the woman sighed. "No one else with a daughter that

moved away like that."

"I see," Marcos sighed, visibly disappointed.

"You know, I had forgotten they even had a daughter until you mentioned the story," the café owner admitted.

"They were more or less estranged," Isabel explained.

"That's a shame," the woman sighed before walking back to give the TV antenna another tug.

"Hey, listen," Isabel whispered, putting her arm around Marcos' shoulders in an attempt to console him. "You did what you could. Reggie will be eternally grateful for the effort alone."

As the café owner continued to twist and turn the antenna, the snow finally disappeared to reveal Senator Cruz standing before a podium inside Rio de Janeiro's Plaza of the Republic, speaking to a gathering of reporters and others.

"I'd like to first thank my family," he was saying, looking back at the row of supporters that included his wife, Juliana, and Paulo. "I'd like to thank my colleagues from the Senate," he continued, "my staff, members of the media."

"I haven't done a single thing right since the referendum," Marcos complained.

"Oh, come on. What are you talking about?" Isabel scolded him.

"I offered no guidance to Reggie as king," he submitted as evidence. "I cost him his job, crown, whatever. I lost my job, my girlfriend -"

Marcos paused suddenly after saying the word "girlfriend." Then, to break the uncomfortable silence, he added: "I hoped that I could at least replace the family Reggie lost, since he no longer believes he's the heir."

"Order up!" the cook yelled.

"The family he lost?" Isabel wondered. "What family?"

"The royal family," Marcos explained, as the owner of the café set their plates on the counter top in front of them. This mention of royalty didn't fail to peak her interest in their conversation.

"Thank you," Isabel told the woman before returning to the conversation. "I don't think Reggie ever had the royal family, so how could he lose -"

"He was the heir," Marcos argued. "He thought he was a Braganza, which would be incredible news to anyone, but it was even more important to him since, after all, he never knew much about his family. Besides his mother, of course."

"Did he tell you all this?" she wondered.

"All of what?"

"How he felt, that he was sad to lose these ancestors?"

"Not in so many words," Marcos admitted, "but I remember the conversation we had that night at his house, after dinner and karaoke. Reggie wasn't happy about being named king," Marcos had come to realize. "He was glad he'd finally found his family."

Isabel was silent, but nodded in recognition of the truth in what Marcos was saying. And, quite honestly, she was shocked at the amount of attention he had paid to Reginaldo's words. Marcos really knew his friend very well, his hopes and his fears. As she pondered such thoughts, Isabel noticed, through the fuzz of the television, a press conference that was being broadcast live. Fearing that it might have something to do with Reginaldo, she got the café owner's attention.

"I'm sorry, ma'am," she called to her. "Do you mind turning up the volume?"

"Not at all."

"You know, Isabel," Marcos said to her, unaware of the attention she had begun to devote to the television. "I was wrong."

"Wrong about what?" she wondered.

Isabel's interest in the press conference had sparked the café owner's interest as well, so the woman stationed herself half-way between the couple and the TV, figuring they would all three have something to comment upon very soon. She wasn't disappointed, for the politician behind the podium soon began to speak.

"And because of my strong conviction," Senator Cruz was saying as he stood before the assembled crowd. "Due to my strong conviction that this beautiful country and its fine citizens have unjustly suffered from a lack of real leadership in the past few years..."

Suddenly, Marcos recognized the Senator's voice and looked up from his plate.

"Oh my god..." he mumbled as his mouth fell open.

"I therefore announce," the Senator smiled, "my intention to run for President of the Republic of Brazil."

"I knew it," Marcos cried, dropping his knife and fork onto his plate. Surprised by the noise, the café owner turned her head.

"It's a long story," Isabel assured her. The woman's attention was quickly drawn back to the TV as the crowd applauded and reporters were invited to ask questions. "Sir," the first one began, "could you tell us a bit more about how you arrived at this decision?"

"I was wrong about my girlfriend," Marcos suddenly declared. The woman behind the counter looked over at him, but quickly tried to disguise her rather blatant attempt at eavesdropping.

"How's that?" Isabel asked him after the café owner had finally looked away.

"I'm not sorry I lost her," he confessed, to which Isabel simply nodded in response.

"Next question?" the Senator asked on the small television located inside the kiosk at Ipanema Beach's Post 9. Unaware of the broadcast, Reginaldo sat with both elbows on the countertop as he settled down to write his final postcard back home to Isabel.

Carta Régia, 26 de março de 1993

Dear Isabel,

What changed from one day to the next after the abolition of slavery was decreed? When the slaves left the tiny quarters from behind their masters' houses, where did they –

"Hey, aren't you the king?"

The interruption came from a young man, seated with a group of fellow teenagers at the kiosk.

"I was," Reginaldo answered as he sipped coconut water from a straw. Actually, it was rather amazing this young man had been able to identify the former king, for many of Reginaldo's friends would be hard-pressed to recognize him without his cardigan and faded khaki trousers, dressed as he was in Bermuda shorts, rollerblade skates for locomotion, and a thin white T-shirt that read COPACABANA across the front.

"Hey, Jorge... Lia," the young man said to his friends. "It's the king!"

"Pelé?"

"No, the other king?"

"Roberto Carlos? Elvis?"

"No, you idiots."

"Then what king?" they wondered, becoming frustrated with their friend's guessing game.

"The guy who got elected last month," he said, seeking to jog their collective THC-soaked memory.

"Oh yeah," one of them finally nodded. "Hey, weren't you guys gonna change the country's name?" he asked Reginaldo.

"We were, but then they kicked us out."

"Kicked you out?" the young man wondered. "Who?"

"Congress," Reginaldo explained. "This Senator guy."

"That Senator?" the kiosk manager asked, pointing to the TV.

Reginaldo squinted to see what was happening on the tiny television set.

"That's the one," he confirmed, recognizing the man on screen as Senator Cruz.

All the time eavesdropping upon this conversation, the other customers now stood up to gather around the kiosk, trying to catch a glimpse as the man behind the counter turned up the volume. Suddenly, a car came screeching to a halt just past the kiosk. All heads turned from the television to the street as the Chief of Police poked his head out above the car.

"Reggie!" he yelled.

"Police Chief Viana!" Reginaldo said with surprise. "What are you doing here?" he asked, approaching the street. "And in a car?"

"It's an emergency," the Police Chief assured him, accounting more for the car than for his sudden and unexpected appearance.

"An emergency?" Reginaldo worried.

"No one's injured," Viana explained. "I just need you to come with me for a while."

"Fine," Reginaldo agreed. "I'll see you all later," he smiled, waving back to the crowd at the kiosk as he skated his way to the car.

"See ya, king! Don't give up the fight," they yelled back.

"The fight?" Reginaldo wondered to himself.

"Rollerblades?" Viana asked him as he stepped awkwardly into the car.

"I couldn't leave Rio without trying it," Reginaldo shrugged.

"True," the Police Chief nodded before pulling back into the midday traffic of the Avenida Vieira Souto.

"I'm not sorry Juliana dumped me," Marcos said to Isabel, moping over his pork ribs. "In fact, I'm very happy she did."

"You probably didn't treat her very well," she guessed, dismissing all tragic pretense from Marcos' confession.

"Treat her very well?" Marcos asked. "Look at what her father's done to Reggie," he said, pointing to the television. "God only knows what he's got in store for the rest of us when he's President." Again, the café owner's interest was torn between the television and these, her only, customers.

"This isn't about the Senator," Isabel argued.

"So, then, what is this all about?"

"It's about what you said the other day," the Chief responded.

"Not the car-jacking idea?" Reginaldo worried.

"No, not that. Something better!" the other proudly announced.

"Oh Lord, Viana. What have you done?"

"Yes, you over there," the Senator said, pointing to the back corner as he continued taking questions from the press.

"Senator," Flavia began, stepping forward. "Can you explain to the public why a financial reform bill, which you co-sponsored, passed through the Chamber and Senate yesterday with less than an hour of debate?"

The others in the crowd turned around and looked back at Flavia. Some furrowed their brows as if to censure her bravado, while others grinned in anticipation of the grilling that was to come. Until now the questions had been nothing more than softballs lobbed in the Senator's direction, but this one dropped in his lap like a grenade.

"Well," the Senator stammered, "it's really not unusual to limit debate on a measure in the interest of -"

"In the interest of the Brazilian people, sir?" Flavia interrupted. "Isn't it true that this bill would allow the Treasury Department to bail out private banks and lenders with taxpayer dollars?"

The crowd gathered at the Plaza of the Republic had begun to whisper amongst themselves as Viana's car skidded to a stop at the corner.

"The press conference?" Reginaldo wondered. "Yes, I know all about it," he told the Chief. "I was watching it on TV when you -"

"It's not just that," Viana assured him. "Look, just wait and see," he told Reginaldo as the two stepped out of the car and waded into the crowd.

"Look," Senator Cruz tried to explain, raising his hands and voice in an attempt to calm the crowd. "It is essential to every citizen that has a savings account in this country that our nation's lending institutions have the protection - "

"Senator, can you provide written documentation of Reginaldo Santos' genealogical connection to the royal family?" Flavia abruptly asked, changing the subject.

"In case you haven't heard," the Senator chuckled, "the monarchy is over."

"Can you, sir?" Flavia continued. "Can you prove to the Brazilian people that Mr. Santos was the legitimate heir to the throne?"

"I'd have to check our records to..." the Senator began when something in the distance suddenly caught his eye.

"What's going on?" Isabel wondered. "He stopped talking."

"I have no idea," Marcos murmured, shaking his head.

When Viana's officers showed up at the entrance to the Moreira Pinto favela, most residents assumed the police had come to interrogate someone, or make an arrest. And when the officers started asking if anyone had anything they'd like to discuss with the Mayor, the residents nearly split their sides with laughter, finding the phrase "discussion with the Mayor" the worst euphemism they had ever heard for jail time. But Viana had prepared his officers to be laughed at, or worse, and ordered them to turn the other cheek, return to their patrol cars, and drive away at a snail's pace back down the hillside. Out of curiosity, the Police Chief reckoned, some would follow. Viana had sent officers to every favela near downtown Rio de Janeiro that he knew of, which was surely fewer than actually existed, but the number of marchers grew steadily as the groups passed through neighborhoods such as Laranjeiras, Flamengo, Catete, and Glória on their way into downtown. And by the time this group reached the Plaza of the Republic, they were an organized army that chanted in unison a phrase they had certainly heard before, but one they had now made their own: Independence or death!

Reginaldo was stunned as he cast his eyes over the multitude. Just listen to the urgency in these people's hearts, in their voices. Marcela was right. A declaration of independence was still necessary, he now recognized, and would have to be constantly renewed. Apparently not all of the great battles had already been fought.

"Viana," Reginaldo said, turning to the Chief after noting that, instead of breaking up the protest, the police were actually encouraging it. "Viana, did you do this?" he asked him.

"I decided to show people the truth, just like you suggested," Viana smiled. "And the Mayor, too," he added. "Last stop: City Hall!" the Police Chief laughed, absolutely giddy.

"I love you, Isabel," Marcos suddenly blurted out, turning from the television and looking directly into the young woman's eyes.

"No you don't," she told him, gently shaking her head. "But don't worry, I know what you're trying to say."

"What do you mean you know what I'm trying to say?" he asked, dumbfounded. "I'm trying to tell you that I love you."

"No you're not," Isabel informed him. "You're caught up in the moment," she explained. "The monarchy being dissolved, our rushing around trying to find Reggie's family, the Senator's press conference, the crowds all over downtown Rio... you know, it's a lot of emotion," she pointed out. "Not to mention the fact that you just broke up with your girlfriend," she added.

"But..." Marcos stuttered.

"How long have you known me? A month?"

"Maybe five weeks," he guessed, trying to augment an otherwise finite period of time. "But a lot has happened in those five weeks," Marcos argued. "We met, we crowned a king, we stayed in a palace, we fought the government and the media, we kissed..."

"We argued..." she pointed out.

"Yes," he agreed. "I was an ass. I yelled, I stormed off, I called the king a baby, I went back to my girlfriend, I yelled some more..."

"Really?"

"Yeah. Bebel," he explained.

"Oh, poor thing..."

"Yeah," Marcos sighed. "Anyway, then I show up all of a sudden in Cruzília, I take you for granted, make you come with me to some diner..."

"The food was good."

"Yeah, wasn't it?" he admitted. "So can't you see that you and I have really been through a lot and become quite close?"

"So tell me that," she said, "instead of brushing over it with some clichéd I love you."

"So that's what I'm really saying when I say I love you?" he earnestly asked her.

"I think that's probably it," Isabel told him. "But it's a nice start," she admitted.

"You're right," he agreed. "It has been a nice start."

The crowd in downtown Rio had now turned its back on the press conference and was instead joining the protest, which suited the Senator just fine, for he seized the opportunity to slip away from the podium. As he turned to leave, two men in matching suits approached him.

"Senator?" Veronica said, stepping out from between them.

"Yes?"

"The Federal Police need to ask you a few questions about the selection of Reginaldo Santos as king."

"For Christ's sake, doesn't anyone understand that the monarchy's over?" the Senator grumbled as he changed direction.

"Please, sir," Veronica called out as the men stepped in the path of Cruz's escape. "I don't think you want to resist in front of this large of a crowd," she told him, glancing towards the hundreds of people that had gathered in the square.

"Oh, for crying out loud," he objected, turning towards his wife. But Melba met his look with one that signaled to him that he'd be wise to follow the young woman's instructions without causing a scene. Behind them, the crowd continued to chant.

"Viana," Reginaldo said, "have you ever heard the story of our declaration of independence?"

"The proclamation at the River Ipiranga? Sure."

"Then you'll remember that Pedro the First was on horseback –"

"Some say he was taking, well, a little break," Viana interrupted.

"I've heard that as well," Reginaldo nodded. "Anyway, in whatever capacity, there he was accompanied by a regiment of his bravest men when they hailed our good leader and –"

"Is this about him not being Brazilian?" the Police Chief asked, recalling Reginaldo's tirade during the radio interview.

"Not exactly, Viana. I see now that it goes far beyond that. So the courier hands the king a packet of mail that apparently contained an ultimatum: return to Portugal, or else. He crumbles up the letter," Reginaldo continued, miming the gestures as he spoke, "rips the Portuguese insignia from his uniform, unsheathes his sword and spurs his horse up a nearby hill. At which point he then rears his horse, waving his sword defiantly in the air as he shouts: 'Independence or death.'"

"Yep, that's pretty much it. Heard it a thousand times," Viana reflected.

"So you know what happened next."

"Sure, we... I mean, they... hey, what did happen next?"

"That's just it. Nothing! Nothing happened next. The officers shout back: 'Independence or death', and they assume they're now separated from Portugal."

"Even if it meant war and bloodshed!" Viana recited the famous line from memory.

"But there never was any war, any bloodshed," Reginaldo pointed out.

"Isn't that a good thing?"

"At the time, I suppose, for the soldiers involved. But look where it's gotten us."

"Uh huh. Wait, where? Where has it gotten us, exactly?"

"In this square, in the middle of this crowd!"

"Right."

"Independence with a shout and Abolition by the stroke of a pen. It's never that simple, Viana. And what did it achieve if even one person remains less than free?"

"I think I see your point," the Chief nodded.

"I read somewhere," Reginaldo reminisced, "that a declaration of independence, or an end to any form of bondage, is not really an end at all. It merely marks the beginning of the struggle for freedom."

"Yes," Viana smiled, fairly certain he understood.

"You know, it really is amazing what you've done here," Reginaldo told the Chief. "But there's no need to take them to see the Mayor."

"No?" Viana asked him, somewhat disappointed. "But what about showing the powerful what they refuse to see?"

"Thank heavens," Reginaldo sighed, placing a hand on his new friend's shoulder. "You no longer have to kiss the king's hand to be heard."

"I thought we were talking about the Mayor?" Viana asked, confused.

"Do you think you could do this again?" Reginaldo asked, ignoring his friend's confusion and looking at the crowd that had by now completely filled the Plaza.

"I guess so," Viana shrugged. "We could probably do even better, now that the residents would trust us," he noted.

"See that they make it to the polls for the up-coming election. I realize now," the king smiled, "that, even though it's imperfect, it's still a pretty good way to make your voice heard."

XXVI

Clara walked home alone from the cemetery that afternoon after laying Jacob to rest. The city hadn't even the courtesy to sympathize with her suffering, for a blue sky stared stupidly back at her when she raised her head, and an ocean breeze blew carelessly through her hair. How could Mother Nature be so blind to the plight of Her children? Clara wondered. She lent the waters to ships that carried them to lands they had no business tilling, Her wind puffing the sails the entire time like the most unashamed accomplice. And on a day that should have dawned as grey as ash, Her sun shone most radiant. Up ahead, a group of slaves had decided to take advantage of the pleasant weather as they set down the load they were carrying and stopped to rest in the warmth of the sun. Clara stared at the pitch-black men, naked from their wastes up with only a loose, sack-like covering over their legs, which was held with a rope tied around the waist. Having relieved themselves of their burden, one of the men immediately began to voice a sort of chant in which the others quickly joined. Clara recognized their song as a hymn to the African deity, Yemanja; goddess of the sea and a symbol of nature's fertility that had no doubt created such a splendid afternoon. Clara stopped to watch them, staring fixedly at the man who led the chorus.

Odoiyá Iemanjá, he sang, staring towards the sky as the sweat poured down his face.

Odoiyá Iemanjá, Yemanjá, mother of the waters

Ero Iyá, peaceful mother

Omí l'ayó mamá, of waters that bring true happiness

Omí tá ni orí, orí, orí o, of waters that illuminate the soul

Iemanjá soro soro, Yemanja leads the ceremony

Ejé balé kara o, her blood falls to the ground and calms

Kamara ikú, so that there may be no death

Kamara arun, so that there may be no sickness

Kamara ofó, so that her children feel no pain.

"Yemanjá?" Clara murmured, shaking her head. "Yemanjá?" she repeated, her cry becoming louder.

She knelt down and scraped the surface of the street, rising to throw a handful of pebbles and whatever else she could find on the ground around her. The men stopped their song, staring back blankly at the woman. They did not cower in the face of the attack, but merely stood there, frozen, and watched with pity.

"Yemanjá? You don't know what crimes the sea has committed," Clara shouted at them, as she continued to spit and curse the goddess with a fury reserved for one desperate mother towards another.

Iemanjá Sabá, Mother Yemanja

Sabá omí rere, mother of distant waters

Sabá omí rere oluwo, mother of the mysteries of distant waters

Odo ri le Iemanjá, the river is the head of Yemanja

Odo fi o fi odo, the river that rocks back and forth

Iá, Iá la ni bu tô, mother that runs like a river

Iá la ni bu tô onirê, mother that runs like a river that has

Iá la ni bo tô, the power to be favorable

Iá kekere, gentle mother

Iá bóia, Iá bóia, warrior mother

Ma re lê arabô, I will shut my mouth when I hear your call

Ma re lê arabô xarenã, I will shut my mouth when I hear your call, your sword that punishes

Ma re lê arabô xarenã, I will shut my mouth when I hear your call, your sword that punishes

Iemanjá arabô xarenã, Yemanja, I hear your call, your sword that punishes

Iemanjá arabô, Yemanja, I hear your call

"CLARA, IS THAT YOU?" Assemblyman Castro yelled downstairs when he heard the back door close. "Clara?" he again yelled.

He's upstairs, she thought. He must want something else, she thought, shaking her head. He can't, he wouldn't. Not today, she tried to convince herself.

"Clara, could you come upstairs for a moment?" the Assemblyman called out.

Without responding, Clara walked through the parlor and made her way towards the stairs when she suddenly heard the bath water splashing about.

"Clara?" he again shouted down.

As usual, the Assemblyman was there waiting for her as she topped the stairs.

"Come, Clara," he said, inviting her into the room. "I need help again with my bath. The wash cloth is on the hook," he told her, motioning towards the sink behind him. "And grab the razor as well," he added, stepping into the tub. "The king's visit caused me to miss my morning shave," the Assemblyman complained as he splashed the warm water onto his chest and arms.

As always, Clara did as he said. She took the cloth from where it was hanging on the wall, dipped it into the basin, and wrung it dry with all the strength her arms could muster. Then, she opened the wooden cabinet and took out the razor.

"I'm sorry about your boy, Clara," he told her. "I really am, you hear me?"

"Um hm," she mumbled, turning mechanically to her left, as if under a spell, and approaching the tub. She came to rest on her knees directly behind the Assemblyman and, as he splashed water onto his face, Clara slowly lifted the razor.

"Clara?" he laughed. "Aren't you forgetting something?" he asked her.

"Huh?" she responded.

"Aren't you forgetting something?" Castro repeated. "The shaving lather?" he reminded her.

"Of course, sir," she vacantly agreed, placing the razor on the floor as she rose to fetch the shaving soap. When she returned, Clara again kneeled behind the Assemblyman and began rubbing the lather onto his face and neck. She studied his features as if blind, moving her hands slowly and deliberately along his chin, over his Adam's apple, and larynx. He was ready.

She grabbed the razor from the floor and opened it, the blade reflecting the light from above as it locked into place. Clara stared into the nape of Castro's neck, and suddenly remembered the shade of her Jacob's pale dead skin. The hue was so alike. Clara began to shake, the razor nearly falling from her unsteady hand. How could she have wished for her son to appear more like this man, no matter the benefit it might have brought him? How could a mother look down at her dead son and want him that way in life?

Curious at Clara's silence and the delay, Castro turned his head slightly and looked down into the tub behind him. And there he saw the first drops of red.

"Good Lord!" he cried, jumping from the tub. "Clara!" he gasped. The slave woman's eyes were now more vacant than before, as the razor dropped from her hand and she slowly began to fall backwards onto the cold tile floor.

"Jesus, Clara, what have you done?" the Assemblyman shouted, staring down at the rivers of blood that now gushed from her wrists. He caught her body and gently laid her out beside the tub, wrapping a bath towel around each of her wrists in an effort to halt the bleeding. Feeling her head upon the tile, Clara opened her eyes and saw her Jacob's smiling face, a sight she felt she had not seen in years. Clara smiled back at him, finally able look her child in the eyes without shame. Soon they would be together.

"Clara!" the Assemblyman pleaded with her to respond. He knelt down above her and rested his head against her breast to see if the woman's heart still beat beneath her dress. "You're going to live. You're going to live," he kept repeating to Clara, as if this would ever console her.

XXVII

The lights inside The Pleasure Palace dimmed as the audience sat in anticipation of the song and dance that was to come. Gradually, they heard a piano start up. Unlike the usual sultry numbers that reign at the Palace, this tune was more lively and it quickly brought the tiny crowd to their feet, swaying their hips in time with its infectious melody. Slowly, the heavy red curtain began to inch its way open. As the opening verses approached, the singer emerged from the shadows and was met by an overwhelming applause. It was Reginaldo, and he sang 'From a jack to a king,' a tune made famous by Elvis Presley some thirty years before.

They were all there, crowded around a single table: Marcos, Isabel, Marcela, Fernando, Luzia, Claudia, Flavia, Gustavo, Milena, Veronica and Bebel. The club had already opened its doors for the evening, but it was early and still rather empty. The fact that his friends nearly outnumbered the other patrons relieved Reginaldo's stage fright as he continued to croon: *From a jack...*

"Can we talk?" Marcos asked, suddenly turning to Isabel.

"Sure."

The two stood and walked towards the bar so that they could talk without disturbing Reginaldo's song.

"What is it?" she asked him.

"What are your plans when you get back to Cruzília?"

"I guess I'll go back to work at the nursery," she shrugged. "Why?"

Behind them, Reginaldo sang on, adding some mildly

complicated footwork during the break between verses.

"I'm thinking about staying with Reginaldo for a while, you know, in Cruzília," Marcos told her.

"Really? What about São Paulo?" she wondered.

"I've got some vacation time, since... well, since the senator is in custody."

"Right."

"So I thought I might give something new a try. Give us a try," he admitted. "If that's ok with you?"

"That would be nice," Isabel smiled.

"Besides," Marcos added, "the night sky in São Paulo is completely without stars. How can anyone stand it?" he wondered, shaking his head.

When Reginaldo had finished, the entire group gathered again around the table to congratulate him on this graduation from karaoke to the real stage; his first ever performance inside a genuine nightclub.

"So, what'd you think? Could you do it for a living?" Marcela asked.

"I don't think so," he admitted. "The moves, the breathing, keeping time with the music while making meaningful eye-contact with the audience. It's a lot of work," Reginaldo concluded.

"Ha!" Marcela cried. "See? I told you so."

"What do you have there?" Isabel asked, pointing to a stack of papers on the table beside Veronica.

"Oh right," she remembered. "A little gift for the king."

"Former king," Reginaldo pointed out.

"A gift?" Marcela confirmed.

"Uh huh," Veronica nodded, grabbing the documents. "I pieced together a Santos family tree, you know, in case the Senator called our bluff," she explained.

"Yeah," Flavia agreed. "Veronica said we would need some proof if we were gonna pull this whole thing off."

"So let's see it," Marcela suggested.

"Alright," Veronica agreed as she began to unfold what was quickly apparent as a design of a family tree. In it, a series of Josés, Josués, and Marias of Fatima, Gloria, Silva, and of course Santos could be seen raining down until they arrived at Reginaldo. However, many empty spaces remained.

"That's fantastic," the others sighed.

"As you can tell, it's not complete," Veronica apologized.

"Even so, it's much more than I came up with," Marcos admitted.

"I had some help, actually," Veronica smiled, turning to Flavia. "See Josué da Silva up here in the corner?" she asked, pointing to the top left corner of the chart. "Well, there was mention that Josué had come from the capital."

"Yes," Reginaldo began to nod.

"Rio," Veronica pointed out. "So I called up Flavia to help me locate Josué's parents and well," she paused, looking to Flavia.

"Well," the journalist continued where Veronica left off, "it definitely would have helped if your ancestors had more distinctive names, like Maximiliano or even Reginaldo, I guess," she laughed. "But I did what I could, and this Maria da Gloria looks like the best candidate."

"It's very likely," Veronica concluded, "that your great-great-great grandmother would have lived in Rio de Janeiro during the monarchy," she told Reginaldo.

"Maybe you're part of that illegitimate line, after all?" Marcos smiled.

"It's very nice, Veronica, Flavia," Reginaldo said to them. "And I really do appreciate the amount of research you put into this, it's really amazing you could find even this much information."

"Well, again, I'm sorry the chart is incomplete," Veronica said. "But, after all, the burden of proof was on the Senator."

"Right," Reginaldo sighed, still quite pensive as he gazed upon his sparsely foliated family tree.

"How about a toast?" Marcela suggested. "Dante, hon'," she called over to the bar, "a bottle of champagne!"

"You know," Reginaldo said after a pause in the conversation, still looking down at the chart. "It really is incredible to see all these names spread out above Mother and me. And I don't want to seem ungrateful, but I can't help finding the Xs the most intriguing part of the chart. The blank spaces, the who-knows-what," he murmured. "And I do appreciate you all trying to make me into a royal bastard, but I've come to appreciate the regular old bastard I was before. But, that's just it," he paused, gathering his thoughts. "I'm not that same old bastard. This experience has changed me forever, thanks in no small part to all of you here."

With impeccable timing, Dante arrived at the table during this pause and poured a round of champagne.

"If you'll all join me in a toast," Flavia said, raising her glass. "Here's to new friends and second chances! Thank you all for both."

"Hear, hear!" the others shouted as they took a sip of champagne.

"To kings with the courage to tell the truth!" Luzia toasted.

"Hear, hear!"

"To kings that like a good song and dance!" Claudia said.

"Hear, hear!"

"To kings that paint a mean toe nail!" Bebel added.

"Hear, hear!" the others laughed.

As the toasts continued, Reginaldo turned the genealogical chart over and began to scribble on the back. Noticing this, the others halted the celebration and craned their necks to see what he was up to.

"I've made some revisions," he smiled, holding up a new, nearly incomprehensible chart that read:

Rafael — Clara

Pedro — Jacob

Jefferson Police Chief Viana Gustavo — Milena

Claudia, Dante & Luzia Mother — X Veronica — Flavia

Fernando — Marcela — Reginaldo — Marcos — Isabel

The others almost inquired about the names up top that they did not recognize, but, in the end, everyone just raised their glasses without saying a word.

Outside the nightclub, Marcela kissed Marcos and Isabel goodbye, as they gathered up the last pieces of luggage and threw them into the trunk of the convertible.

"What's this I hear about you staying in Cruzília?" she asked Marcos.

"It's true, Marcela. I'm off to try country living for a while," he confirmed.

"Isa, honey," she said to Isabel. "Buy him some shorts. Or sandals, something! Please. And burn the ties and those dreadful blue dress socks," she added with a grimace.

"I've already gotten rid of them," Marcos assured her. "Good bye, Marcela."

"Maybe we'll see you one day in Cruzília?" Isabel speculated.

"Stranger things have happened, hon'," she sighed. "Stranger things have happened."

At last, Reginaldo and Marcela were left alone to say their "farewells."

"Pretty good performance back there," she admitted. "I could've sworn it was Elvis himself up on stage. Well," she added, tapping his belly. "Elvis in the latter half of his career," she laughed.

"Thanks, but I think I'll stick to karaoke at the Apolo."

"That's probably best for the tourism industry."

"You know, Marcela," Reginaldo began. "That chart... the one I made..."

"Yes?"

"It was my way of saying that I no longer miss that other family, royal or not."

"Well, just remember Reggie," Marcela smiled, pinching his cheek. "You'll always be my king, no matter what the government or the history books say."

"And you, Marcela," he sighed, "will forever be my drag queen."

"Oh, Reggie," she laughed, shaking her head. "You finally got a sense of humor."

"Rio is good for something," he winked as Marcela gave his face a light tap.

"Your carriage awaits, King," she told him, glancing towards the car. "Now get the hell out of here before someone spots you with a lounge singer."

"Ah! You mean actress," he corrected her, index finger raised in the air.

"You always were naive. Now go," she said. "And don't forget to write."

"Take care of yourself, Marcela."

The former king climbed into the back seat of the convertible as Marcos and Isabel waved a final goodbye.

"Oh, I forgot to mention," Reginaldo shouted, turning back towards her. "Before I was deposed I granted you and the girls royal titles. You know, one of the perks of the position," he smiled. "Anyway, the paperwork should arrive soon," he told her.

"Titles?" she wondered.

"Good bye, Lady Seville!" Reginaldo waved, as the car pulled away.

"Oh, Reggie," Marcela sighed to herself. "A Lady?"

"Marcos, you mind if we make another quick stop?" Reginaldo asked his friend.

"Of course not. Where to?"

"Downtown," he told him.

As the convertible pulled up alongside the National Library, Police Chief Viana was already there waiting for them.

"Greetings Chief," Reginaldo waved, bounding from the car. "Thanks for meeting me here."

"I do owe you this favor," Viana pointed out.

"And I am grateful. Viana, you remember Jefferson, a friend of mine," he said as they approached the roving snack vendor. "Jefferson, you remember Viana."

"Howdy Cap'ain," Jefferson greeted him.

"Actually, it's Chief," Viana corrected him.

"Chief?"

"That's correct," Viana confirmed.

"Jefferson, Viana just happens to be the Chief of Police."

"You don't say."

"And I've brought him here for a couple of reasons," Reginaldo explained. "First, you now have a permanent vending area here if you like," he said, pointing to the corner of the busy intersection. "No more cops hassling you. Isn't that correct, Chief?"

"Stay as long as you like," Viana nodded.

"Second..." Reginaldo began, but then paused suddenly. "Did you bring it?" he asked the Police Chief.

"Oh, right," Viana remembered. "One second," he told them as he headed towards his patrol car. Seconds later he came walking back, rolling along beside him a rather odd looking contraption.

"What in the heck is that?" Jefferson wondered.

"That, my friend, is one of modern technology's finest marvels," Reginaldo explained.

"Oh yeah?"

"Uh huh."

"What's it do?" Jefferson asked.

"It makes hot dogs!" Reginaldo excitedly declared. "Look," he said, bending down to demonstrate its wonders. "With a minimal amount of heat produced by a gas-lit flame, the weenies are slowly heated as they rotate inside the glass dome," he continued, narrating his way along the height of the machine. "And the best part," Reginaldo concluded, "is that it uses a minimal amount of energy since the glass covering allows the sun to do most of the warming. We've put the city's stifling heat to work!" he celebrated.

"And you're giving this weenie cooker to me?" Jefferson asked.

"The city's already paid for it," Viana confirmed. "Including a starter tank of gas," he added, opening a tiny door underneath.

"It should increase revenues," Reginaldo guessed. "And with a guaranteed spot smack dab between the library and the museum, you should be able to cultivate quite a loyal following."

"I reckon so," Jefferson agreed. "Although you leaving takes away 'bout half my business," he chuckled.

"Jefferson," Reginaldo proudly declared, "your hot-dog stand will always be proof that my month here in Rio wasn't a waste of time. Good luck, my friend."

"Good luck, Cap'ain Reggie," Jefferson graciously smiled, placing a hand on the shoulder of this, his most loyal, customer. "I think I speak for the whole city when I say that us vendors are sad to see you go."

The two men embraced.

"You too, Viana," Reginaldo sniffed.

"What?"

"C'mon," the former king insisted, wrapping a free arm around the Chief of Police's shoulders and drawing him into the group hug.

As Marcos' convertible pulled back into traffic, Reginaldo saluted as they passed the *Museu Nacional de Belas Artes* for the last time. Inside, two employees were putting away the exhibition pieces from the time of the monarchy. The first one, that is.

"This one's also for the Archives," one of the employees said to his colleague.

"You've wrapped it already?" the other asked, surprised.

"No, it arrived this way."

"Arrived all packed up? Where'd it come from?"

"I don't know," he shrugged. "Read the card."

"Berrini," the employee read on the small card attached to the package. "Fernando Berrini. Says it was commissioned by the

Ministry of Culture. And it's going straight to the Archives?"

"Apparently so."

"Let's open it," the other said with a sly grin.

"What?!"

"Come on, let's open it up just a bit and see what it is."

"I don't know..." the one hesitated.

"We'll wrap it back up with the others when we're done," the other assured him.

"Alright, but gently, gently," the employee kept repeating as his colleague began tugging at the edge of the heavy brown paper.

The first tear stripped away the uppermost part of the cover and exposed Reginaldo's nose and eyes and the crown resting upon his head. A second tug in the opposite direction revealed the head and upper torso of a beautiful woman dressed in a simple, yet elegant, pearl-white gown that formed a stunning contrast between the burgundy of the king's cloak and the deep black of her skin. Both subjects stared back stoically from the canvas. Yet, if one were to look more carefully, you would almost swear that they each betrayed the tiniest hint of a smile, as if acknowledging a joke shared only between themselves.

The End.

Printed in the United States
56550LVS00002B/104